EXPLORER RACE
SHAMANIC SECR
SERIES

Shamanic Secrets
Lost Wisdom
REGAINED

Shamans and Healers through Robert Shapiro Bring Back Lost Wisdom

Other Books by Robert Shapiro

EXPLORER RACE SERIES

1. The Explorer Race
2. ETs and the Explorer Race
3. The Explorer Race: Origins and the Next 50 Years
4. The Explorer Race: Creators and Friends
5. The Explorer Race: Particle Personalities
6. The Explorer Race and Beyond
7. The Explorer Race: Council of Creators
8. The Explorer Race and Isis
9. The Explorer Race and Jesus
10. The Explorer Race: Earth History and Lost Civilizations
11. The Explorer Race: ET Visitors Speak Volume 1
12. The Explorer Race: Techniques for Generating Safety
13. The Explorer Race: Animal Souls Speak
14. The Explorer Race: Astrology: Planet Personalities and Signs Speak
15. The Explorer Race: ET Visitors Speak Volume 2
16. The Explorer Race: Plant Souls Speak
17. The Explorer Race: Time and the Transition to Natural Time
18. The Explorer Race: ETs on Earth Volume 1
19. The Explorer Race: Walk-Ins
20. The Explorer Race: Totality and Beyond
21. The Explorer Race: ETs on Earth Volume 2
22. The Explorer Race: ETs on Earth Volume 3

SHAMANIC SECRETS SERIES

A. Shamanic Secrets for Material Mastery
B. Shamanic Secrets for Physical Mastery
C. Shamanic Secrets for Spiritual Mastery
D. Shamanic Secrets: Lost Wisdom Regained

SHINING THE LIGHT SERIES

Shining the Light I: The Battle Begins!
Shining the Light II: The Battle Continues
Shining the Light III: Humanity Gets a Second Chance
Shining the Light IV: Humanity's Greatest Challenge
Shining the Light V: Humanity Is Going to Make It!
Shining the Light VI: The End of What Was
Shining the Light VII: The First Alignment; World Peace

ULTIMATE UFO SERIES

Andromeda
The Zetas: History, Hybrids, and Human Contacts

SECRETS OF FEMININE SCIENCE SERIES

Transformation

SHIRT POCKET BOOKS SERIES

Benevolent Magic & Living Prayer
Touching Sedona
Feeling Sedona's ET Energies

EXPLORER **RACE**
SHAMANIC SECRETS
SERIES

Shamanic Secrets
Lost Wisdom
REGAINED

Shamans and Healers
through Robert Shapiro
Bring Back Lost Wisdom

LIGHT
Technology
PUBLISHING

For information about special discounts for bulk purchases,
please contact Light Technology Publishing Special Sales at
1-800-450-0985 or publishing@LightTechnology.net.

ISBN-13: 978-1-62233-049-2

Light Technology Publishing, LLC
Phone: 1-800-450-0985
1-928-526-1345
Fax: 928-714-1132
PO Box 3540
Flagstaff, AZ 86003
LightTechnology.com

For Ono Teave

Contents

Preface

Isis

August 25, 2016

Over time, as is typical with ancient knowledge and wisdom, at least 95 percent of such valuable knowledge and wisdom has been lost, primarily because civilizations have been interfered with or died out for natural reasons and perhaps did not have any means to keep the knowledge going other than verbally within their own culture. So this is to be expected.

The value of these books, of course (aside from the obvious), is to perpetuate this information in written form and, at some point, in digital form so that it is available for those who might wish to call on it in the future. For example, the idea of moving stones in certain ways to purify water will come into practice, in time, in places where water purification is needed on a large scale or even a commercial scale. This is actually pretty urgent. Because of underground mining and fracking, the water table is not getting any lower in many places and is perhaps higher in others, and the water purification underground is not working because of the chemicals and the pollutants injected underground to bring up or make petroleum products available. This is essentially poisoning the underground water systems of the entire planet, so a means to purify water in a way that is spiritual and has physical results is essential.

Then there's this, and ultimately this is the most important aspect of these Shamanic Secrets books: Children being born now and people who were born some time ago and are in, say, their twenties, thirties, and even forties are coming into a greater sense of being able to perform many of these things. The children are especially capable because they will have no qualms. They are not as conditioned to automatically disbelieve things because they are not exclusively mental. So the young people (now especially) — including teenagers, those in their twenties, and some in their thirties — are evolving into that attitude, and the young ones will be born with it. Thus, they will most likely be able to bring about a more benign and benevolent life for people on Earth.

In reading these Shamanic Secrets books, and this one in particular, keep these things in mind. You don't necessarily have to do any of them, but know that this is *lost* wisdom that once worked very well in other times and can work just as well in your time. Good life.

Introduction

Speaks of Many Truths

June 27, 2016

This is a time on Earth when people are being rent asunder by so many things. Dramas in their lives are overwhelmed by dramas in the lives of others or are sometimes attached to the dramatic events of the day. In times gone by, there were people, places, things, groups, and others that provided knowledge, wisdom, comfort, and ease through life.

This book is entirely about finding comfort and ease through life. You don't have to struggle. You don't have to find substitutes for things you don't have. You don't have to get along without things you need. You need food, comfortable shelter, good health, and time to enjoy life. This book does not provide all the answers to all your questions. It is the beginning of much more to come.

Some of you are interested in how others lived their lives in the past, but most of you, especially those who need something, want something, or are desperately trying to acquire something, are interested in how people from the past acquired those things. Some of the suggestions will seem fantastic or impossible to you. Don't assume that. Some of you will find you can produce, in some way, a portion of what those shamans from the past were able to do. This might be easier for those of you already on your spiritual path. Even if you are not on any particular spiritual path, don't assume you cannot do these things. Always remember, though, to say these words before you do anything:

> "I ask for all the most benevolent energies that are available to me to be all around me and all about me now."

Then wait. You might feel benevolent energy or even sense warmth in your body. That will be your body's acknowledgment that this engagement, this time spent with these beings, is all about love, support, and compassion for you, and they will be there to help you to create things of love and support and compassion for yourself and others. This is a time when you can act to transform things in ways that might seem impossible. The impossible can be done (as you will read in these pages) as it has so often been done before.

I wish you well in your studies in this book, your activities, and life itself. Remember always that your spirit and your soul — your personality as you know it without all the slings and arrows and experiences you've suffered through in this life, the lack of knowledge you've endured, all the answers you've wanted, and all your needs that went unfulfilled — are immortal. Remember that your spirit and your soul are immortal. So if it's not in this life, you will know, experience, or have all you need in other lives, and it will all happen in the most benevolent way for you.

Good life.

CHAPTER ONE

Bring Life Back to Your Drinking Water

Howannie

June 9, 2014

This is Howannie. You would spell it H-O-W-A-N-N-I-E.

Welcome.

It's two different meanings in your language. It means either Cloud Woman or literally "from the clouds." So you want to do a book. What do you want to do it on?

Well, there's more energy coming in every day. People are changing. We're in a difficult time right now on Earth as we attempt to return to our natural selves and be benevolent. We would like advice on how to live, practical information, on ways to survive and thrive and awaken at this time on Earth. Isis said that 95 percent of the wisdom gained by ancient peoples has been lost due to various situations: wars, lack of students, the teachers dying before teaching someone, accidents, and so on.

That's good. That's a practical book. Of course, you will have to recognize certain basics — that everything is alive and everything has feelings, whether you see and feel them or not.

Yes.

How Howannie Was Named

How about an individual subject question? It's a good overview, what you said, but I need to have something specific.

First, can we talk a little bit about you?

I was born on Earth during a transitional stage of the planet. There were not many people living on Earth then, human beings, you understand, perhaps fewer than a thousand. We did not consider our-selves a tribe. We were just the people, meaning human beings, yes?

To live, we had to pay attention to life around us. We also had to wel-come life from above us. In those times, there were many visitors coming to the planet with lightships and sometimes solid ships — all manner of vehicles. Some were too big to set down on the earth. Others were so small that they would be unnoticed. You could walk right past them and think it was just a stone or something. And there are in-between sizes. I think if it had not been for these friends from above, human beings might not have survived on the planet.

Now, as to why I was called that name: When I was born to my mother, the first thing I did (I don't remember doing this, but they told me I did) was flip over on my back, open my eyes, and look straight up at the clouds. Even though they picked me up and cleaned me off and so on, I kept want-ing to look up at the sky. There were beautiful clouds on that day, big puffy clouds. It was a beautiful day with clear air. So that's how I got my name.

What came to pass was that I seemed to have an ability to communi-cate with all visitors from afar who visited Earth then, and they did not have to use devices. Of course, they didn't know that at first and used their devices, but then I started talking. I was about three years old then, I think. I commented on things they were thinking but not saying. That's when they shut off their devices, and we conversed.

It was what you call telepathic. I could understand not only what they were thinking but also what they were feeling. Often I was able to reassure my people that things were safer than they seemed, that the nonhuman life forms, while sometimes frightening looking, were actu-ally very friendly and were frightening in appearance only. So they did not have to worry.

To show them, I would walk — you would say toddle, but I was walk-ing pretty well by three years old — over to, say, a lion or a big tiger. The being would nod or lie down, and I would hug that being. They had big ears, or I'd stroke their teeth. They had big teeth. Then the beings, wher-ever they were from, would smile and feel comfortable on the planet.

So it is with children, you know, that there is a — how can we say? — a feeling of compatibility. These beings — tiger-like beings, lion beings — were actually the same age I was. We had all been on the planet for three years, so we felt a kinship, and I was able to impart that feeling of kinship to the visitors — whoever they were, wherever they came from and at any time. This is how Earth gradually came to be identified (what you call Earth now) as Eden, which is closer to the meaning of the intention of this planet.

I think you have been told that the intention of this planet was to be a host to the Explorer Race and all that you are doing here. But the planet had her own intention, which was to welcome all the life that could survive and thrive on Earth, on Eden. That's why she came into existence. She liked that, so she welcomed the big, the small. It didn't make any difference.

Now, you are thinking, "How long ago was this?" It's a little hard to factor it in your years now, but I'm going to give you something you can understand. It was about 400,000 years ago. Understand that it doesn't even compute in your own time because 400,000 years ago according to the time you're in now could have been 400 years ago. I'm saying 400,000 years ago so that you can get a mental idea, even though the time moving back (even in a linear way with certain flexibilities) has nothing to be built in and would be different.

You were one of the first groups of humans that came to the planet, then?

I cannot be certain we were the first, but we were early.

Do you have a memory of where you come from? Were you looking up at the sky as if you were from some place there?

It wasn't about remembering. When you come to such a place, you would describe it as heaven on Earth. I think that when some people die, they want to see what heaven on Earth would be like. It was like that. All life forms got along with all other life forms, and when it was necessary to consume another life form, one would wait for volunteers. But humans did not eat life forms in those times. We ate plants, like that. At those times with my people, we did not eat other life forms. Later generations started eating water beings but not land beings. I think when it came to the time when people started eating land beings, my people were already gone from the planet.

Did you incarnate more than once?

No. But I was born at the time when all life got along well, so this must be why I am here speaking to you now, because I understand how it can be done. Keep in mind that even though I could do this, everybody else I knew in my people also got along with all the other forms of life.

It wasn't just something I could do to help them get along. They already got along. The only thing that was different was that when visitors came from other planets, I was able to help them understand Eden. I think it's important to make that clear.

That's beautiful. Have you incarnated in other places many times since then?

No. I stayed on Earth as a spirit and walk among you here, among life forms. Not so much with human beings now, but sometimes with children. When they are very young, they see me in different forms of garb, but the one you would recognize is a Native American woman. I've stayed on Earth all this time, but most of the time, I'm not with human beings. I'm with the nonhumans because they are still the same as they were in Eden. There's no difference except sometimes they do things that are extreme in reaction to what is going on around them. Generally, when they are in their own company and human beings are not nearby or not a threat, they are exactly the same as they were in Eden. So I am there.

You Must Feel Peace to Impart It

How can you advise us to get back to where we started?

It will all be in the question. I understand you are a good questioner. Perhaps you can form questions, and I will share based only on that. It is a traditional thing with shamanic, mystical people that one only teaches what the questioner asks. That means the questioner is open to learning. That's why it works that way. If the questioner hasn't asked something, then we're sharing knowledge or experience or our life stories and so on. When it comes to asking questions, the questioner must be interested, and then we are open to whatever wisdom can be imparted.

But I feel that's not fair to the readers. I might be totally oblivious and unaware of something that they need to know, and I can't ask if I don't know it exists.

Right. Then you know how to do that. You can speak on this machine, this computer thing, to your readers. Ask them what they want to know. Tell me their responses. You don't have to say too much: "We're making a book, and if you could speak to a wise woman spirit and mystical person," (however you want to describe me, but don't give my name at this time), "what would you ask?" Then you might not ask exactly what they asked, but you'll get an idea what they want or need to know. Go to your readers and ask them.

That's a very good idea. Okay. So even though you don't interact that much with humans now, you're aware of everything — the difficulties we face and where we are in our awakening, right?

I don't follow everything you do, but I have a general knowledge of what you are doing. You might wonder how that is possible. Usually when I visit human beings, it's only little children who see me and are happy and comfortable with that. But I hear about it from the nonhumans. Nonhumans keep an eye on you. You say "animals," but I'm not comfortable with that word. It suggests a separate class of being, and they are the same — you understand? — as good as beings.

Yes. We have talked to many of them. We have a book called Animal Souls Speak *and one called* Plant Souls Speak *[from the Explorer Race series]. Yes. We talk to everybody [laughs]. I guess you are worthy. How can one person now living on Earth make a difference toward peace?*

Yes. You must live it yourself, to begin with. It is not easy to do. The first thing to do is to simplify your life as much as possible so that you have time to focus on the feeling of peace. If you do not have time, it will be difficult to be peaceful. While some people can be fooled, not everyone can, certainly not children — especially very young children. They will know whether you are peaceful or not.

Of course, there are others who try to create the absence of violence, which might not be peace, but it is a step toward that. There are many who work in these ways. Since you asked about peace, I feel that it is good to practice the feeling in yourself. You will have to imagine it since many of you have never been in conditions that were totally at peace.

I recommend practicing this feeling if possible. Give yourself time, as quiet as possible, to relax and be supportive in the feeling of peace. You will not be able to impart it if you cannot be it. At times, you will be able to do this. If you know how to feel peace, you might be able to bring up that feeling when you are in a situation where there is conflict. Spiritual people have done this for thousands of years in your time; focus on their feeling of peace.

Don't send the feeling out. I think people get confused about sending something. That's not what you do. Become peace as a feeling to the greatest degree you can, and it will naturally emanate from you. You say "radiate." It will naturally do that, but don't send it out. If you send it out, you will not feel it as much. You have the responsibility to do something about peace: Feel it yourself. This is not a selfish act because the more you feel it, the more it will radiate. That's what I recommend.

It is a good beginning. Many times, you might be around people who argue. Perhaps you'll be in a public place — let's say an airport — where people often feel unhappy or stressful. There you are, and if you sit near people who are arguing or snapping at each other, then go into that feeling of peace. The more you feel it, the more you will see it radiate in all directions.

It might be interesting to see what happens, but if you are listening (listen only with, as you say, half an ear or maybe just a quarter of an ear), you might notice things calming down. If you notice it, that's fine, but all the while, you feel peaceful because if you start listening, the feeling will go away. That's your responsibility, and it's what I recommend.

The reason I say it's your responsibility is that if you wish to do something about peace, then you will have to claim this peace for yourself: "I am going to do what I can for peace." Of course, many times you will be in a situation where you can create peace some other way, but this is something any individual can do. The older you get and the more conflict you've experienced, the more difficult it might be to get there.

There are many great meditations and ways to meditate. You could learn whatever one you want. It can be religious or philosophical, whatever. Focus on the physical feeling of peace. It's not a thought. It's a physical feeling. That will be your responsibility.

You do not need to say anything. In this way, it is beyond language. You don't have to speak anybody's language. You know when people are arguing even when they are speaking in some other language because you are able to tell when people are angry with each other. So feel peace then. Just feel peace for your own sake and for the sake of others. Feel it physically. That's what I recommend.

Water Contains the Energy of Life

Human beings are 60-some percent water, and obviously we need to replenish water all the time. There are so many other liquids on this planet that people sell to make money. How much water do we need each day to be healthy?

Water is different in your time. It is handled by human beings and machines, so of course it loses its life-giving quality. Water is essential for your body. But in my time, and even still in some places on Earth, at some springs — some, not all — water is life. You've read this many times. But what you don't always understand is that you don't just need it to survive physically. Water has the energy of life within it. It is literally life-giving.

In my time, you didn't need to eat very much because the water not only hydrated your body but also gave you life. Therefore, I cannot say how many glasses but handfuls. Put your hands together, and drink that. It would be maybe, in my time, four to six handfuls a day. You'd have to measure how much it is for you, but in your time, you'd probably need twenty-five handfuls a day because the water does not have much life.

Sometimes you buy bottles or containers of spring water, but even those have been handled a great deal, filtered, as you say, and put in something that water isn't naturally in. Glass would be better, but even that is only occasionally touched by earth, all right — Eden in her natural state.

Water filters through the soil but mostly through rocks in underground springs. The water constantly flows over rocks and minerals and is filtered, yes, but it's more than filtered. I'm going to have to use this word. I don't know another word. It is "inseminated" with life-giving qualities. When it comes to the surface, I cannot guarantee it will be safe because there are so many pollutants in your time. But in some places, perhaps where it comes to the surface, it still has so much life that the water itself would be able to sustain you for a time without food. So I answer your question in terms of the water you drink: at least twenty-five handfuls a day.

How can we compensate for this lack of life? Everything is alive. Can we talk to the water? Can we do anything with the water or to the water? Is there any way to get life back into the water?

Ideally, you'd have a natural stone dish, perhaps carved, or a bowl. It might be possible to use a bowl that has been made by somebody who uses clay, and then it gets hard and is glazed — all of that. It might be possible to use such a bowl, but then you would have to pick out the stones, and if you pick the stones out, you could only pick ones that have volunteered. Do not just pick up a bunch of stones and toss them in the bowl. That won't help you at all. It might make you sick, actually.

It's time-consuming, but this is how to learn. Let's say you walk out on a trail some place, for those of you in the country, and you see a stone, a small stone or something not much bigger than the first knuckle on your thumb. Okay? Something like that. If you have small hands, the knuckles of the first two fingers, to give you an idea, a small stone.

If you see one you like, stop and squat down if you can. I know a lot of you would want to go to a creek, but I don't recommend that at this time. This is how to learn what stone will come with you. Do this on a trail somewhere, maybe. So this small stone, yes, put your finger in your mouth and get a little moisture, and then with your finger or thumb, reach down and touch it to the stone. Then give the stone a little time. It's not a clock time. You give it as much time as feels right. Feelings are everything here, physical feelings. Don't rush the stone. It will take time.

If you need to use the clock, it could take up to fifteen minutes or half an hour. It might be less time than that. After you have introduced yourself (that's how you introduce yourself), ask the stone whether it will come with you. Just ask it out loud, "Will you come with me?" Notice how you feel in your body. If you get a comfortable feeling or warmth, then the stone will perhaps come with you, but that's not the only way to know whether the stone wants to come with you.

Then pick up the stone. Be very careful when you pick it up, all right, so that you see the exact position the stone is in. Stand up to see how you feel in your body. If you feel excited, put the stone down. It's not about excitement. It's about being polite. You are asking a life form to change its life for you. That's a lot. So see how you feel in your body. If you get uncomfortable, put the stone back down in the exact position it was in to the best of your ability. Then if you get a good feeling — warmth, say — that's your second confirmation that the stone will come with you.

If you have a camera with you, and many of you do these days, you will perhaps take a photograph of the stone. If you do not have a camera with you, then make a sketch or take a note of where the stone was because even though the stone will come with you, it might at some point wish to go home. If it wishes to go home, it will want to go back to exactly where it was.

Some stones will be happy to stay with you for four or five years, maybe longer, but other stones will not. They'll want to go back. Obviously, you will want to pick up stones that are possible for you to take back.

Remember, you're asking another life form to change for you. So you are responsible for that life form's happiness. It is not like your child but a helper, someone who will help you feel well. All of the steps in this process must be followed as I'm recommending not because I say so but rather if you want it to work, then I recommend it. Then you go all the way back to your home to get to that bowl.

You'll be feeling other feelings, and you'll be doing other things. Carry the stone some place personal. A pocket over your heart is a possibility, but I don't recommend it at that time because you don't know the stone that well yet. It might be better to have a pocket over your abdomen but not right over where your mother's cord entered your body, not that. That's too personal. Put it somewhere, maybe, just below the bone in a sensitive area where you go from bone to a softer part in your body. Do you know what I mean?

Under the ribcage, you mean, or under the sternum?

In the center of the ribcage. It's right under there. If you have a pocket there or you have a way to keep the stone in a pocket there, that would be a good place, but not where the cord went into your body from your mother. Okay? That's too personal.

Carry the stone with you on the way back to your home. From time to time, stop in that journey, and look at the stone; feel the stone. Ask, "Do you still want to come with me for a time?" You say, "For a time." You don't say how long. It will be up to the stone to say how long. If you still get the good feeling, then the stone comes with you.

Let's say you can't get back to the house right away. Then you can (if you like) wash off the stone. If you're going to wash off the stone, it would be good to use spring water. So acquire some spring water from as close to the area as [possible from where] that stone was. If there is a creek nearby, then some of that water will be sufficient. Make sure you mark it [the container] so that nobody accidentally drinks it [this water]. Then you can rinse off the stone with that.

If there is a creek nearby, you can even rinse off the stone before you leave the area, but always ask the stone's permission. This is a relationship. And if you get the good feeling, then it is all right. Don't just put the stone under tap water when you get back. That will be foreign water to the stone, and the stone will not recognize it. It will be as an insult. All right? The stone will eventually transform that water but not so soon.

I recommend that you do that with at least eight more stones. You want to have at least nine stones. It will take a while. But if you want to put life into water, it will work. So have at least nine stones, and follow that process.

I'm going to jump ahead to having nine stones. So you have the nine stones in the bottom of the bowl. It doesn't have to be a bowl, and it doesn't have to be a big bowl. It can be a container of any size. Do not use a bowl that you will tip up to your lips. Although, it's possible. When you do that, the stones will move around, and when you put the water into the bowl, the stones will probably want to stay in the place you put them.

When you put each stone into the bowl, you might have to move the stone around until you get that good feeling in your body. When you get that good feeling in your body, that's the stone telling you — telling your physical body — that this is exactly the position the stone wants to be in.

It might be good to have a big bowl. You can have the nine stones in that bowl, and you can have more. That's fine. But nine is enough. The reason you may not want to tip the bowl up is that after doing that, you'll have to move all the stones back into position. So if you have a big bowl, that's what you want to do.

Then take tap water, all right. But don't pour it directly into the bowl. Use your hands. Turn on the tap, and fill your hands. Then very gently pour the water into the bowl. You can release it moving through your hands, whatever you want. Obviously, your hands and the stones need to be clean, all right?

If you want to clean the stones, I'm not sure how you're going to go about that. The point is to put life into the water. So I'm not sure how you can clean the stones to make sure they're safe to drink. You might have to ask somebody else about that. It is acceptable to use alcohol because alcohol comes from a natural element, I think, or a natural place.

Don't use anything chemical except for alcohol, 100 percent alcohol. But if there is some water in the alcohol, that may be okay. Use a cotton swab if you want to or a cotton ball, whatever you have. I am not an expert in the waters you drink. Okay? You might need to consult an expert about cleaning the stone. You have to ask the stone's permission before you do that. Every step of the way, you must ask permission. Then, of course, the bowl and the stones in the bowl and so on must be clean.

So drip the water in from your hands, or you can let it run on the side of the bowl if the bowl is slanted and come down to the stones. The reason you don't want to dump it in there is it will move the stones around. Be careful the stones don't move too much. Don't put anything in the bowl that will cause them to roll.

It would be best that the bowl is not glazed, but most likely, it will be. Leave the water in the bowl for about twenty minutes. It doesn't take long. Say, "I'm asking that you speak to the stones." I'll have to get the exact words. You really want to say something that sounds like it flows in your language. So you would say out loud, or whisper if you like, "I am asking, stones, that you share your life-giving quality with this water."

Then wait about twenty minutes. Fifteen minutes might be okay, but twenty minutes is the sort of time you can wait or just until you feel good or can get back to the bowl. After that, see how you feel. Look at the bowl, and note how your body feels. Look at the water to see how your physical body feels. If you get a good feeling, then make a cup with your hands. Put your hands together, you understand? Or put your hands (clean of course) in the water, and make a cup out of them. Pull it up, and drink the water from your hands. That's how you put life into water, and you're done.

That's beautiful. The same stones will transform the water over and over again?

Yes. But there will probably be a time that it would be good, after about six months, to ask. When there's no water in the bowl or maybe just a little bit at the bottom because it has evaporated, again you touch your finger to your mouth and then touch the stones individually. Otherwise, you're talking to them all.

You will have to touch that in your mouth and touch the stones individually and then ask, "Are you ready to go home?" Or you can ask, "Will you stay longer?" If they all will stay with you longer, then you can continue. You might wish to clean the stones again. I don't know what you will use. If you don't need to do that and it's just you drinking the water, maybe you don't need to do that.

What about the people who live in a city who can't just go out and find stones?

I do not have a solution for that. I am telling you what you can do that I know will work. I don't have the solution for that.

What is wrong that you won't be able to talk again?

It is a problem with the channel physically. It might be me. We will see in the next day or so. If it is not me, then we will talk again, but if it is me — and it could be — then we will not be able to talk again. So I will have to stop now.

Well, I hope it works out so that we can talk again. Thank you very much.

Yes. Goodbye.

Goodbye.

CHAPTER TWO

Look to Plants and Animals for Health and Wellness Clues

Min

July 9, 2014

Welcome.

Thank you. Question?

It seems that we have lost the traditional wisdom that people knew on this planet about how to live benevolently, and we would like to recover it. What's the most important wisdom that humans have lost that would allow them to live comfortably and benevolently now?

A sense of fellowship with every human being, every animal, and every plant. Such awareness allows for community of all living things. When there is such community, answers to questions, spoken or unspoken, are often readily available just by observing life around you. If the answer is not available through your fellow humans, perhaps plants or animals or even cloud patterns might give you an inspiration by what they do so that you might try something that could work. You may have to build on it, but sometimes just a simple motion by animals or by the way a plant blooms and stimulates your senses or the shapes in the clouds will inspire the answer you need.

This sense of community is not something that is difficult to recapture. It is something that is available now, and there is no need to feel that it is lost. It is readily available and still being practiced in many places. It is true that in many places it is not, so the key is to look past your differences and to understand that the foundation of all life is very similar not just because the material, the matter, that you are made up of is the same — light, soul, spirit, yes, and Mother Earth, yes — but also the nature of life is not as complicated as it seems. When you set aside technology and perceived differences, you can find common ground without too much difficulty. That is what I recommend.

Where do people start? Most people live in cities and urban areas nowadays.

That is your perception because that is where you live. You can start by being friendly, in a safe way for you, with your neighbors. You can start by considering the possibility that fear is something you have learned, but love, happiness, and friendship are things you are born with. So find something you can all laugh about. Find something that you all feel good about, and build on that.

The changes we need to make have to begin with each person. We have talked about being optimistic, about being empathetic, about being benevolent. But when you look out at the planet now, that doesn't seem to be working.

It is working. When you talk about things like that, it goes out to the individual person, and each one very often puts it into his or her life. If you say it doesn't seem to be working, you're watching too much news. You are reading too much news. The purveyors of news find that it is to their benefit to spread around that which is dramatic even as other purveyors spread around news that is more communal. I am not saying there are not dramas that need to be reported, such as the weather, for instance. But I recommend you read different news. You don't have to stop reading what you read now, but I recommend you start to read news that is communal, that is neighborly, and that reports the daily affairs of people's lives that are not as awful as you might think when you hear about dramas elsewhere. If you hear about such things, then you can say your prayers in whatever form you use in hopes of bringing about something better.

Plant Community Gardens to Improve Food Sources

With the state of our food right now, especially wheat and other genetically modified foods [1] and the use of growth hormones, how do you recommend we get our food supplies, given that most people can't go out and plant a garden? How do we deal with the condition of the food now on the planet?

Many people who can plant gardens are not. Sometimes during difficult or hard times or in times of great need, people who hadn't considered

---

1.   In 2014, agriculture studies found genetically modified wheat in crops in Oregon and Montana. See http://www.npr.org/sections/thesalt/2014/09/26/351785294/gmo-wheat-investigation-closed-but-another-one-opens.

planting a garden try it, and very often friends and neighbors give advice according to their experience, and everybody learns together. I recommend planting gardens — yes I do. Even if you have only a couple of containers on your porch, you might be able to grow something. Start that way. Don't automatically assume the worst. Typically, things are not as complicated as they seem. Understand that it is important not to see these experiments in food crops as hostile. I am not saying such foods are good for you or for life; they are an aberration. However, the intention is to create as much food as possible, given conditions that are not optimal. That was the original intention. Granted, that has been distorted by competition and its practice, but I think for starters that if every other house (to say nothing of every house) in your neighborhood started a garden in the backyard that took half the yard, you would find that the children would want to participate. You might have to keep the dog out of the garden, but the children might want to take part because they are in school and are learning, and the idea of doing their learning might be beneficial. Don't make it complicated.

I am not saying anything here, so far at least, that is something you don't know. It doesn't have to be sweeping change. Don't concentrate on the enemy who is doing "this" or "that." Focus on what you can do. When your crops come in, be sure to share them. It would be best if neighbors planted different things or at different times, or both, so that everybody can have a share in what might be available and will grow in your area.

Many people want to live benevolent, comfortable lives of service. How can we, in these busy times when everyone works and rushes around, be of service to others at the same time? Is there anything in your experience in the traditional ways that would help us be of more service to others while still meeting our responsibilities and obligations?

You understand that I know almost nothing about your times. I am, you would say, a medicine woman from maybe 700 years ago in your time. I only have a glimmer of what your time is like, not the vast wisdom you seem to want.

Plants and Animals Can Guide You

May I ask where you lived when you were a medicine woman? Was that your last life?

I am alive in my own time.

You are! Where on the planet?

We don't have a where as a name. It is land, and I am looking up at the mountains now. It is springtime, and I am looking up because this is the process that can be used for such communication. I am watching the clouds in the sky pass the mountain, and the land is flat.

You don't know what part of the planet you are on?

I will pull back and see whether I can tell. You would call it North America. You might also call it Canada.

Are you the medicine woman for a tribe?

No, I am a medicine woman who travels with a small group and teaches, as needed, the value of understanding the plants and the animals and that the plants and animals have their own lives. People might have questions — and questions in our time are largely based on survival or well-being or how to feel better after an injury, like that. If no one has an answer, you can ask for an answer from the sky or an animal or a plant. You might do that either for someone who needs it or for yourself to see what any animal — it could be a beetle, it could be a deer, and if you are near the water, it could be a water being — might do that would inspire you to know what you need to do. In this way, it is the other being's job, you might say (though they are there to live as well as possible, and in that sense, everyone's job to do something that involves his or her own life).

Other beings cannot live your life; they cannot tell you what to do in your life because they are not living your life. But they might do something that is a little different for them. They might turn "this way" or "that way," a way that they wouldn't normally turn, because for some reason it might inspire you. They might even do something that would cause you to laugh and in that moment of laughter, lift your spirit and your feelings, and you might get an idea of what to do. That's what I remind people: It is not the animal's job to stop being an animal and to become a human. They must be who they are. It is your job to not only interact with them in a benevolent way, as you say, but also let them be who they are and be inspired in what you need or even just want to know from how they act. Such a way of interacting with them can bring about peace and knowledge, and when practiced for a time, wisdom might even follow.

I watch where I put my feet so that I don't step on anybody, if it is possible. The land is somewhat dry at this time of year, so it is easier to see the places where I put my feet. It is easier to see when there is motion and then not step there. If there is a lot of motion but it is safe for me, then I might expand my being, meaning become more present to myself, and this sends out a signal that someone is coming. I do so in a way that is friendly and kind so that all beings, whether they are very small (many-leggeds, for instance) or a little bigger (maybe four-leggeds or for that matter, two-leggeds), who are perceptive and who feel safe and even happy that someone is coming. This is a good thing.

What a wonderful way to live. Were you trained from childhood? How old are you?

I am about two-thirds of the way through my life, but in the terms of your question (a moment, because we don't do what you do with years; we don't think about it), I am, what you would say, almost but not quite twenty-seven.

So your lifespan is under forty years?

That is very long. I don't think I will live that long. You know, not living that long is not so bad. I have heard of someone who lived a long time and had long white hair and a lot of pain. That doesn't happen to most people I know.

So how does it work for your people? Does death come through an illness or an accident or some other event?

I can't speak for everybody. For most of the people I am aware of who have died, it has been something unexpected, such as an injury that doesn't get better. It usually isn't something long and lingering.

Are the people you interact with at peace? Are there wars or anything like that? Is survival about getting enough food and water and a safe place to live?

Well, they are not all at peace. They are human beings, as you would say. Sometimes they get angry or upset, so there is that. If I see someone who is angry or upset, I don't go near that person.

Do you understand how to heal with plants?

Yes, I understand a little bit. We don't have that many plants around at this time, and I do not pick the plants. If someone nearby needs care and there are plants in the area that can help — and there are not too many plants right now because of the time of year, the dry time — then I will go to the plant and just breathe in and out with it, just looking at it first. If I can breathe with it and I get a good feeling, then yes. If I don't get a good feeling, then the plant is tired and is doing its best to survive and cannot share its beingness with me. Eventually I might find one that can, and then I breathe in and out while I look at the plant. When I feel a lot of that plant's energy in me, I walk over to the person and hold my hand, usually my right hand, with my palm facing the part of the body that doesn't feel well, and I breathe toward the person. I remember the plant, close my eyes, and breathe that memory of the plant. Then as I breathe out with my hand over the person, I will — it's hard to describe, but it is as if the memory of the plant is radiated toward the part of the body that is not well. Sometimes that helps. If the person is meant to live, then this often helps. If the person is not meant to live, then it doesn't help, or something else might help them more, but this is what I have to offer.

Seasonal Wanderings

Do you travel around from one group to another in a regular way, or do you feel a need and go other places? How do you decide where to go in your travels?

I can't wander far. I don't know how many miles, as you would say. There are only three encampments that I know about, and I walk between them. The advantage of the three, even though they are spread out, is that each is within a day's walk, no more than that. Then I stay there for as long as I am needed or if they want me to stay for some reason. I don't usually stay for too long. It is good to go to the different ones because you never know when you are needed.

How long have you been doing this?

Using your years as much as I can understand them, when I was working with my teacher, I began traveling with her when I was seven years old. That might seem to be very young for a child to be away from her mother, but it was all right in this case because my teacher was my grandmother. So when my mother couldn't go with us, and often she couldn't because there were other children to consider, I would go with Grandmother. When I came back, I had lots of stories to tell my mother and my brothers and sisters. Some things I wouldn't tell because Grandmother would say, "Now, that's a secret just for us." When she would say that, I knew that it was not something to share with others. I never asked her why — you never ask your teacher why — you just know your teacher is giving you this wisdom. I traveled with my teacher until I was about thirteen, and then she moved into the beyond. After that, I traveled on my own.

Do you have any means of transport, such as horses?

We walk. That is our means.

Are these encampments permanent? Do your people plant food and hunt there?

The encampments stay there except when the cold comes. Then we go to a place that is warm. I cannot explain why this place is warm, but the people from the encampments go there. It is a cave at the foot of a mountain, and it stays warm all year. It is very big, and one has to go a ways in there — not too far — and it is comfortable. It is not what you would call hot, but it is warm and comfortable and very, very big. Of course, it is not very bright, but after a while, your eyes get used to it.

Altogether the encampments, at the current time, have about eighty-seven human beings, and this place can accommodate us. It has lots of clean, fresh water, and there is — this is hard to describe — something in the cave that is like food. We can eat it. It is a little odd looking, but it serves us well. I don't know what you would call it. It grows on the walls, and it is kind of crumbly. At first, we were afraid to eat it, but I saw one of the animals come in and nibble at it, and then she looked at me, nibbled at it more, and looked at me again. I had with me something that would make me feel better if the cave food wasn't meant for humans, so I ate a little bit of it and was all right. It turned out that we could eat a little bit of it, and that was enough. It was not exactly like a mushroom, but it tasted like a mushroom.

Are the walls of the cave damp?

No, but nearby there are walls that are damp, so perhaps it is damp behind that wall. It is a big wall.

Maybe there is a hot spring back there that gives you warmth.

When the cold goes away, the food rebuilds itself on the cave wall, so there is no danger of us eating it all.

Amazing. So for all your life, you have gone there every winter?

Yes.

The Joy of Passing on Knowledge

Are you married?

What is that?

Do you have a mate?

Oh, a mate. Yes, I had one, and I had two children, but neither of them survived. It is possible another mate could happen, but it hasn't happened yet.

What are the greatest joys you get from the life you are living?

Teaching the youngsters in the ways of the knowledge. I have one now coming along, and I think pretty soon she will be old enough to travel with me if her mother says it is all right. Her mother is my sister.

Does this ability run in your family?

Yes. I think maybe that is not unusual. It is not just the sensitivity and the ability but also the knowledge. I do not know whether doctors, as you say, are healing in those ways in your time. Perhaps they are.

What are some of the other ways you heal in your time?

I shared that with you already.

Yes, the plants, but are there other things you do?

Plants. What else would there be? It is what I said. There is nothing else. That is what I do.

The knowledge of what plant to go to for what purpose is the important part, and that is what your grandmother taught you, is that right?

Yes.

Do you ever get inspiration to use a plant that she didn't teach you about or to use a plant for a new purpose?

No. I use what she taught me because I know that it is safe. At times, others have suffered to get such knowledge because when you don't know, you don't understand the language of the plants or the animals or the clouds in the sky. You have to learn the languages first, and others who came before me learned the languages. Sometimes they didn't survive because they didn't know or they made mistakes. Now that is known in my time, so why would I want to go against that?

But you said that there are so few plants.

It is not that there are so few plants; it is that this is the dry time.

So in the time when there are more plants, do you cut some and save them for the dry season, or do you only work with breathing with live plants?

I never cut anything. Plants do not say, "Destroy me. Hurt me." They, like you, want to live and be whole, complete, and exist as well as possible.

How many plants would you say you work with or that you know the healing qualities they possess?

Sixty-seven.

But no one writes that down, and we wouldn't know the names you call the plants, and you don't have cameras to take pictures of them. You recognize them when you see them, right?

I recognize them, yes. And I don't need any of those things, whatever they are, that you are talking about. I have knowledge and memory. I have my senses, and I pass that on to the students. If one or two students are very good at it and want to know, then I will travel with them — one is for sure, and another one, maybe.

Are you the only medicine woman in this group of eighty-seven, or are there more?

I'm it. It would be good if there were more than one, so I am hopeful that the other child will become interested too, but if not, at least there is one to pass the knowledge on to. Some things can be shared with people, but other things are known only to the person who wants to do the work. That is what my grandmother told me.

Do you ask for the rain or the sun? Do you work with the elements?

No, someone else does that, a man. It doesn't have to be a man; it just happens to be. I have heard that a woman did it once, but the student eventually came to be a male, and now it is a man. He is open to teaching a girl child. In that case, he would have to have a young woman come along because, you know [laughs], men have these urges.

A chaperone, right. That would seem to make the process more difficult.

Yes. It wouldn't be more difficult. It would just have to be done that way.

You know of sixty-seven healing energies. Have you used them all in the time you have been the medicine woman?

No. I have used about sixteen, but I have knowledge of the others.

So no one has developed the disease or illness or discomfort that calls for those others?

No, and that is a good thing. But it does tell you what you can do. If there is somebody who has a special affinity, a special feeling, for plants and animals or maybe even for helping animals like that, he or she can do what I do. With permission from the plant: Breathe in and out with the plant and then hold his or her hand the way I described. Maybe someone in your time is already doing it. You might not know about it, but my hope is that it is already being done. In that case, find that person, and ask him or her to teach you.

This turned out wonderfully well. Do you have the ability to look beyond the life you are in? Can you tell whether you came back to Earth in another time or place?

I do not know about these things. I have found that this job requires me to be present in my time. The more present I am, the more I can help. Grandmother taught me that daydreaming is okay when you are a child, but when you are a medicine woman, it is best to be present,. This way, you can tell when someone is experiencing something that is not safe or is coming into something that will not feel well, and in that case, you can find the plant. When you find it, you can do what I taught you. Then you can hold your hand over the person in the place where he or she needs it, and perhaps that person will not have that thing happen, be it an accident, a disease, or something else unknown. Maybe it won't happen, and that would be good. To do that, you must be in your self, be in your beingness, and you must be aware. You must be present, and in this way, you cannot daydream. When you sleep, you can have all of the dreams you want. I think that is enough for today. If you wish to talk to me again, you can ask for Min. That is the only part of my name that I can share.

Okay, Min from Canada. You have been wonderful. Thank you very much.

I am from there, but we do not call it that. If you ask for "Min from Canada," you won't find me. Just say Min.

All right, thank you very much. Good life.

May you have the most bountiful and benevolent good life.

Thank you.

CHAPTER THREE

Share Your Healing Wisdom with Others

A Shaman

July 14, 2014

We would like to speak to a shaman, alive or in spirit, who can bring us some of the traditional wisdom that has been lost as to how to live benevolently and healthily and how shamans healed the people in their groups on the planet.

Thank you. Greetings.

Greetings.

You are living in artificial times, eh?

Yes.

We are living, my people, in the early days of human population on Earth, as you say, about 40,000 years ago in your time, and there are not a lot of people. The reason I'm able to speak to you is from awareness. It's all my people can do to survive, and I don't want to distract the being I guide from anything he needs to do to help these people to live. If your people today saw him doing what he does for them, you would probably think he is crazy. The reason I bring this up is that a lot of people in your time are inspired to bring back the skills of times past. Sometimes you'll see children doing things like this that you describe in your book.

I'll describe what the person I guide is doing. Right now, he's about middle-aged for his people, which means he's about seventeen years old. He spends most of his waking time (when he isn't helping to cure any maladies) crawling around in the dirt not unlike a child would do to play.

When he walks to a place where the energy feels right to him, he'll hunker down. He won't put his knees on the ground right away. He'll turn around (he's very flexible), rotating to his left, which feels right, in a very slow circle. When he feels he's in the right direction, he'll get down on all fours, as you say. But he won't put his hands on the ground. He only gets his elbows and his knees down on the ground. He gets as much of his body down on the ground as possible without touching the main part of his body because he uses that to sense what he is and isn't looking for.

He'll crawl on the ground, and he'll look very closely at the dirt or the sand or whatever is there. Little stones, perhaps. If something feels right to him, he'll touch it. Then he'll very lightly — because he knows to be careful — taste it, but only very slightly. If it feels good to taste, if it feels good to touch, and even if it doesn't exactly look good but as long as it looks okay at least, then he'll pick it up. Perhaps it is a stone. He'll pick it up, and he'll hold it up to the top of his head and gradually move it down to slightly below his navel, what you say is the belly button, not much farther than that.

If it feels good all those ways and all those touchings, then he'll put it in a little pouch he has. It's an animal skin pouch. He has it tied to something that is also tied around his waist with an animal skin like a cord, and then he'll continue. He'll do that every day. Over time, he has gathered about thirteen little piles of dirt, which he keeps very carefully in those little pouches, and about fifteen stones so far. Sometimes it has to do with how the dirt smells, how the dirt feels, or how the dirt tastes. He only tastes it if it feels right to taste.

When he tastes it, he'll know how it can be used. This skill has allowed him to serve a great many illnesses, meaning to cure them for others. For example, sometimes people in your time get something you call arthritis. This is rare in his time, but they still might get it. They get it in their knees, for example. Then he'll have the person lie on his or her stomach, and he will apply this dirt that he acquired to the back of the person's knee where it's flexible. That's the most important part, the flexing part.

Anyway, he knows to put the dirt there. He'll rub it in very lightly there, and the person will lie there with that. He'll usually apply it like that three days in a row, essentially just rubbing enough so that it stays there. The person won't brush it off afterward, and generally speaking, that will work.

When he puts it on, he sings a little bit. It's hard to describe what he's singing because it's not about the tune. It's about the sounds he makes. He has learned this from his teacher. The teacher before him did not do the dirt thing and did not do the stone thing that I'm describing to you. He recognized that talent in the student. The teacher before just did the singing thing. This is how the knowledge grows over time, you see. It grows. This is really how people accumulate skills, so I wanted to give you an example.

I'm not saying that people in your time should do this because in your time, I'm concerned that the dirt is not as clean as it once was. There are many people, and there are fewer nonhuman beings, so there is that. That's actually a problem that a great deal of things are in places they're not supposed to be. You understand?

Yes, pollution.

Yes, that's it. So to sing a song — the singing, the words — know that sometimes with certain types of healing, it might be the tones. Very often, it is the words that do not have to be words in your language. It might just be sounds, you say. Sometimes people, I think, are taught that making tones, just sounds, is enough. But there are things that sound a bit like words. Maybe they sound like words from another language, but it's not a language you know, and it's not a language anybody else you know knows. Maybe no one's ever heard of it, but the thing to check is to see whether it works, it helps people.

Remember always that it's about helping people or sometimes helping animals, if you ever see a farm or even pets. I'm going into this because in your time, children are born with some of these old skills, and that's why I feel that this book is very important. Other things have been touched on at times, and some things might get repeated, but I do not know what you know.

I will say, so you know who I am, that I am the one who taught this middle-aged seventeen-year-old. I taught his teacher. I am the spirit of that being. I linger close and inspire the seventeen-year-old, the ground seeker, you might say. I inspire him in his dreams.

People in those days knew how very important dreams are as a place of teaching. Dreams are more pure in those times because people don't tell each other scary stories. They would never do that. It's one thing to tell a story that's a warning — watch out for "this" or watch out for "that."

That's real, you know: Be careful of "this or that" animal, or don't touch "that" plant or something. People don't entertain or frighten others just for the sake of it, and there are no entertainments that do that, either.

So dreaming is very pure. What you experience in your dream is at the very least 85 percent teaching from spirits, guides, and others like that, and some of it is just recollection. You visit the spirits of those who passed over sometimes, maybe grandfather or grandmother or uncle or auntie or brother or sister, who knows. Mom or dad, it's hard to say mother and father, say, formally.

Ongoing Education

Where on the planet did your student live, and where did you live when you were in a body?

The very far south in what you call South America. Not quite as far south as you can go, but almost. If you go down the west side of South America, around there. I don't know the name, so that's the best I can tell you.

By the beach, by the water, or in the high mountains?

It's not by the sea, but you could walk to the sea in about a day if you wanted to. It was problematic because you had to be near fresh water. You always have to be near fresh water. But you could go up to the high places and see the ocean.

How many people were in your group?

It varied. I think the largest it ever became was about forty-seven.

So you were the medicine man or the healer? What did you call yourself?

We don't have titles.

Were you the only one who was the healer for the people?

No, we always try to have at least two because somebody could die, and then what happens? Even the very young who are just beginning to learn teach somebody younger than they are, so the teaching is constant. Even if someone shows a little bit of interest, the person is taught. Eventually, you might (if everyone survives for a while) find that some people are better at it or they like it, so they are taught more. But the teaching is ongoing, just like teaching to hunt or to fish, you would say. We consider that hunting. It's ongoing, the skills there. All the skills for life to keep you healthy and happy, if you like — well fed, sheltered, all of that — are taught all the time to everyone, even babies. Mothers sing to them, you know. Or they sort of stroke them gently and sing to them. I can't really describe it. It's not exactly a language, but it's a song expressing feelings or a picture in a mother's mind or memory.

Were you taught how to heal with the dirt from the land by your teacher?

No, the seventeen-year-old was. You wonder why I'm not saying a name; it's because people didn't have names. We didn't need them. So, no, that method of healing is completely unique. That's entirely new. No one had ever done that in that group that I'm aware of.

He figured it out for himself?

He didn't figure it out. It came to him. It wasn't a thought. Thought is not a factor so much. It's instinct. When he started doing it, nobody stopped him. I looked after him, seeing, you know, watching. The elders watched him so that he wouldn't get in trouble. He would just play in the dirt like a child. But he was older. He had shown signs of being interested in learning the old ways of healing. This is something he developed on his own, and it will be one of those things that is passed on. It's already being passed on. I didn't do that at all.

What did you do?

I learned a bit about the plants nearby, what was not safe and what was safe. What you couldn't eat and what you could eat. I watched the animals, of course, but you can't always tell. Sometimes animals can eat something that people don't do so well with, so you have to take a chance. Anybody who works with plants is a kind of person who is willing to take a chance, and you have to begin with very tiny amounts. If the tiniest amount makes you feel bad, then you know that part of that plant is not safe to eat. So I was primarily focused in what's safe to eat and what isn't.

But you had a teacher who taught you some of that?

My teacher taught me where the water was safe and where it wasn't. People think in your time that if the water is safe to drink, then it's safe. But in our time, it's not just whether the water is clear and clean, which for the most part mountain streams are, but how the water feels. If the water is turbulent and full of life, that is good. But if the water is still and not so full of life or even if the water is doing something — maybe going around and around in the same space — sometimes that water is safe to drink, but other times it isn't. So it's all about feelings — how did this feel? — and every day it changes. You don't find a place that always feels good in the water. You find a place that feels good that day or that time.

The water specialist, you might say, is the person who finds out where the water is safe to drink that day. Of course, you watch what the animals do because when it comes to water, you can be pretty sure that the animals and the people will drink the same water safely. So we would do that. There was also an agreement with the humans, all right? If animals were drinking water, they would never be harmed or hunted during those times because they would be showing the people, the humans, where the water was safe to drink. It was a safe passage time, and always they would be honored. You would not do harm to them. You would demonstrate that you love them without touching them, in whatever way was the way your people did. So it was very important to find that. The water person would be busy every day.

Now, that was you.

I learned that from my teacher.

But with the plants, you were interested enough to learn on your own. No one taught you that.

I can't say that. Somebody else did. It was one of those skills known by others but not about the plants I was checking. No one had checked the plants around the water. They hadn't done that, but since I was around the water frequently, I thought I would explore the plants there too.

I knew that my job was very important. When I checked to see what could be eaten and what couldn't, I was extremely careful because even though there were a few others who had skills with the water, I was the most skilled at that time. Everyone knew that each person was very important because whatever he or she had learned and was doing or whatever that person was learning was important for the people to survive and live well and live as long as possible. All people knew they were important, so there was no doubt about that.

So you found new plants that your people could eat?

I found one. I don't think it exists in your time.

Specialties and Responsibilities

Who did you teach the water specialist skills to?

I taught that to my students.

To the student who taught the songs to the seventeen-year-old?

Everybody learns different things. You do what you do.

You had several students?

It's everybody. You teach anybody, whoever is there. You learn and you teach the same day. You learn and you teach. You make sure that you're teaching something that you know yourself, but you learn and teach whoever will listen, which essentially would be anybody. Whoever wasn't doing what needed to be done in that moment could listen, and people would listen. It was a way of keeping the skills alive because you never knew who was going to have a problem or die, could run into an animal that, you know, would kill him or her.

When someone died, there was someone to carry on the water skills?

You couldn't have the skills die because if the skills died, then you'd have to start all over again, you see?

So when you leave the planet, when you leave your body, then you have someone trained in water and also the one you taught the singing.

As well as the plants. You might have one skill and teach twenty people. Some people will retain it, and some people won't because they're learning other things all the time from everybody else. Everybody teaches everything they know all the time.

To everybody.

Yes, to whomever will listen or whomever can. It's not a matter of being bored. These are all survival skills. You want to survive. You want your family and everyone else to survive. This is like a family. Everybody wants everybody to survive and live well. So all people learned as much as they could learn all the time. Usually, there was one or more things you were good at. But you would have some knowledge about other things, so the knowledge would not die out. Do you understand now?

Now I understand. Okay, so you had provided the teaching so that when you left the body, someone or several people were able to carry on and work with the water and the plants and the singing.

Oh, the plants person, the specialist, simply added that to his or her knowledge.

Right. Then that person taught others?

Yes.

Group Survival

Did you stay in the same place, or did you travel around?

We stayed in the same place. I want to give you an approximate area.

We stayed within maybe — it depends because it wasn't a square or a circle or a shape but generally speaking — a square mile to three square miles but not all of that space, okay?

For food, you found plenty of plants in the area? You didn't plant anything, did you?

No, we hunted, and we gathered.

Then you fished.

Absolutely, but never any more than we needed. The changes in the weather were acceptable, so it was warm enough.

So you didn't have a cold winter, then?

At that time, where we were was warm enough. It may have changed. I don't know.

So you never met another group of beings like yourselves, or did you?

They'd have to be traveling by, and no one traveled by.

So all your life, you saw those forty to forty-seven people but never anyone else?

It wasn't that. Forty-seven was the largest number there ever was. It wasn't during my time, though. I don't think there were more than thirty-five during my time, and that was just for a short time. But it got down to about thirteen at one point, and we were a little nervous. It happens.

No one ever struck out across the area, no one ever explored to see whether there was anybody else out there or looked to find a trading trail or any other encampment or anything?

You are thinking like a person of your time, and of course that makes sense with your work. Keep in mind that the only trails that existed were trails that animals made, and they were not very big. You wouldn't want to meet some of those animals. There were a few people who explored, as you say. Those were the people who never came back. Perhaps they found something, or perhaps something found them. After that happened twice, that was the end. There was no reason to go anywhere, and we felt if there were other human beings out there, we would not reject them. We would be open and welcoming as long as we felt that in them, but nobody came along.

It's completely different when you're in survival every day. You don't wander off some place. You stay with the group because within the group, there is a degree of safety.

Can you look from spirit and see across 40,000 years? Are there any descendants of your people still alive?

I don't wish to say.

How would you deal with broken bones and things that we would consider you needed a medical doctor for?

Very often people died from broken bones, so we were taught to be very careful. Broken bones were very serious. People would generally die from that.

What weapons did your hunters use?

That wasn't my specialty. Sometimes rocks but you need to ask the hunters. That wasn't my skill.

Okay, what would they bring back, what kind of animal?

Something that resembled a deer, sometimes smaller animals, and sometimes animals who got hurt. They had broken bones. If they were recently dead, that would be considered a good thing; they would bring that back. But if they were dead for quite a while, they wouldn't bring that back.

You fished also?

Yes, that was the main source of our food, and then just with our hands.

So what about cloth? Did you weave anything? What did you wear for clothes?

Most people didn't wear clothes because it wasn't really necessary, but at times, animal skins could be used. Nothing was ever wasted.

From your vantage point and spirit now, did you have other lives after that on Earth?

I am still in the form of spirit after my life, so I can't say that I have because I'm still in that form.

You're at the time 40,000 years ago?

How could I know your times? I am in the form of spirit. I was and am. When I died, when my body died, I went into spirit, but I lingered. I'm still in that form, so if you're asking whether I've had any more born-into-a-body lives since then, I haven't.

So you've been in spirit for 40,000 years and still on Earth?

Yes.

Who do you interact with?

I can't say.

But you interact and teach now, or do you inspire beings?

Right. I teach a little bit.

Visitors and Lightships

It's a long time ago. That's an area that had visitations from other planets. Did you ever see or interact with beings who were not born on Earth?

You mean the people in the lightships? Yes, that's what they called their vehicles, the lightships. They would visit with some regularity.

They could not give you anything to aid your life?

Why would we want that? What they had aided their lives. How could it possibly aid us? Well, they had some pretty neat toys, and they were for their civilization. We would sing songs, maybe tell stories a bit, not the way you do. We would sit down and remember something we had seen or done. And they, the visitors, had a way of knowing that. Then one of the visitors would sit down in the same way and remember something he or she had seen or done, and then we would know. It was very nice. Sometimes they had children, and our children played with them. It was nice. It was always just a pleasant visit.

How often did they visit when you were alive?

That happened about seven times when I was alive. That was pretty often.

Did they call themselves anything, or go by any name?

No.

Didn't that seem like a tremendous vast spectrum of knowledge? I mean, from a light-ship to surviving alone there on the ground?

It was very clear to us that if they were there as people like us, they would need every bit of our help to survive. They would be completely helpless. Yes, so we would have to teach them continually. They knew that, and they respected us.

Aha! And they never said that they had seen another encampment or another group over the hill or down around the corner or something like that?

No.

They never mentioned that, and you never asked?

Why would we?

Wow. Well, I'm curious. I would want to know what else was out there.

But you are a person of your time.

Family

It's true that our children were also curious, but we had plenty to show them. So their curiosity was fulfilled. The world that we lived in was teeming — is that your word? — with life. I think your world is different. So a child would not have to go more than a tiny distance, one or two paces, to see something completely new every day.

Like what?

Little creatures moving about, doing things, surviving. Some of them have managed to live on in your time — not with any great ease, I might add. You don't seem to recognize what great teachers they are. I think you called them ants. They are survivors, fortunately. Watch them some time, and you will learn how to live.

Were you male or female in that life? Did you have children?

I was male in that life. Everybody did. Oh, I see what you mean. Everybody's children were everybody else's children. Whichever woman brought life — she was everybody's wife, she was everybody's mother, and she was loved and nurtured. It wasn't like a family separate in your time. There are mother, father, and the children. It wasn't like that. All children were everybody's children. All women giving birth were beloved by everyone. All elders were loved by everyone. It was a family.

I see. So perhaps children didn't know who their biological father was?

Yes, it wasn't important. It was a family.

An extended family. So there was a lot to take care of, then — the children, the mothers giving birth, the elders. There were more people to take care of than there were people to take care of them, right?

No, everybody had skills. Obviously the babies needed to be taken care of. By the time they could stand up and walk around, they were already being taught. Everybody learned everything all the time, and everybody did everything all the time to help everybody live as well as possible.

And since you didn't live that long, the elders were not old and decrepit, so they didn't have to be cared for, right?

To be an elder in those times was, say, thirty-five or forty years old. You felt like you lived a long life. Keep in mind what I said before. People died most often from infection, so think about those times. How easy is it to get an infection in your time, huh? So there wasn't much to support that cure. There was always the ongoing thirst to try to find the right plant so that the infection would not kill and so that broken bones would mend safely. Always that was going on in the search.

Despite all your searching, you never found a plant that would be an aid to infections? You never actually ... ?

I didn't myself because I was looking at the plants and the water. But the plant people were always looking for things to mend wounds that people died from.

Did they find anything?

They found a few things, but they didn't always work. No one ever found anything that would mend broken bones.

Well, I don't think there is anything. You have to set the bone and allow it to heal by itself.

But that was not known in those times.

The area you lived in, was it lush with many plants, or were there just a few here and there?

Of course it was lush. It was not exactly what you would call a jungle, but it was very dense with plants and life forms and water and humans.

So despite everything, it was a happy life, then?

Mostly happy, yes, but when somebody was suffering or dying, then everybody was serious. Sometimes there'd be tears and weeping when loved ones died, but you had to live, so you went on.

Healers of Other Worlds

The dirt thing, I've never heard of that. What was in the dirt that was the healing factor?

I understand you live in your times by chemistry, chemicals. "This" does "this." "That" does "that." But sometimes it depends who has stepped on the dirt. Maybe you think that healers exist only in the human world? Maybe the healer from the many-legged world stepped on that dirt. So it might have been exactly the same dirt made up of exactly the same stuff. In one place, it works, and then in another place, exactly the same dirt doesn't help at all. So it was important. That's why the person — the dirt specialist, the grounder, the ground man — would pay particular attention to the track in the dirt, what track was most important.

Sometimes he might know about a certain beetle that walked in that dirt and maybe even an individual if he knew the beetle well. When he met a beetle and there was an acknowledgment, he could tell sometimes that it was a healer or a teacher. He could acquire a feeling and would watch where that being walked and then check that dirt.

There are many-leggeds who are particularly admired because they had so many legs, so they must have been doing something right. With all of those legs, they could go places and do things the human beings could not do, so they were much admired. They were watched. Not all many-leggeds would make the dirt healing, but some of them would. Very often, that dirt, like I said, would be used on the legs of the human being because it felt right. So that gives you an idea of what he did.

So the healing many-leggeds would leave an energy there that would then be transferred to the human?

It would be left on the dirt, and the dirt would be acquired. It would be all right to do that. If the dirt didn't want a bit of dirt to go, then the ground man would leave it.

He was that sensitive?

He had to be. Beings had to be sensitive to do what they did so everybody could survive and thrive. I'm sure that there were other people living other places who knew how to set bones and all of that, but we didn't live that way. There were no animals around there who set the bones of other animals. Everybody learns from the animals when living that way. If you want to know who is living well and thriving, just look at the animals. If the people aren't suffering and dying, you don't need those skills. But you understand what I mean. If you saw people, human beings who were suffering and dying and not doing well, you would pay less attention to their skills than to the skills of animals doing well.

Did you have stories that were passed down from the elders to the children about where you came from?

No. They knew where we came from; we know where we came from. Earth, that's where we were born. Also, I can see I haven't made it clear to you yet. We didn't have words; we didn't speak. We didn't have a language. We didn't talk. Talking wasn't our way. So when the visitors came, that's why we didn't talk. We could tell that they were talking.

You were telepathic, then? So you could still communicate with them?

Not in a way you think. You think of telepathic as seeing words.

So pictures or feeling?

Pictures. Feeling has to do with your instincts. You don't need to be telepathic for that. You do that maybe even in your time, but the people might have forgotten. I think they notice it when they're around somebody else based on feeling. For themselves, they radiate strong feelings, and other people demonstrate that they notice it as well.

That's fascinating. You didn't speak. I wonder why.

We didn't need to. I think sometimes people speak words because they've forgotten how to truly communicate, which might involve, say in a family, a touch, a light touch. If they touch each other, that is affection, and I think some other touches are understood. Mom and dad touch you gently on the head, and maybe you lean into their touch because you know that's affection. There's no doubt about that. Instead of touching a child with love like that, if you just sit down in front of the child and say I love you, it doesn't work as well, eh?

So you taught by example, then?

Always. Everything.

Wow, that's truly unexpected. I didn't know that.

There's no reason you should, so don't be critical of yourself. We are talking about living in a way that you have not lived but in some things you have experienced. So it's not foreign.

Pay Attention to Your Children's Gestures

What did you look like? Were you short, tall, dark skinned, light skinned?

Well, we were fortunate in that our skin did not get uncomfortable in exposure to the sun. I remember seeing babies when they were born, and they were, well, if this is correct — how do I describe it in your terms? Well, I don't know your color descriptions; I suppose beige.

So light brown.

Light brown, yes. But exposed to the sun for a lifetime, you get darker brown. I'm sure everybody looked darker brown, but the way the babies looked when they were born was light brown.

How tall were you?

If we were really tall, we might be around maybe a little less than five feet tall, four feet nine inches, four feet ten inches. That would be tall. But the average height might be around four feet two inches.

Which was helpful then because you didn't have to eat so much.

That's right, the food could go further. Plus the food was full of life. It wasn't sick. I think the food in your time is not well, or you're not eating things that are helpful and good for you. So you eat more because even though you're eating, your body craves food that will actually nourish it. It's why you eat more, but you're not eating something that your body needs. When you eat what your body needs, you don't have to eat so much. Your bodies feel as if, "Oh, this is enough." Of course in your time, you have to eat differently from us because you have to try to eat things that are safe. Unfortunately you are in a time when there are many things you can do to grow foods, yet your food is not as safe. But the people who grow the food seem as if they're doing the best they can under the circumstances. It's almost inconceivable to me how many people you have.

Right, 7 billion.

Well, the people who grow foods are doing the best they can. I can see why they must feel very rushed to grow as much as they possibly can.

They've sort of modified the food in a way that it's good for the people who sell it but not so good for the people who eat it.

I think it is not meant entirely to be cruel or greedy, though — maybe in some cases but not always. I think it's meant to make it possible for a small amount of ground to raise a large crop for places where many people live. In my time, Earth was something you shared with the other life forms. In your time, it seems to be a little overwhelmed with human beings. But I think it will change in some good ways in time.

Yes. That's what we're working on.

So let me just say this: When you see children doing things that alarm you — and by that, I mean your little children crawling about — it is good to keep them safe and not let them eat things that you know are not safe. Pay attention to what they do. They are in that time of discovery; babies are babies for the first few months at least. I think they are exactly the same in your time as they are in my time.

Try to notice what your babies do. You love the babies, of course. Try to notice what they do. They are being their natural selves, and if they're doing something that looks completely safe and is, you say, cute, that's fine. But think about it. What does it mean? Babies are not just born completely helpless. They are born as teachers, and very often, they're demonstrating something in their gestures. Not always, but very often when they're lying on their backs, they're doing something as a gesture that might be helpful.

It could ultimately be that as you observe it, you see it as an exercise program that you do in order to feel closely connected to a spirit or to God because the baby is demonstrating something, not just what babies do to feel themselves. "This is my body. What is it?" And they touch their toes to their mouths and so on. But sometimes babies lie where you have them, and they start kicking their legs. Usually when they're doing this with enthusiasm, it means it might be a good thing for you to do — not always, but observe and consider: Is baby doing something because it needs help? Is it hungry and so on? If it is just lying there, it is not crying, and everything is all right, maybe the baby is teaching a benevolent life to you.

How beautiful. Thank you so much for coming. Thank you.

Work as a Group for the Benefit of All

An Ancient Wisdom Keeper

July 17, 2014

Greetings!

Greetings.

We don't really have names in my time. Give me a moment to adjust. I'm speaking from my lifetime, for the sake of accuracy (which I think the others might do as well), about 400,000 years ago from your time. I am in a region that you call Siberia in your time. It was not quite as cold as now. It had a warm season, so we could come down from the mountains, you might say, and be comfortable and then other times, go up to the mountains, as desired.

I want to talk about how I was trained by my master teacher on how to know whether a course of action — a decision, like that, something along those lines — could be answered with, "Yes, proceed," or "No, that's not so good, at least not at this time," that kind of thing. Something could be decided utilizing the element you are presented with, meaning Earth, her ways. So what I would do — I did not make decisions other than minor ones, and I did not receive acknowledgment of right and not so right, meaning to try something else or to wait to interpret that, unless it was snowing.

I would ask a question. I wouldn't necessarily speak it out loud. I might just think it, and then I would wait. I put my hand out, which was covered in fabric, not really like the fabric you have, but something a little courser. It was long enough so that it covered my hands. Then I would wait to see the snowflakes that landed on my sleeve.

If they were very plain or even not really a snowflake, I would assume that I needed to make a different choice, or it would be some other course of action that might be better, or maybe it was not to do what I was proceeding to do or considering to do. But if the snowflakes were very beautiful and complex and even had that really marvelous appearance, that meant it was not only good to do but also worth celebrating how good it was to do. It meant, "Yes, wonderful, marvelous!" That is what that would mean. And that's how I would make the decisions that I would and then recommend them to the other elders of our group.

I wanted to mention that. I don't know whether that would work for your people in your time because you have to be totally in balance, yes, but there has to be a feeling present. You cannot do this when you're angry. You cannot do it when you are distracted, thinking about other things. You must be totally focused on what you are asking about. In the case of somebody who is not well, you can picture the person and then ask whether it would be good to do "this and that" for the person, and then accuracy would be more likely. As I say, you could have other choices in your time, but that's what I did.

How many days a year did it snow, or how much of the year? Was it half the year, three-quarters of the year, or something like that?

Oh, I understand your calendar. We used the Moon system as the calendar, but we didn't use it to keep track of time. We used it to understand the nature of life, such as when it would be good to plant things or when it would not be good. I think you have this knowledge in your time.

Yes. I just wondered how often you could use that system and what you did when it wasn't snowing.

What I did when it wasn't snowing was wait. But if a decision, or a question, for instance, had come up before and the same circumstances were repeated, you see, then I would use the decision that had been made before.

Ah, so you only checked on new things?

Yes, exactly. That's what I didn't make clear.

How many people were in your group or tribe?

It varied during my lifetime. Not counting my earliest years (since I didn't notice such things), it varied from a low of 17, I think, maybe 16, and at one point, 247, but that was unusual. There was a group that joined us for a time, but I considered them part of our group since we merged, and they were as friends and family. Then they moved on after a while, but I'm going to include them.

Did you have one function, such as the medicine man or the healer? What was your responsibility?

The wisdom keeper.

Were there other people who had specialties?

Yes. Other people knew about plants and understood the flow of water. You might not have known that, but sometimes it's the way the water flows and what it does. In a stream, for instance, and even in a river, if you know how to do it, you can ask those questions, and according to the way the water acts near you — not far away, but near you — you can get an idea of whether the answer is yes or no. This was not my specialty. We had someone who could do that, and because of the nature of the terrain, there was always water.

Even when it was snowing?

Well no, not when it was really cold. That's why it was handy to have our wisdom keeper.

What kind of wisdom did you keep?

Whatever we needed to know — survival skills, how to know what to eat, what not to eat, and the plants that were also involved with that. When it came to hunting, there were parts of the animal that weren't good to eat or were unsafe. This usually depended on how the animal had lived its life. Obviously, there are some parts that you wouldn't eat. It depended on whether the animal was sick or maybe had had a hard life. Sometimes a hard life makes you stronger, but other times, it's just crushing, and if an animal suffered, we would not consume such a being.

Sometimes the suffering was not obvious, but the hunters had skills to know how to hunt and how much to acquire as well as how to bless the animals so that they would not only be strong and independent but also bountiful. Still, sometimes animals were sad because their lives were so uncomfortable. So even if the hunters could only find one animal, if that animal was sad, they would not take that animal.

Each Person Contributes to the Group

What kinds of animals were there? Do you have names for them, or would we recognize them?

Well, there were some four-legged ones that had horns. I don't think the names translate to your language, but looking at your animals, they were something similar to antelope. In those days, I think that it was possible to travel between Siberia and your continent. You had to go at the right time of year. We didn't do that, and I think that's why sometimes animals that are not necessarily found on your continent or our continent in your time were found more frequently in my time or in times before. We didn't know much about the times before. The only way you could know about that is if you had generations that went back. I don't know how far they went back. It turns out that our people did not celebrate the past.

So you don't know where your people came from or their history or anything?

No. Well, our people did not celebrate their past. You could, perhaps on another day, speak to a different member of my group, the storyteller. The storyteller might know.

But if he did, wouldn't he tell the stories to the rest of you?

You have to ask the storyteller, but everybody had their own things that they could do. They had their own set of principles that they would follow for that, as long as everybody agreed on the principles. But generally, I think that for some specific types of things people do, there were some secrets. For example, your teacher would teach you, and you would pass it on to your student but not necessarily discuss it with everybody. So I think the storyteller would be your best way to know.

Your teacher is no longer living, I assume.

No. Teacher was very old when I was trained.

How old was "very old" in your culture?

You would say twenty-eight.

How old are you now?

In my time, you're asking?

In your time.

I am thirteen.

When did you start to train with your teacher?

When I was two.

You could talk then?

Talking isn't everything.

He would show you things?

Yes, I would be with him, and he would be doing things. Your children in your time are exactly the same. The reason I know this is that children are not different. They are around in your time, and even at two years old, they can sort of get around on their own. If they are with older ones, they will pay attention. They will watch, and they will do. It was the same in my time.

Did you live with your teacher full time or just spend some time with him?

Oh no. He was not a relation in that way. He wasn't mother or father, no. But there weren't walls where we lived, so there were no great secrets.

Did you all live in a huge tent or a building or something?

When it was warm, we lived outdoors under the stars in night and day. When it was cold, we lived in a cave. It was a very nice cave. It had fresh water, and it also had a heat source. It was steam. There was no smell. It was just warm. So if you went far enough back into the cave, it was very warm, and during the daytime, a little light would seep in. So it was a nice place to be in the cold times.

I can imagine. You gathered plants. You didn't grow them, right?

We did not at that time grow them, no. But when the others who came to visit and stayed with us for many years — I mentioned them before — some of them knew how to grow food. They explained about seeds, and my people tried to learn that. But during my lifetime, they weren't very good at it, but there was some success. So think that probably later on, things might have gotten better.

When you grow things, you have to stay in the same place and protect those things, and in my time, that would not have been considered honorable because the animals, the other life forms, have to go places. Very often, it seems to me, they needed to go right where we put the seeds down, so it wasn't very practical. We honored them. We hunted not all of them, but some of them, yet they understood that we honored them. We didn't think of them as lesser beings.

Did you move around during the warm season? Did your camp go from one place to another?

Yes, we did.

How many miles? Did you travel a great distance, or did you remain close to the cave?

I don't think we traveled in any specific direction. No more than four to six miles.

So you ate animals and plants that you found in your area that were safe? That was your diet, right?

Yes, yes.

Knowledge for Health and Well-Being

What were your healing techniques? What did you do when someone was sick?

Mostly it was a feeling. I would ask to have the feeling that corresponded to the healthy, strong version of that person, and I would hold my hand over that part of the body. Of course, some things didn't work as well when it was a terrible injury — broken bones, pierced skin, something. That didn't always work. But when it was a disease, something internal, that method usually worked. I think a lot of it had to do with the feeling. It helped to have been raised together like that because I would know what that person felt like when he or she was healthy. I could bring up as an inspiration, you would say, what the person felt like when healthy in that part of the body. I would remember because part of my training was to become acquainted with how everybody felt when healthy.

Could you feel everyone's feelings in the group if you chose to? If someone was happy or unhappy or uncomfortable or inspired or whatever, could you feel it? Were you an empath?

No. I see that I haven't chosen the right words. I would picture somebody's belly, for instance. The feeling I'm talking about doesn't have anything to do with whether the person was happy or sad. It's how that belly felt on the inside.

Oh, I see, the organs. Okay.

Yes, or any other part of the body, whether an organ or not, how it felt. I don't know any other word.

How it felt and expressed when it was healthy. Amazing. I understand. So what happened when the other group was there? Did you learn a lot from them? Did they have knowledge you didn't have that you were able to gain?

No, because my teacher taught me what I was supposed to know. My teacher didn't teach me what they knew, so I didn't do it. I had to use what I knew and what worked because I knew it did. Later in my life, going to a later moment, that's when they were there.

So your family is communal. Do you have a mother and a father and brothers and sisters, or is everybody sort of everybody's brother and sister?

I have, of course, a mother and a father. Everybody does. In your time too, I think [chuckles]. You for sure, I can say (unless you are made in a machine), have a mother and a father.

Right. But I just talked to someone a couple of days ago who didn't know who his father was.

Though the being has one.

The being has one but didn't live in the kind of family that had a mother, a father, and children.

It's all right. You don't have to … I was trying to make a joke, but it wasn't funny.

Oh, I see [laughs]. All right. Did you live in separate groups with your mother and father, or did everybody live together?

Everybody lived together, but when it was time to sleep, for instance, we would sleep with our mother and father and brothers and sisters. We would wake up and talk about things, but other than that, you know, if we were talking … but talking is not everything. That's just to give you an example of what I think you were asking. However, the rest of the time we'd be with everybody.

It's a very nice way to live.

We liked it.

What was the biggest danger that your people faced?

Well, really big animals, of course, and storms that lasted longer than we hoped they would last. You get used to planning ahead in times like that. Hunting in the winter is not always something we could count on, but part of the reason we lived where we did was that there were other life forms we hunted that would come through because of the heat in our cave. There were other caves where the animals would live or just be at times. I don't know whether they lived there all the time. There was a heat source there and water too. So probably somewhere there was something very hot, but the surface was just comfortable. So there were animals around. The danger, though, was storms that were strong, and you didn't eat for a while. When you could eat, you ate everything. When you didn't have food, then you went hungry, but at least we had water.

How long could a storm last?

It could last for a long time, days. There'd be a lot of snow, too much to go out. Even though we were in a sheltered area, there would still be snow.

Did you weave? You said you had something on your arm that was woven. Did you weave fibers?

No. The cloth came from the others who visited. They apparently had some source, and because I was an honored person at that time, I was given that. But during the other times, I had a garment that my teacher had. Teachers only wore this when they had to ask a question because they could see the snowflakes on that. The fabric was dark, and we could see the snow. But I don't know where he got it. It was very warm and comfortable, though.

Was it an animal skin?

No, I don't know where he got it. It was fabric. He said it was special, so it was something I only used for such an occasion, a spiritual occasion. Sometimes we wore animal skins, especially if the animals had fur. That would be warm, you see.

So what were your greatest joys?

Life, love, good times — what can I say? It's no different in your time, is it?

[Chuckles.] No. Did you have a spirit teacher? Could you talk to your teacher after he left his body?

Yes. He was my master teacher through my life even though he had died. I spoke to him, and I would see pictures of what he would do in that situation. He didn't speak to me. When I said, "Speak," he said, "think."

Then he showed you a picture?

He showed me what he had done. If it was something he didn't know about, I wouldn't see anything.

So you'd have to figure it out. Did you come up with some stuff on your own?

Sometimes I asked medicine women, and sometimes I asked elders. When they didn't know and it was an important decision, and there wasn't snow, I just made my best guess.

Did that usually work?

Sometimes it worked, and sometimes it didn't.

But you added the ones that worked to your store of knowledge, right?

Always.

Do you have an apprentice now? Are you teaching someone now?

I'm going to skip to the time when I was twenty-eight, and now at twenty-eight, yes, I have two. It was always good to have more than one when you cannot be certain who will live and for how long; therefore, I had them. So I have two, a girl and a boy.

Is there something magical about twenty-eight?

You asked me a question, and I went to the time I was twenty-eight.

You don't understand something. I'm speaking to you from when I was alive in my own time so that I can give advice that is valid in the physical world in your time, even though it might not be something you can use for whatever reasons. But obviously it is 400,000 years later, so I am also alive in spirit, and it won't help to tell you what goes on in spirit. How can that possibly help you in your physical world? Do you understand? I think some of the other beings will do that also. They want to be relevant.

Relevant, yes, we appreciate that. Did you reincarnate into that group? Did you come back to have more lives in that group of people?

No. But I am not going to talk very much about my spirit because it is forbidden. I think it is in your time too.

It is? All right. Let's see, you have water. Did you bathe in the stream in the summer, and how did you bathe in the winter?

Carefully [chuckles]. You wouldn't ever stand in a water source. We would scoop a little water out. As we were washing, we'd scoop a little water out. We wouldn't keep scooping while we were washing. It wouldn't be proper. It's hard to describe. Sometimes we wouldn't use water. There was a place in the cave that had a powdery soil. Sometimes we would use that. So most of the time, we only used a little bit of water, just briefly.

So there was a limited supply of water. Is that what you're saying? You had drinking water, but you had to be careful with it?

No. It was about being respectful of the water. It is alive.

So the water as snow is what gave you your answers, right?

Well, you can put it that way, but everything is alive. The snowflakes were alive. They just didn't live very long. They changed form quickly. We as human beings live longer, but we change form too.

So did you have other healing techniques besides presenting the body with the energy of itself when it was healthy? Did you do other things?

No. That's not what I was taught. There were many people, and I had to know how each and every one of those bodies felt. How could I have had time to do other things?

That's amazing. You have to be able to feel the energy of everyone's body, remember it, and bring it forth. That's a special talent.

You can do that in your time. You'd have to have people who are dedicated, who do only that.

Specialize in Your Interests

Do your people have descendants on Earth today?

Yes, but not in a situation like that. Some are in Siberia, some are in northern Europe, and I think a few are further south on your continent.

If you can't answer this, say so. Do you sort of watch over them now?

No. I am answering on the basis of your question, not because of my interests.

Could you say what your interest is in spirit now?

No.

At some point in that life, did you marry and have children?

Yes.

Did you train your children or others from your group in your skills?

It depends what they seem to be interested in; that's what they learn to do. It is not my job to teach them something they're not interested in. Is it different in your time? I notice the method is still the same. They are interested in something but not everything. It might take a wise, experienced person to know that, to notice what they are interested in. But you have to observe and have lived life and be around children, maybe remember being one.

When you started teaching, were any of the students you taught your children?

If one of my children is interested in what I am doing, not just curious — curious is fine — but interested to the point of starting to imitate and so on, then yes. But sometimes, children are interested only for a while, and then they get interested in other things. That happens in our time too. So it depends who stays with it. When someone stays with it, whoever that person is, then he or she becomes the student.

So when you were two years old, you were interested in it. You focused on it, and you stayed with it, obviously.

I was interested in it before I was two years old, but my teacher wasn't sure of me until I was in that range between two and three, as you would call it. Then the teacher was sure, and I was with him more often. And even though I was with him, my mother was nearby. There were no walls, and lots of others were around. He didn't show me anything that was secret. When there was a secret, it was shared in quiet times and not spoken. He would show me something, but he might hold his hand up, one hand up in front of it, and then show me something so that others could not see.

Anytime anybody did that, held one hand in front of the other hand, others would turn away, knowing that was meant only for the teaching going on. It's a way of honoring; it's not that a person is being excluded. It's that if you know too much about too many things, you forget. That's why it's good to specialize. You know as much as you can remember about one thing.

That's remarkable. So you would have watched the plant person teach someone, but it wouldn't be good for you to retain it because that would interfere with your focus?

The more I started to acquire knowledge and wisdom, the less I looked at things like that. Others' teachings are interesting, and if I weren't doing my own thing, then, yes, I would have looked at a lot of things. I was trying to remember my own wisdom, so I didn't look at that much. We would smile to each other, interact socially and so on, but not necessarily study each other's work.

I haven't asked. Are you a man or a woman?

Male.

You don't look to the past, so you have no idea how you got to that place or where your ancestors came from or anything like that?

It's not necessary to remember these things. One can be grateful, and we are all grateful for having this wonderful cave and this fresh water. We all have so much to remember. I am not the only one who has things to remember. Everybody has things to remember, and there's only so much remembering you can do when the information you have is wisdom, and you have to apply it. At other times, you wouldn't want your mind full of things that weren't needed to be remembered for the sake of others.

So you have language, but you have never had anything written down?

We don't have that much language, but we have some. We have some sounds. You have many sounds, perhaps, but we have some sounds. Are you asking whether there is anything still in existence? No. Not that I know of. But it is possible that there are somewhat similar sounds.

Did you ever experience beings from other planets, perhaps lightships? Were you ever visited by people from other planets?

We weren't, but the visitors who came to stay with us, the other group, they said that they had seen lights flying overhead, different colors. So I'm describing terms that you use, okay? Blue and green were the most frequently seen.

But they had not communicated with the beings in the lightships? They had not seen them.

Not that I can recall, no.

A Typical Day

What is your typical day like? You're not healing people all the time.

Well, when somebody is injured, I wake up even if it is a time when we sleep. Of course, we'll sleep when we're sleepy, if we can. So I am either learning, remembering, or doing for others, as well as living, eating, sleeping, and so on.

How often are people sick or diseased? How often do people need your services?

Just about every day. It is unusual to have a day go by without being needed.

Wow. No days off?

No [chuckles].

When you move around in the summertime, do you all go together? Does everybody stay together for safety?

Oh yes, absolutely.

What kind of weapons do your hunters have?

Spears with, you know, the pointed thing, and there is a rock. Someone in the group knows how to make such points from certain rocks that are found. There is not a lot of it, so they are careful. That person was trained by a teacher to know how to put the points on that.

What does that person use as a tool to put the points on the arrow?

They use other rocks, and then they chip away the rock, which gives it a very sharp edge. You have to be very careful not to waste the product. It has been found in the cave. There is some, but sometimes we have to dig around to get it out. Sometimes we have to use sticks to dig around so that we don't get hurt. Generally the stone is found just smooth, and we have to break the pieces off. It takes time, and it doesn't always work so well. So they're always working at it.

The only place you can find the rocks you need for the spears is in the cave?

That's the only place we know for sure. When we move around, we're always looking down. We have to make sure we place our feet somewhere good, and we're always looking for signs of that rock.

What color is the rock?

Part of it black, and part of it is a lighter color. It is sort of layered.

Someone reading this might know what rock that is. What do you use for utensils? Do you make baskets? What do you use to hold things?

We don't have baskets. When the visitors came, they had a few, but not many. We don't have much of anything to hold things.

Did the visitors say where they had come from and where they were going to — give you an idea of what else was out there?

I know you're speaking as a person who has time to think about the past. They said they had come from "that way." It doesn't mean much to you, does it? They were pointing, but you can't see what picture I am showing you. It won't do you much good. When they left, they went the other way. They didn't go back.

Did they come from where it was colder or warmer? Or that doesn't relate, either?

No, they came during the warm time. I think that's why they could get there because it was easy to travel then. And they stayed for a while.

Did the animals and people you said went to our country go in the summer or in the winter when things were frozen?

They might have gone in the winter, but it didn't happen during my time. But I'm able to look at it from my now perspective. I see that it looks like it's snow and ice.

I would have thought that it would have to be ice so that they could get across some of the water.

The land might have been a little different then too.

I wish we could get you to draw some pictures [laughs].

I don't think it was different in a big way, just a little.

Inspire the Children

What would you tell people who live now? What wisdom would you like to pass on to them?

Pay attention to the children. What do they like? What are they interested in? What are they naturally interested in, and how long does it last? I'm not talking about facts and history and that. I'm talking about what they are interested in doing. For example, they might be interested in fishing. How is that done? Maybe their grandfather or grandmother is showing them. "How did you do that?" If that lasts, then this might be something they should pursue. They will be able to feed their families, maybe their friends, and maybe others. It is a way to be — something to do. They might be interested in animals. There are important things to understand. Just because they're interested in one thing one day, don't think that that's the only thing they'll be interested in. When they're very young, they have many interests. I would suggest not to expose them to too many things. Try to expose them to things that are physical and needed and not just facts.

If they're exposed to stories, let them be stories about your family, what your people are doing. Tell them stories about what their brothers and sisters and your sister's children are doing, what people in your family are doing, not to make them feel as if they should be doing that too, but to inspire them. You know, "Your sister is doing 'this,'" and "look, you're good at 'that.' Maybe you will do that in your life and enjoy it. If not, you will find something else you're interested in, and then you will do that." I'm saying don't complicate their lives with too much, and pay attention to who they are, what they like, and what they're good at.

Do you fish in your time?

Sometimes.

In the streams? In the rivers? Do you have rivers nearby?

Not always, but sometimes. To me, a stream is not a big thing. There's not many fish. We only fish when they are abundant, and then we fish with just our hands. I am not the fisherman, but this is what I know about it. The people doing that, the hunters, will ask one of the fish elders to come to consult with them. They will ask, "Do you have enough to spare?" If the elder indicates no, then none is taken, no matter how hungry we are. Then we get along as best we can.

If they have enough to spare, they might be willing to sacrifice. Whoever is willing to sacrifice will swim close enough to us so that we can scoop them out of the water. Then we must kill them swiftly so that they don't suffer, and they must not be killed in front of the others, their own kind. We take them away and do that so that their loved ones do not see it. That's the way it's done.

Would you say that on most days you get enough to eat?

No, I think everybody is pretty hungry on most days. Some days we get enough or even more than enough. But the days when we're hungry, the storyteller helps us to [chuckles] forget it. Then we sleep a little more if we can't get out and about for some reason, for instance, because there's a storm. Generally when we're hungry, the hunters are off looking — not just looking. It has to be done with respect, and before they go out, they do things. I don't know exactly what, but they do things, and in the same way when they hunt fish, they'll ask, and an animal will come to offer itself. It is the same way. This is part of the reason we did not have a big number of people. The others came and stayed for a while, but they moved on because they could see that where we were living, there weren't that many animals. There weren't that many fish. So they didn't stay. They stayed for a while, and then they respectfully moved on. I think they were looking for a place that had more food, and we didn't have a lot.

It wasn't possible to send people out to see whether there was a place that had more food?

How far could we go, really?

Yes, and you would have all had to go for safety, you're saying?

Yes. We could have sent a few people out, but they would have had to go during the warm time and they could carry a little food. Sometimes the hunters went out for days on end but only at times when they felt that there would be enough to sustain them or they could survive on what they caught.

Speaking from your spirit, did you only have one life in that group?

Yes.

Do you feel that what you learned there was very valuable? Was it a life in which you were of service and learned a lot?

Yes, and because of this book, we have the chance to share a little bit of not only what we learned but also what we believed, such as my talk about the children. They are the important ones because they will make a life and live the life they make and help others to live as well as possible, and what better things can be done? And that is all I have to say.

I honor you for coming. Thank you very much.

CHAPTER FIVE

Collect Healing Energy from the Stars

A Shaman and a Pleiadian Elder

August 11, 2014

Very well.

Welcome.

I will speak for a bit. In my time, I knew the lights of certain star positions. I can see the one you now call Pleiades. We used to call it the Sisters, and through that one, the Sisters, I am sometimes able to see other star systems. First, I will say what I do. We have been fortunate here in my time. It's about 80,000 years ago from your time, and we are high up in the mountains, very high. There are not too many of us here, just a few hundred, but we have visitors regularly from the Sisters. They call it the Sisters, at least when they speak to us. Perhaps when they speak to each other, they have another name.

The visitors showed us how we can maintain good health by looking at that star system and singing. I cannot reproduce it here because this voice cannot go high enough. But it is very high tones, you say. Perhaps it could be reproduced by a child. In our time, we are not very tall. Many of us can reach these high notes, mostly the women and young girls. They had been trained, but not like teacher-student. They were trained through hearing the songs sung by the visitors from the Sisters. These beings are formal with us because I think they think that we are formal. The first time they came to see us, when the door opened and they came out of the vehicle, we sang to them. It is a song we like. It isn't our song [laughs]. I think they think it is, but it is just a song we like. We learned it from the birds and other animals that come to visit us. It's a combination of the tones they make, and it's a way of honoring them for visiting us and sometimes providing us with food, which we appreciate. Mostly we live on what you call plants.

The birds have brought us some seeds at times. At first, I think people thought the seeds were meant to be eaten [laughs]. The birds were determined, though, and they kept bringing the seeds but just a couple at a time. Finally somebody figured out they were meant to be planted [laughs], and eventually the crops grew. I'm not sure what they're called in your time, perhaps oats, but they have life-sustaining energy. It has helped us a lot.

When the visitors came, we sang the song. It doesn't take long, a minute or two, and they paused and smiled. Then they all came out of this ship, at least as many as we ever see, which is sometimes four, sometimes five. On this occasion, it was five. They all came out of the ship, and they lined up, facing us in a straight line. The beings put their arms around each other's shoulders, and they sang to us in these very high tones. We were a little surprised because the men were able to reach those tones also. They were quite a bit taller than we are, but they were friendly, so there were no worries on either side.

Then they came and greeted us, and they offered food for planting. They had something that would grow into a bush, which we found out about eventually. They shared the fruit from the bush. I suppose in your time you would refer to the fruit as nuts, but we didn't have that term then, so anything that grew on a tree or came up with seeds and so on that could be consumed, we just referred to as fruit. We liked it very much, and they gave us enough seeds for us to plant. Then we had this wonderful nutrition; you'd say food, yes. So it was a wonderful thing.

Make Pleiadian Connections

Of course, living in our time, we sometimes needed medical care. Occasionally, somebody would trip over something and get hurt. So they talked among themselves the first time, and they sat some of us down. At that time, we were all youngsters, and one or two parents sat in. The visitors were perfectly happy with that. They were able to communicate in our language. We're not quite sure how that happened. Sometimes we saw their lips moving, and we heard the sounds. At other times, their lips didn't move, but we still heard them. I'm not sure what that's about, but anyway, it came across.

They told us how, by looking at the Sisters in the sky (which we could see very easily), we could learn to bring about healing energy if it was needed at any time. Some of the children were interested, and some weren't. But there were only two or three of us who were really interested, and I was one of them. I was very young at the time. To use your years, I was four years old. After we started meeting with the visitors, we started living to an average age of about 131 years, averaging it by your mathematics. But before that, we didn't live that long because sometimes people would get hurt and then get infections, and then they would die.

Before the visitors, I'd say maybe the average age was about twenty-eight, so there was a big difference. I'm not sure why they came to visit us; it would have been rude to ask, so I don't know. We were happy they did, though, because they would tell stories sometimes, and we would tell our stories of various things we've done or experienced, sometimes funny things. Sometimes things don't seem funny when they happen, but later they seem funny because many people have had those experiences as well.

Anyway, I was able — because of being 4 years old at the time and very interested and learning well — to become what you now call a shaman. There were two others; they were both girls. One was 5, and the other was 6. They also became shamans and lived about the same time I did. One lived to, I think, 127, and the other to 128. So because I was a little younger, I outlived them a little bit, but [laughs] it's not a contest. I was able to pass on a lot of the teaching to students.

The visitors came quite regularly for about, well, you would say five or six years, and then there was a long gap. We thought, "Well, they have other things to do," when we didn't see them for about twenty or thirty years. Then they came regularly again. That cycle repeated about two more times, and then they stopped coming for a long time. I think they might have come again later, and I'm not sure why it is they came like that. But that's what they did, and we were happy for that.

I can share with you in your time one of the healing methods they gave us, only one. It will only work if you can go outside and look in the sky and see what you call the Pleiades (but we just say the Sisters). If you can, look at it — don't stare at it because it might get too bright — and while you look at it, slowly sing any song or any tune that doesn't have words. Don't whistle, though, just sing, and go up to the highest notes you can make. Some of you won't be able to go very high, and I understand that. Sing the highest notes you can make, and sing the melody of whatever tune you are singing, but don't say any words. It's very important not to say words. Just hum; that's all right too, but it might be easier to hum with your mouth open to get the highest notes while you look at the Sisters.

I have found in the past that this could cure some stomach problems — in our time, you understand — and it could sometimes cure pains in the neck and the back of the head. I've also found that it can cure some nightmares, the kind of thing that doesn't go away easily. It doesn't work for everyone all the time, but I found it to be the key. Even one time when a person seemed to be going, you would say, crazy, the person went out and did this three nights in a row and then was okay. The person was, what you would say, balanced by the singing. So this was something that really worked.

Now, the reason I can't share anything else is that this is the only thing I am guided in my time to share, okay? I am guided that it is the only thing that is, you say, relevant in your time, so other things won't help you. But this will help you, I feel. Some of you might find that it makes other illnesses feel better. I'm not saying you shouldn't go to your shaman and get treatment, but I am saying that it might help with whatever is bothering you or won't seem to go away or you have too much of. That's what I recommend.

An Isolated Group

Now you're going to ask where we are, and I really want to tell you, but they have informed me that we have, what you say ...

Descendants.

Yes, thank you. We have descendants living in your times in those places and nearby, so it wouldn't do to reveal it. I am sorry. Still, I feel good about passing on the healing method, and I hope you can use it.

There are those of you who cannot see — either it is always cloudy where you are, or maybe you just cannot see as well as you once did, or maybe you never could see very well. But if you can have someone aim your head toward that star system, the Sisters, that could work. We don't have people like that in my time. Everybody can see, but I understand this happens in your time.

Also, where we are, it never — oh, it rains and so on, but when it isn't raining, the sky is very clear. You might not always have that. Some of you might have a cloudy sky all the time. So for you, if you can find out where in the sky the Sisters are — if it wasn't cloudy you could see the Sisters — then try that. Also look in that place, and then try. I cannot guarantee it, but it is worth a try; it is always worth a try.

Excellent. Thank you. Did you ever meet any other humans on the planet?

We were, what you would call, isolated. I don't remember ever meeting, in my entire life, anybody who wasn't part of our regular community. I think that this is because it was probable that people lived at lower, what … ?

Elevations.

Yes, but I think no one really knew we were there. It wasn't unusual for clouds to be below us, so to speak, you know, down around the mountains. So people probably didn't even know we were there. At least in my time, we never saw anybody else, just our own people. Except, of course, the visitors when they came.

Yes. Did you have a history about where you came from or stories about where your ancestors came from?

We didn't have a history because we tended to be very present in our own time. But the visitors told us that some of our ancestors were from where they came from. So it's possible that some of our ancestors — that's how they said it, *some* of our ancestors; they didn't say everybody — some of our influences, you would say bloodline, apparently came from the Sisters. I suppose that's why they came. They probably wanted to see what was going on in other places.

Ah, so you could have been relatives?

Yes. Perhaps they thought that. They seemed to be happy to be there. They were always happy to be there, which is very nice.

But then they didn't come for a long time, you said. They were very tall, and you were only about 4 feet or so?

Oh, we were, well, a little shorter than that sometimes and a little taller than that sometimes. They weren't very tall. In your time, they would probably seem to be average height, but they were tall to us.

When you began living so much longer, did your population expand?

No. No, because we were wise. Our elders said we would have only so much food to go around and only so many shelters. We were not inclined to build many shelters. There was loose stone, and we made stone houses and so on. Of course when it rained, we got wet, but eventually it would stop raining, so there was that. But our elders spoke very strongly that it would be best to be careful about that, so we were. I don't think, at least not in my time, our population was ever less than 84 and never more than 191. I'm going to round that up and say a couple hundred.

So you restricted your reproduction, then?

I suppose that would be a formal way of saying it, yes. [Laughs.] You don't mind my little joke?

No, absolutely not. Why can't you share any other healing techniques?

Because they're not relevant in your time. My guide tells me that it wouldn't be good to tell you because people would try them, and they wouldn't work. People would be disappointed.

Animals Provide for People

Okay. You didn't move around? You stayed in one place, but were you able to get enough food from that place to sustain all of you?

Yes, we were able to do that. We had a few areas that you would call plateaus, and we had some crops before the visitors came. But they provided a lot of variety, and I think they understood what kind of food would nourish us. I think that's why they might have focused on proteins, and the protein really made a big difference. We lived a lot longer [laughs].

I think another thing the visitors liked about us — I'm not sure, and this might have had to do with their philosophy — is that we didn't eat the animals. Sometimes the birds would leave eggs, but we didn't understand at first that they were contributing to our food supply. We didn't know what to think. [Laughs.] Eventually the visitors explained that some of the birds felt that we could consume the eggs. Apparently they were leaving eggs before the visitors gave us the fruits because they thought we needed protein. We didn't know the reason; however, the visitors seemed to understand the animals very well. They could communicate with the animals exactly the same way they communicated with us.

Many times they would talk to the birds, and when the birds would speak back to the visitors, they would move around, like you say, become animated. They would move their heads in certain ways, and they would move their bodies in certain ways. I think they did it because they were passionate about something. That's the word you use. The other animals did it too. That is my best guess that this is how the visitors came to understand us better — from the birds and other animals. They seemed to consult them more often when they first started coming and not so much in later visits. I think that perhaps the animals were teaching them what we needed or something about us. In the beginning, they asked us a lot of questions, but after they started talking to the animals, they didn't ask us as many questions [laughs].

Ah, because they already had the answers.

They had the answers because the animal knew us.

Can you say what kind of animals and what kind of birds?

Well, I think in your time, one of the birds is considered something like a hawk or maybe an eagle. Another animal, I don't think you have it in your time, was a cat — dark-colored fur. You would call it a big cat, but it wasn't huge. It was a nice being. None of the animals ever bothered us or looked at us as food. The cat was a very beautiful being. Sometimes it would bring a family along — other cats, little cats. [Laughs.] That was nice. I think you still have cats, yes?

Oh yes.

Do you still have these birds? Those are the ones I'm allowed to mention. They don't want me to mention animals that you don't have because then you'd feel sad. I have discovered in my life — and this is important advice to you — it is not a good thing to feel sad about something that you can't do anything about anymore. If I share something with you, such as telling you about animals that you don't have any more, you would just feel sad, and there's nothing you can do about it, so it isn't a good thing to share. You could probably live a lot longer and a lot happier if you didn't get sad and unhappy about things that you can't do anything about anymore. [Laughs.]

That's very wise. Thank you.

Community Skill Sets

Did you have a system of apprenticeship with your shaman?

It's not an apprenticeship in the way you think about it in your time. It is just that we tried to notice who was interested in whatever, you might say, the job was. Whoever of the children was interested would be encouraged to, you know, be with us. Mom would bring them over when they were really little, and when they got a little older, we would know for sure whether they were interested because they would come over on their own. It wasn't a big area, but it was big enough. Sometimes they would have to travel a ways to come over, and when they did that, we knew they were interested. We shared with them whatever felt right for their age.

We also answered questions based on their personalities. In your time, you would say you wouldn't tell them everything all the time. It's like that. Sometimes you take into account their ages, sometimes their experiences, and sometimes whether they're boys or girls, all of that.

Did you weave plant fibers? Did you have clothes?

Oh yes, we had clothes. In the beginning, it was kind of minimal, but it wasn't ever very cold. I don't know how to explain to people who live high up in your times where it's cold. As I say, we lived high up, but it never got very cold. So we didn't need that much. After a time when the visitors came, they explained another crop we could plant that would provide a certain juice that was helpful and nourishing, but it did not necessarily taste very good. You can believe me when I say that [laughs]. I don't know what it's called in your time or whether it even exists. My guide is telling me it doesn't exist in your time. Maybe you're lucky.

The fibers, as you say, can be put together and become a cloth. It's not the same, but it resembles what you call linen. We didn't need a lot of garments, though, so we didn't grow very much of it. As I say, it was comfortable.

That's unusual. Now anything that's high up above the clouds is cold.

Not in that time. I cannot say for your time. It's different in your time.

Yes, it must be. What about pottery? Did you fire clay? Did you work with making your own utensils?

No. We didn't do that. I think a couple of times the visitors left us these things that you would call cups. We used them sometimes for the water. When the water came down, we collected it in pools, and we would drink from them. They gave us a couple of these cups. They were made out of something you call metal. I don't know what kind, and I don't know whether they still exist in your time, but they seemed very sturdy. We all shared them. I mean, really, how many cups do you need? We could share them. I think the most we ever had at any time was three, but somebody dropped one, and it went way down the mountain. We didn't go get it, and we were kind of embarrassed to tell the visitors that. They just laughed and said not to worry. They could see it, and it had fallen into a crack. They didn't think anybody would ever find it. At first they were alarmed. I'm not sure, but maybe they didn't want people to know they were there. But they figured out where it had gone, and apparently it's not going to be found, or if it is, maybe it'll be okay.

It sounds as if they didn't want to leave evidence of their visits. Someone finding metal from 80,000 years ago would face controversy.

It sounds like that, but they left those cups with us, and well, we liked them. They were comfortable to drink from.

You stayed at your elevation. You didn't ever go down the mountain?

No, never. Why? We were happy. We had all we needed.

Did any of your children become shamans?

No, they didn't. [Chuckles.] Isn't that always the way? I was able to train a couple of people, one girl and one boy, and of course, the other two in my time, the women, they were able to train people too, so we always had an abundance of people who could do these things. I think we also had other people who could do these shamanic things. There was always more than one person who could do something. Sometimes if there were enough people doing something but there weren't enough people to do the other things that were needed, then people would learn more than one thing, but only if they could do that. There seemed to always be a couple of children around who could learn more than one thing. I was never good at that, but several others were. They could learn two types of jobs at the same time. Well, the one that comes to mind, a girl — obviously a woman when she grew up — learned what I could teach, and she also learned how to farm. She could do both very well.

Did someone specialize as a plant person who knew which plants were healthy, you know, safe to eat?

Well, the farm person would do that too.

Ah, the farm person. Was your specialty healing?

Well, healing and balance, meaning helping people to be balanced in all they did so that nobody did anything extreme. Sometimes the healing took place in the form of a group activity. Sometimes being together and singing the songs that we all liked or telling stories that maybe we heard twenty times already but we enjoyed. Someone might even tell the story a different way so that we were never (this is something you are in your time) bored.

Oh [laughs]. That's interesting.

Shaman Mountain Living

Did you hunt? Did you move?

No. I'd be hard-pressed to say how many acres or square miles we lived on because there was not a shape like that. So I don't know how to describe it. There was enough land sort of sprinkled around from one spot to another that we could live on and sleep on and eat from and just be together. It was adequate, you'd say. It's adequate. It wasn't ever more than we needed, but it was always enough. That's another reason why we maintained a certain level of population and didn't go over that: We didn't have any extra land. [Laughs.]

Yes, when you live on mountaintops, it's different from being on flat land. Did you live as individual families, or did you all live together?

We lived as families, but we did things together — mother and father and children. Sometimes there was a grandfather, and when we lived to be older, even a great-grandfather and occasionally a great-great-grandfather. I didn't get to that level, but I did get to be a great-grandfather.

What about language? Did you speak a language that still exists today?

I don't think so, but I cannot be certain. My teacher tells me that elements of the language still exist today in that area where we lived, but it's not the same language we spoke. My teacher let me listen to a little bit of it. I recognized not exactly words but some sounds that were apparently parts of words. To us, they would have been whole words. But I think that in your time there is maybe more going on.

More complex, yeah. Who is your teacher — in spirit or embodied?

In spirit.

Did you have someone while you were alive in your body who you could ask questions of?

Yes. Teacher answers, yes.

How were you introduced to this being?

When I was born. When children are born, you know, they can talk to beings. They can talk to spirit, and elders know this. At least in that time they did, and maybe some elders or wise people in your time do. Then you try to introduce them, but of course they have guides that watch over them, and they know who to listen to. Sometimes I think in our time, maybe in your time too, the elders or wise ones are teaching the babies something the babies already know, and if the babies could talk, well, the babies would teach the elders. It used to be one of our regular jokes, but I think that it's true.

Yes. Well, they're still in their soul personalities when they're born and for months or a couple of years afterward.

Yes, quite awhile, and it's a good thing because it helps you to understand why you can't do things you can do when you get older. As a baby, you sometimes get upset because you're used to being able to do something in maybe another life or in spirit, and you can't do the things that you expect to be able to do, you know. I mean, you expect to be able to do some things, but you can't.

So sometimes you might get upset, and then a guide or teacher is there to help you. Of course, your mother is there, and frequently others are there just to hug you and let you know you're loved. Then even though you still can't do what it is you want to do, you feel batter.

Yes. You had midwives, right?

Do you mean a woman who helped women give birth? Yes. That was another important job — very important.

Would you mind if I ask to speak to one of the Pleiadians on that ship that visited you to ask how you got there and where you came from and some things like that?

Well, it's up to you anytime you want to do that.

I would like to do that for a minute if you don't mind, just to sort of finish up?

Well, I have to say goodbye, then.

What would you like to tell the people who read this?

Try to pay attention to the simple things. Notice always what the animals are doing. Yes, it's important to see what your pets are doing because they are your connection to the actual world — you say the natural world. It's even more important to see what the wild and free animals are doing. Don't interfere with them. Watch what they are doing if you can, but don't stare at them. The polite way to do that is to just take a quick look for a second or two, and then look away. Otherwise, it's impolite. You might make them nervous or upset. They can feel somebody looking at them, and they're afraid that somebody could be dangerous. Then they won't act like they normally do. If you take a quick glance, try to remember what it was you saw. You can do a quick glance like that maybe twice a minute. But maybe wait. I'd say even wait for a whole minute. I think you know when a minute goes by. That's what I recommend.

If you can pay attention to what they are doing, you will find out that they often help you to avoid dangers, such as many times when you have seen birds suddenly fly away, and you don't know why. Then within a few minutes, there is thunder and lightning or other danger, and you didn't even imagine that was going to happen. So always pay attention to what the animals are doing, and you will be happy.

You're wonderful. Thank you very, very much. Do you have a name?

Have a good life.

✳   ✳   ✳

I am an elder in the Pleiades.

Oh, thank you.

I think you asked a question for which there was no answer. There was no answer because they don't have names.

Oh, I see. I thought he was already gone and didn't hear me.

He heard you, but there was no answer.

Right. Of course.

An Extended Stay

So can you tell me whether some of your people started a group on the mountaintop, or how those people got there?

There were people there already when we visited the first time, and two of our people wanted to stay. They weren't allowed to stay permanently, but they were allowed to stay for a while. One was a woman, and one was a man. They didn't have to have, what you might say, a reason. They felt very attracted to being there. So they stayed there for about eighty years. During that time, they became involved, and as a result, there were some children born who were part of our people, understand?

So the genetics were there. This was the case for quite a while. This initial visit, when the two people stayed in that group on your planet for about 80 years, happened about 1,000 years before the time of that person who spoke to you. So part of the reason when we went back 80 years after that first visit was we were interested to see the two who stayed there. We were interested to see how that affected things among the people they stayed with. It was controversial for them to stay there for so long, affecting the genetics.

Yes. What did you find?

That really they had to do it. They were elderly when they stayed there. But elderly or not, they could still produce children, which is the way it is for our people. They returned, but the two people didn't want to leave your planet. They wanted to stay there until they died, so they were sad to go. They were sad about it for a while. But when they went back, then they were happy because they saw their families.

They died shortly after they got back. But when they left your planet, they didn't know what it was going to be like for the people they left there. The people there are very much as the shaman described. They were sad to see them go, but once they were gone, they were not sad anymore because they couldn't do anything about it. That's part of their philosophy, to let go of sadness.

This is probably why, when we started helping them out a bit, they very quickly started living much longer lives, because they have a healthier way to live. This sadness thing that you have in your time — dredging up memories from the past that make you sad and people telling you things from the past that make you sad — this is very bad for your health.

Why did the two people have to return to the Pleiades?

It was felt by their families that they should return. Their families wanted to see them, and their bloodline had — how can we say? — more influence with them. They weren't forced to leave. But you know, when the loved ones you were born to want to see you … well, it was a tough decision for them.

Because they also had loved ones there on Earth who had been born to them.

It was very hard. As a result, no one has ever been allowed to do that since. They can visit, but they can't stay because it can create too much sadness. And we think when they got back home to our planet, even though they enjoyed it very much, you know, being with the loved ones and so on, we felt that they had died before their time because of missing the people they left behind on Earth. It's not been allowed since for our people to do that.

They also had a harsher life there during those eighty years, right?

No, I wouldn't say that. It wasn't harsh. It was just different.

So when you went back 1,000 years later to the time of the shaman who just talked to me, what was the genetic result on Earth?

We didn't notice much difference. There wasn't anything observable, and we weren't geneticists. We didn't go around taking samples of their bodies. We were just asked to see whether there was anything different based on comparisons from before to when we started going there again. "We," speaking for my people, you understand?

No difference was noted, nothing obvious — no change in personality, no apparent differences. This is why the assumption was that the people who stayed there for the eighty years — it was then that it was understood. It wasn't understood at the time, but then it was understood that those two people must have had lives in that place before, and that's why they felt that they had to stay.

Oh, I see.

You would say it was karmic, but we don't believe in that. It was their lives; they felt they had to be there. It was a wonderful thing for them to stay, but the way it turned out was kind of sad in the end. I will say that when they died, they didn't suffer. There's no suffering. Still, we felt that they died before their time.

They had those memories pulling on them that they couldn't do anything about of the people they left behind.

But once they died, I am sure they went right back there, to those people on Earth.

Did you look into how those people got there in the first place?

No, that's not our job.

Can you look into it? How did they get on top of the mountain with no other people around them?

Just a moment. You know, I'm not allowed to tell you, and I think I know why. I think it's because you have people like that in your own time, and they have secrets. And I think there is a similarity between people like that. But that's as much as I can tell you with keeping the people in your time safe. I have the choice of fulfilling your curiosity, which is completely understandable, or keeping people safe. Well, you know what I'm going to do.

You weren't allowed to see completely?

I wasn't allowed to see completely, and the answer to your question was a very firm no.

Well okay, that's very good. You've added something to the story because each of these people we talk to, it's like a whole world unto itself, you know. It's not familiar to us.

This is where we feel happy to cooperate in the creation of this book because it might, in some ways, support people in your time. I believe that it is your desire to provide such wisdom.

Yes.

So we are happy to support that.

Oh, I thank you very much. Is there anything you want to tell the people who read this?

No. Is that okay?

Yes, that is okay. Thank you and good life.

Yes. Good life. Good life.

Thank you.

CHAPTER SIX

Use Lightning Energy to Free Spirits from Earth

A Contemporary Andromedan Descendent

August 13, 2014

Yes.

Welcome.

Thank you. I realize that you desire shamans from the past. Well, this is an exception.

You're from the future?

No. I'm from the present, and because of circumstances that I cannot explain to you at this time, it is possible to communicate in this fashion. I'm alive on Earth now.

Oh, wonderful, okay.

I'm conscious of some of the issues that are disturbing your people — of course, I will only discuss things that are in alignment with this book and these times. One of the big things that people are truly afraid of is not just that fictional things (stories or movies), unfortunately, try to scare people but also something that goes way back. So I'm going to tell you about it, and then I'm going to give you something you can do. You don't have to do much; you just have to do a little.

Now, in places where people are truly terrified of ghosts (which is something that people are much more frightened of these days than at any other time, though you wouldn't think that was so because of the confusion between what people say and what they do and also because it's so popular to dream up fictional stories about this and to make money scaring people), sometimes people think it's perfectly all right to scare children. I really do not understand that belief. Nevertheless, this is something uncomplicated.

At times, there are restless spirits on the planet because of circumstances in life in which souls do not immediately traverse from the bodies of their formerly living selves to the afterlife, moving beyond Earth. There's also another situation in which beings are sometimes released. There's a whole group of spirit beings who go about trying to release beings who have been stuck on Earth. Usually this happens in scenes where there have been battles — "scenes," meaning areas where there's been much suffering and wars and whatnot. There has been a need to send spirit beings from the angelic, or Creator does this. I don't know exactly. I have seen them, though.

They usually have gold lights. Sometimes there's a little green light with them and occasionally other colors. You can see them if you know how. They'll always move slowly. They won't usually look like human beings, just flashes of color. They free spirits who have been stuck because when there is so much energy of violence, sometimes bodies fall in layers or fall into holes and get lost for one reason or another. It's complicated, but what happens is spirits come and free them.

Most of the time they immediately go on to the afterlife, but sometimes they have attachments; they want to see where their families are. Of course, if this had happened a long time ago (as it often has), the families are gone, and they continue looking. Sometimes they just wander about when they cannot find them. If they wander long enough, they could get stuck again because there are energies floating around that they might not be able to shake off. This is because they are no longer physical, so they do not have the capacity to work hard or run hard or do something like that. And the energy is transformed from the physical that way. So there's something that exists now, and this has existed for a long time on Earth. It works not only for human beings but also for others.

Ask Lightning to Help Animals Move on to the Afterlife

In some circumstances, other beings, meaning nonhumans, might be stuck here at times too. You call them animals. They don't mean to get stuck here, but something happens, and there needs to be a means to release them. As I have mentioned before, it has to be able to happen quickly so as not to allow any circumstance whereby they can wander off. So that is the job that lightning does. Very often when you see a lot of lightning in various places, there have probably been battles there in the past. Sometimes the battles have been in your history, so you know what they were, or you can guess. Sometimes they weren't in your history, you don't know about them, or perhaps they happened in a lost civilization, meaning that something sudden and catastrophic happened, and many were wiped out. Rarely but sometimes in those situations, a being gets stuck, and lightning will come. It will land in the exact spot where that soul is wandering around or is stuck, and the soul will immediately travel up the lightning and move on to the afterlife.

It's important to bring this out to you now because at this time, you are going through a transitional stage on your planet, and you are being touched sometimes by loving beings from the future or angels or guides or other benevolent beings. You would say "benevolent," yes?

There are other benevolent beings who help you, perhaps with healing or something else you need. Sometimes they just take away nightmares when you are sleeping, and sometimes they put words in your minds so that you understand the nightmare. Maybe the nightmare is trying to tell you something. They help the way guides help, so people sometimes feel very light touches, but since there is so much fear about ghosts, they think [those touches are] ghosts, meaning (in your terminology) scary spirits, okay?

I want to give you something you can do, all right? I assure you that these benevolent beings never mean any harm. I'm not talking about something that touches you and causes harm. Generally speaking, that doesn't happen, but it might happen in some extremely rare cases. So this isn't just for such rare cases. It is also if you are personally concerned that ghosts might harm you, or maybe you feel something isn't right, yet no people are around, and you can't understand what it is. This is what you can do: The next time there is a thunderstorm and lightning nearby, ask the lightning to pick up that spirit and take it to the afterlife. This doesn't mean that if you feel that energy in a room in your house, the lightning will have to come inside.

When lightning strikes the earth, it tends to move laterally. It comes down, but it tends to move laterally, and it can come in energy immediately in the electrical lightning bolt itself into rooms. If you've been near lightning, you know that you can smell something. The odor can penetrate. In short, it might be able to do that job without having to smash through your roof and break up your house. So this is what you can do. You don't have to go outside. Simply make your request from inside. Look up at the sky if you can. If you cannot see, then just tilt your head up toward the sky (because that's where the lightning will come from) and simply say,

> "I am asking that lightning, when it comes, remove frightening spirits who might be causing harm to me or others, and do so quickly in a most benevolent way."

You're going to say "in a most benevolent way" at the end because (even though lightning will do what it does in it's own way) by saying this, it's done without having to cover all the varieties of possibility. It suggests that you don't want the lightning to crash into your house or your apartment. Of course, it wouldn't do that in most cases. But if you've ever had the situation when lightning has visited you — having come through your roof and crash through your house — this happened because sometimes a spirit has been there crying out for help to be rescued but was not able to leave. It will then be evacuated up that lightning bolt. When that happens, sometimes people feel (even though they may not be happy about the damage) a sense of lightness afterward, and the house feels better. This is especially noticeable to people who understand and feel energies.

I wanted to come through and say that today, obviously, since this is happening now. I'm not going to say who I am and where I'm from, but I will say that I live in a place where lightning happens. I have learned from my teacher how to work with lightning and honor and appreciate it for its gifts.

Mitigate Ghosts Using Moonlight

It might surprise you to know the percentage of people on the planet right now who are afraid of ghosts: about 17 percent. That's a lot, and in some countries, it's much more than that. In some places, it's 80 percent. So this is really important.

Is there anything that we can say that will cover not just our immediate area but areas where they don't even know that it's possible to ask for this kind of help?

You understand there are some places where lightning doesn't generally happen, yes?

No, I didn't know that.

Yes, there are a few places like that. If you look around, you'll see. It might happen once in a while but not as a rule. So in that case, I recommend this. You can do this when you feel spirits are frightening people and you're not sure whether they're benevolent or not. You think maybe they are and that people are just frightened because they don't understand. Perhaps something touches them lightly, and the actual touch does no harm but because they're afraid of ghosts or somebody else is causing them to be afraid, then their fear makes them uncomfortable. So you can make a request similar to the lightning request.

I recommend you do this with the Moon energy because the Sun energy might actually amplify these spirits. It works best during times of the full moon, but it doesn't have to be completely full. You can also make the request a day before the full moon and the day after. So you have three days to do this during the times of the Moon's cycles. Go outside at night if you can. If it's cold where you are, then dress appropriately. It doesn't matter. You don't have to do much. It's just saying something and looking up to the sky where the Moon is. Then look down at the earth. Do that three times very slowly so that by the time you look down at the earth, you have a latent image in your mind's eye of the Moon. All right? Don't stare at the Moon. Just look at it enough so that when you close your eyes and look down at the earth, that afterimage is sort of blinking in there, if you understand. Then say,

> "I am asking that troubled spirits who might be causing harm to me, my friends, or my community now be benevolently helped to leave and move on to the afterlife."

Do this, and it will attract the spirit beings who are sent out and are "here and there" all over the planet to come to your location very soon, if not immediately. Within a very short time, they will clear the area of any spirits that might be causing harm. But if they have already done that and you feel it has been done — maybe you feel sensitive, and you can feel the change of energies — yet people are still receiving these light touches for some reason, then you can reassure them that those are benevolent beings. They are probably angels or guides or the like, and let them know that the others who might have been lost or unintentionally causing fear will be gone. They will move on to the afterlife.

Will this work also for those who aren't causing any harm and are just stuck but aren't troubling anyone?

No.

Can you share something that we could say to help those beings?

No, because there are human beings who have been trained and know how to help them get clear. It is a long process to teach human beings to do that, but once they learn how to, then they can. That kind of teaching has to be done in person.

Andromedans Share Light Expertise

Is there anything you can say that will contribute knowledge about how you were trained by an elder? You were trained by someone, right?

Yes, by an elder.

He was trained by someone — or she? Can you say whether you're a he or she?

She trained me.

She trained you. Are you a male or female? Can you say?

I am one or the other. [Laughs.] That was a joke. In other words, no, I won't say. All right, I can see you're having trouble, so I will tell you a little bit. Don't you usually ask where we are from?

Well, maybe you could just answer it, then.

I am getting there. Give me a moment. I am trying to help you. So about 800,000 years ago, my people were not on the planet. They were in a distant star system, and they were invited to come to the planet. We traversed the distance in a vehicle. It was not our own creation, but someone said that they thought that our work with light might be conducive to adapting to the types of light on Earth. They thought we could help, so they essentially asked for volunteers. Some people volunteered, men and women who were not yet married and didn't have families. Of course, they would leave their parents and grandparents behind because it was a one-way trip. So the request was made, but the ship didn't come for five years so that goodbyes could be made.

The people traveled to Earth and quickly learned how to work with the sunlight, of course, and there was the moonlight. There was the starlight. These things are found in other places, yet you take lightning for granted because you're used to it. It happens on Earth. There's a tendency to think it happens other places, but in my travels — my people's travels and my soul travels — and according to what my elders taught me, the being on the ship said lightning is rare. It's not found very many places.
Oh, I didn't know that.

Lightning is very unusual, and we believe the reason we were asked to come is because of our work with light, that we would be able to work with lightning, which no one who was born and raised on Earth until that time had been able to do effectively. Some people had visited and were able to do things, but they did not live there. They went back where they came from. So our people started lives on Earth, and we were immediately taught how to work with different forms of light. Of course, we already knew how to work with the sunlight and the moonlight and the starlight and all of that, but we had to learn a little bit by experimenting, you'd say.

It took about two generations, a little more than two generations, to learn how to work with lightning. But we were able to do it, and we have been able — my ancestors have been able — to pass this on to the current generation as well.
That's awesome.

The reason I came through today is my people are still doing this, but because of changes on Earth now, who can say what will come in the future? It is just good for you to know that you can do these things I've shared with you, even if you do not do everything that my people have learned how to do because I cannot share it all here. I've shared what I can share. You can do this one thing, and it will help you feel more at peace.
Well, thank you.

Andromedans Volunteered to Work with Light
Can you say what star system or galaxy your people came from?
Andromeda.

How many came? How many on the first ship?

Six.

Was there someone who taught them a little about lightning after they got here, or did they have to learn it all by experiments and trial and error?

They learned it all by experiment. There was a little bit of instruction, but the instruction came from the elders before they left Andromeda, and it was not understood that working with lightning would be their main focus on Earth or what the desire was for them to do with lightning. So a little more was explained to them about what they could do with the Sun and the sunlight, things with the Sun. When they first came, these volunteers thought the lightning was associated with the Sun. It wasn't until toward the end of the second generation when they realized that the lightning did not come from the Sun but rather came as part of Earth's living system. That made it easier to understand what to do because initially they were working with the lightning as if it were part of the Sun.

How did you work with light on your home planet? What sort of things did you do there?

People did not need to be cared for in the ways people do on Earth. Mostly it had to do with balance. Sometimes there are people who need more light, meaning something simple — daylight, yeah? So we learned how to extend the day for those people, but everybody else was happy without much daylight, yes? And there was night light. Do you say "night light," or do you have another word? You say "dark night?" We call it night light because there is light; it's just not as bright as day. We learned how to extend the daylight for these people but not to disturb the other people. Other people experienced more daylight even though everybody else was experiencing night light.

It's very complicated, and I cannot explain it to you at this time. I wouldn't want anybody on Earth to do it. I have not been taught this, but I know that it can be done. It could cause problems on Earth, so I won't explain it, but that's one of the things we did.

Were the first six left with some technology, or were they just sort of dropped off? How did that work?

When the six people were dropped off, as you say, they were not given much technology, just food and instructions on how to get along on Earth. They were guided as to which animals could support them and teach them and how. There was somebody on the ship who gave them this teaching, so the assumption was that this person must have been on Earth for a while. But the person was not from there, so there was some teaching there — getting along, surviving.

Did they move around, or are you all still at the same place where they started?

We are generally in the same place.

What an amazing history.

Well, you'll have to think about it. These six people left their families, their lives, and everything they had ever known, so of course there was a lot of missing loved ones. But the three men and three women made families of their own, and so life went on.

Without teaching us how to do it, are there other things you can say about what you do with lightning besides what you shared with us?

No.

I assume that what you do helps the planet in some way,?

No, it helps the people. I don't think it helps the planet. Earth does this on her own, helps to free spirits. I think the lightning does other things. It might help Earth balance herself. I'm sure there's no doubt of that, and she moves of course. She breathes to an extent, and she uses her elements — rain and wind and so on — but she might need to affect her polarities or charge up places or stimulate herself, I assume. I think she does other things, but in my experience when observing lightning, I can see — as I've been taught to see things beyond what is physical — every time I have seen lightning strike the ground, I watched the spirits go up. I think that this is something that happens all the time, and it's a good thing. Otherwise the spirits wouldn't have another way to get there. So it shows you how loving Mother Earth is that she would help because she can.

Well, this is marvelous. It's totally new information, which is what I love.

Well, I'm going to say good night.

Is there anything you want to say to the people who read this from the perspective of your training or wisdom?

The times you are living in are fraught with temptations. Sometimes it is just something innocent, a little too much of "this" or a little too much of "that." But very often the temptation is to do something that you later regret. You have all had these experiences. If you feel something coming on — especially if this has happened before and you think to

yourself, "I know I'm going to regret this," yet you go on and do it —
keep in mind that you are perhaps perpetuating the problems. So my
feeling is you should pause and consider. Good night.

That's marvelous, thank you very, very much. Good night.

Good night.

CHAPTER SEVEN

Accept and Maintain Your Physical Body

Grandmother

October 9, 2014

Welcome.

Thank you. I can tell you some of what we do. For one thing, it's important to know that some shamanic things, depending on the group of people, will always be secret and meant only for the students — the apprentice, you would say; they are not meant for the general public. So whatever comes through for this book is to help people who are choosing or considering or are on the path of the shamanic way to be inspired. It's to remember, perhaps, or to have pieces added to the pieces they already have to achieve something. You are not going to get things that are profound and secret because those are meant to be done in the most careful and specific ways. That kind of teaching cannot go out to a general audience because the teacher, the practitioner, cannot be with every single person who reads it, and that's what is required to get the work done in a way that is safe not only for the person who is performing the work but, just as important if not more so, for the people or beings who experience the effects of the work.

This is also for the reader so that he or she knows why he or she sometimes only gets what very distinctly feels like part of the puzzle. You get part of the puzzle because if you are meant to do this work, you will find the teacher you need, the teacher will find you, or you might have a vision of the next step on the path for that work. The purpose of the book is to achieve something, but it is not to be a substitute for person-to-person teaching.

Each Person Has a Tune

I will share a little something. I am not that far back in terms of your time — only about 175 years ago in what you call the steppes region [possibly referring to the Great Steppe region in Eastern Europe and Central Asia]. What we did then, though it might be a lost art or misunderstood in these times, was every time a child was born, the shaman (though there might have been different words) would get very close to the child after the child was cleaned up and had lived on Earth for at least three days. The first three days are important so that mother and child can bond in the same physical world. Bonding goes on when the child grows in the mother, but this isn't happening in the same physical world because the mother cannot embrace the child in the same world.

So the shaman — whether it's a man or woman doesn't matter (some places would only allow a woman in this situation, but occasionally it would be men) — would get very close to the child and smell the child just at the top of the head or occasionally around the ear — one or the other. Then a melody would come forth, a tune. Not words necessarily, but sounds. And that is what you call a baseline or foundation element of that child's health and well-being and life.

The child's physical mother would memorize the tune, and the shaman or the shaman's student (sometime there would be more than one student) would also memorize that tune. It would just be a few notes. It might not be even a full bar, musically speaking, but just a few notes or tones. Sometimes there would be other sounds. It might have been a word in the local language, but more likely it would be — how can we say? — in a secret language, a very spiritual-sounding language. It might sound like something you ought to be able to translate into your language, but there's usually no direct translation. This is the way that life was cared for.

Throughout a child's life, as he or she grew up, he or she had that tune. Sometimes, the physical mother would incorporate it in lullabies, but if she did, she would always stop the lullaby, make the tone or tones, pause again, and then go on with the lullaby. This was to make it clear to the heart, soul, and mind of the child that it was his or her tune. As the child got older, he or she would be taught that tune. And if ever that child was not well or was injured, he or she could sing that tune and it would immediately connect that child to his or her physical mother (even if the mother was not on the planet anymore) and to the mother's mother. It would also connect that person to the shaman and to the time and place of birth when the shaman, mother, and baby connected, which would have been the most perfect balance of his or her life on the planet. So that is something I can share with you. There might be a few people left in that region who remember that or who have been told about that and can recall it.

I assure you that the tune thing made complete sense to almost every mother on the planet and to a great many people who work with animals, as this can be done with animals as well. It is done, even now, with dogs and cats and birds in your time. They do it. Where do you think it was learned? It was learned by observing wildlife. Someone didn't just have an ET sit down to teach that. It was learned by observation, so it's important to know that it's being done even in your time.

Bring Warmth to Your Body through Memories

Does your tribe still exist on the planet?

We are an extended family now, and there are certainly survivors. I don't think they would consider themselves a tribe at this time but yes.

You were in the steppes. You lived in an area that had cold weather, right?

Yes, I did, and there were times when we did not have the right garments. So when we made certain tones and absolutely focused on one thing, which was to be warm, then we could bring our body temperatures up somewhat. This is not something a shaman would do for others. The shaman would teach others to make the tones, but people had to focus on being warm. In your time, the easiest thing to do would be to focus on being warm. Don't pay any attention to being cold. Just focus 100 percent on being warm. You can remember being warm. If you can't remember, then get under the covers for a while in your bed, get warm, and pay attention to how your body feels. Then come out from under the covers, sit in a chair or something, and practice feeling that way in your body even though you do not have the blankets for warmth. You can do that now.

Did you have to do that very often?

We did it when it was cold. We had things to wear, but we didn't have your modern types of garments.

What about animal skins?

Often, garments were passed down. As a matter of fact, even now you do that, but it's not as widely practiced as it used to be.

But you hunted animals, and you used their skins, right?

Yes, but they're not very warm. They will keep you warm up to a point, but you know, in that kind of snow and cold, you have to practice and focus on being warm.

So how many months a year was it that cold? Was it half the time?

Something like that or a little less than that. By "that kind of cold," I mean bitter cold.

Yes, South Dakota cold.

People Come from and Return to Light

Had you always been there, or had you migrated there?

You mean our origins? Our origin beliefs take us back as far north as you can go on this planet, where we lived as light, sometimes within the Earth and sometimes just above the northernmost portion as radiating light. You call them that?

Aurora borealis.

Yes. That's where we came from. We came from the light. I think probably all people come from there — maybe not always the same place, but certainly from the light. In my time, I saw many people die, and their bodies remained on Earth, but what goes on is light, and I have seen this light go on. So I have reason to believe that this is not only something from my people. I have seen other people, not just my people, die, and I have seen the light go on from them. So I believe that everyone is that.

But most don't remember like you do.

It is not popular to remember. Your time is more focused in being busy. Some people practice religions, but all religions do not remind people that they are of the light. When the light of day happens, this is to remind your physical body that you are in residence only temporarily — every time the light of day happens.

That's beautiful. So your people interacted with others, then? You said you'd seen others die.

Sometimes. There was not a lot of interaction, but sometimes we encountered travelers. We tended to stay in the same area, but sometimes people came by in various states of being, usually going somewhere, migrating. Sometimes there were old ones, and occasionally the old ones would do as all old ones do — die but continue on as light.

That seems to be a strange place for people to be traveling through.

It's not strange at all. Wherever you are in the world, there are always people traveling, even in the distant past, thousands of years ago, people traveled. Why? I think it's because people are curious. They want to know, "What's behind that rock? What's that sound? What's that smell?" And they'll go find out.

Why do you think you were in a place that was so inhospitable? Couldn't you have gone some place warmer?

We were always there. Why leave? We had comforts there. There were (what you call) hot springs. There was a deep cave, and we would go there sometimes. It had great beauty and sparkling things, glowing things. There was always enough light so that we could see our way. Why leave? It was a beautiful place.

What was your food? Did you hunt? Did you have agriculture?

We hunted, yes. We had some other food that you would probably consider mold that grew on the sides of things. I don't think it's safe for you to eat in your times, but we were able to eat it. And we found something in the cave too.

How many people, roughly?

Oh, rarely more than forty. I think there were almost fifty once, but it wasn't unusual to be around thirty. That's why I like to say it's an extended family. It was not a huge number, so we didn't decimate the local animal populations. We had to be respectful of them. We wanted to be. They taught us many things, and we paid attention to what they did. It's always good to pay attention to what the animals do in your time — not just your pets but more importantly the animals that are still free.

Were you the shaman for your extended family?

For our people, yes, during that time. I was taught by someone, and then I taught someone. It's passed down but not necessarily through lineage. It depends on what a person shows he or she can do — what that person is interested in, yes, but also what he or she can do. You might be interested in something but not have the capability, or you might not be able to do it well. More important, there might be something you can do better. If there's something you can do better, then do that. But if nobody else can do the shamanic work, then even though you can do something else better, try to do both (if you can) until somebody comes along (is born) who can be the student. I remember that.

You are now in spirit?

Yes, of course.

Have you incarnated since?

No. I stayed in the region to watch over the survivors and to sing to them at night. Sometimes they wake up, and they remember a tune. If it is a pleasant tune, very short, it is probably their personal song.

Do you sing their songs to them?

Sometimes, especially if they need it. Sometimes the old ones do. They don't have that knowledge anymore, but they remember in their deep sleep that it exists.

So 175 years ago is really very recent. Do you mean they still remembered some of the old ways, so they could teach you as a shaman, but they had forgotten some of the old ways?

No. Because of events in your world in the past 100 or so years — wars and fighting and struggles — the people were dispersed or harmed, but some of the bloodline remained. There were survivors. And even though they may not be producing children who are completely in the bloodline, some of the bloodline is there. Those are the ones I sing to sometimes or watch over to the extent that I am able to help them — not as their personal guide, but I have decided to be here in spirit to help as long as the bloodline lasts. Should the bloodline ever thin out past a certain point and I don't feel needed anymore, then I'll move on. When I move on, I'll return to our place of origin, and you might see me in the sky.

A Shaman's Responsibilities

You said there were wars and your people were dispersed. That happened after your life, right?

Yes. When I say 175 years ago, that is when I died. Generally speaking, when people tell you that they lived so-and-so long ago for this book, that's when they stopped living.

How old were you at that time?

Well, in your years, I was a little bit between thirty-eight and thirty-nine.

Was that considered old at that time?

No, it was about midrange.

What did you die from? Was there an accident?

I was helping some people who were in distress. It was during a rock fall, and I was trying to save a couple of children. I managed to save one.

But the rocks got you?

Yes. It was a worthy effort. I had a student pretty well trained by then, so I wasn't a great loss for our people.

Were there other healers or medicine women? What other assets did you have to keep the tribe safe and healthy?

There was a medicine man. It may not be obvious from the voice of the channel, but I am a feminine being.

Oh! That didn't even occur to me.

Yes, I understand your confusion. There was a medicine man who understood such things as the plants around there. That was something that could be passed on too, knowledge, and of course, it was passed on.

Did you have children?

I did not. I don't know why. I couldn't. But I had a husband. He was sad when I died, and I was happy that he joined with another. I wouldn't have wanted him to be lonely.

Do you remember lives before that life?

I try not to distract myself. I've had dreams, and I think they might be past lives, but I don't focus on it because I have enough to do. Oh, you're talking about during my life. Yes. Obviously in spirit —

Yes, in spirit you would know, but —

Yes, during my life, I had dreams, but I didn't focus on them because we didn't really write anything down, so we had a lot to remember. The work that I did wouldn't be written down. Why would it? Suppose something we wrote on became damaged and someone read it who was not part of our people. That person could make a mistake. No, it had to be done exactly right, and at the same time, it had to be flexible because the students would be different. Each had his or her own thoughts and feelings, and the teacher would have to anticipate. Sometimes, though, because people are who they are, there were surprises. So you can't write something down and anticipate surprises from people, especially with children.

How old was your apprentice when you started to train that person?

Oh, I would train more than one because we could never be sure who would survive. That was always the case. Is that the case in your time? Sometimes, children die, and yes, it is a sad thing for parents and others, but —

So you train two, three, or four, something like that?

I trained, at various times, several. Sometimes it started as young as two. I didn't speak as much as I would sing. I would play with the child, but mostly I waited until he or she got to be a little older — not too much, though, because little children show what they're interested in very, very early. Some things won't interest them; other things will. Pay attention.

Yes, I've heard that many times.

Connect with What Ails You

Was there anything else that you or anyone in your tribe did that would apply to our time now and that we could learn from?

There is one thing that I have had insight on now that you can do in your time. You will have to do it carefully, but I think it is safe. Start with some minor disease, the kind of disease that people get over without any treatment — without any treatment at all. Do you understand?

Such as a cold or something similar?

Yes. You'll get over it. You don't need to do anything. Or perhaps you have an injury that you don't treat to get over it or even some temporary discomfort you don't treat but you get over. Maybe you lie down for a while or something. If you feel that this discomfort is caused by something external to your body — I think you call it a germ — try to make contact with it. Don't be direct. Don't try to touch it or something. Some of you might try that, especially in the world of thought you call science. Don't ever do that. Rather, try to sing or make tones that you feel will reach that life form. Then just make those tones.

If you are physically comforted by the tones and you feel a connection with that germ, as you call it, then it is possible that it will be comforted as well and will feel who you are. Perhaps it will be able to do something with its own existence to not cause the discomfort anymore. If you have success with that, then you can go on and very gradually work on other germ beings. They are alive. You can work with them, and perhaps when there are discomforts that are more extreme, the germs might change the way they are. It is easier for life forms like that to change the way they are than for you to change the way you physically are in your now time.

Keep in mind that life's not about how long you live but how much you enjoy it physically. You can have many wonderful things in your life, but if you are not feeling well, you may not be interested in them. It is this way for all who get on in years. Choose right now to love your physical body. Respect it, and recognize that your physical body can change. There will be one threat or another. This will go on indefinitely. If it's not "this," then it will be "that."

It is a time of testing what you can do. What will you do? How will you help? How will you be a good example to others? How will you ensure that your help is something they might respect? You cannot suffer and be unhappy and tell someone else, "I've got a great cure for you." You must show that you and your body are in agreement that what you are teaching can benefit at least some of the people. No one thing will benefit everyone. There will be many things always.

I feel you have much to offer, and I thank you. Do you have a name?

Grandmother.

Grandmother! [Chuckles.] All right, blessings from my heart. Thank you.

CHAPTER EIGHT

Focus on the Positive to Bring It About

A Modern-Day Shaman in South America

October 30, 2014

So then, you wish to have things you can do to change your world, eh? I will give you something you can do. It is not complicated, but you have to be able to focus on something you want that would be good for you — not revenge or something harmful, but something you would like in your life. I don't recommend asking for an object. I recommend asking for what the object is intended to do.

Let's say you want to have a new car, but what's that car going to do for you? It's going to get you to "this" place or "that" place. It's going to simplify your life, or it's going to make your life more fun. So what you need to do is to focus on that outcome: "I need to have more fun. "I need to be able to move from place to place freely, comfortably, and happily." Focus on those kinds of thoughts. Bring up the feeling as if that were something you could have. One thing at a time, all right? You'll have to learn how to focus on that one thing because if your mind wanders and you're thinking about lots of things — meaning accidentally not wishing to think about it — what will ultimately happen is you will come up with something you are afraid of or cynical about or disappointed by or angry about for the work to function and to bring it to you, or at least create circumstances whereby you could have what you want and need. If you bring up your fears accidentally, it will bring that to you, so you see why you must stay focused.

It is not complicated. Learn how to stay focused on something that you want. Don't just ask for money; ask for what that money is going to be used for, all right? It's important to understand that something that is desired is most easily manifested in multiple ways with the simplest possible execution of it, of an idea. If you need something, go to what you actually need, not the thing that's between you and the need. Right now, most people in your time are working for the thing that's between them and what they need. Perhaps you understand.

Now, this is what you do. Once you are able to focus on something like that for just thirty seconds, see whether you can focus on it for forty seconds. That will be your goal. You may be able to achieve thirty seconds, or you may not. When you can do this for at least twenty seconds, go outside (you must be barefoot, so if it is wintertime, you'll have to wait until it is warm outside) and find a place on the land that is comfortable to you. It must be comfortable to walk barefoot, so no anthills, no uncomfortable grasses. Dirt would be best, but if there's no dirt, then find what you can find. It won't work very well on pavement, so try to find a place that is dirt.

Focus on that practice you've been developing to bring something about for yourself, and then step on the land, all right? Take steps with the front of your foot down so that the ball and toes touch first, and then bring your heel down. Walk only on land that feels comfortable and safe for you. This does not mean that what you need will come up for you or that the opportunity will come up for you only in that place. You're giving a message to Mother Earth, and Mother Earth is soil, dirt, sand, and water — the beach, for instance. Walking on grass or anthills doesn't work.

Now you're going to ask who I am. I am a shamanic person alive in your time in South America.

Well, welcome!

Hold an Image of Happiness

Now, there's more. You will find that with your families and your friends, there will be a tremendous need to release something, to let something go, to let something out of your life. Perhaps somebody is being abused that you know of or somebody has a destructive habit that is harming him or her and perhaps even others. There is a way you can help to remove that from a person's life. It is different and won't be easy, but you can use a similar process.

Do not think about the self-destructive or the harmful behavior; that could create complications and bring that into your life. Focus on what would be better for the person. You could picture them living in harmony in some way or laughing or happy in some way that is not harmful or that is perhaps even a good thing, a fun thing, and a pleasant thing that doesn't harm anyone. You see? You focus on that, and in this case, you do something a little different.

Find that place on the land that is comfortable for you specifically — on the dirt or on the sand, as I said before. Before when you put the front of your foot down, you walked forward naturally. This time, put the front of your foot down and hold that picture or image or thought that transforms the issue or situation: the person is better off, not doing harm, happy in his or her family, safe, and so on. You have to have the image of that; saying the words is not enough, I feel.

Try to hold an image, a picture in your mind's eye, and fill your body with that image, something that if you were in that presence, you would be happy to experience. It could be something you would be happy to experience for them — happiness, joy, peace, calm, whatever. You'll think of something. Then with the front of your foot down, walk backward. That helps to bring something about while removing something that is harmful to your friends or family.

What about doing that for one's self?

It's not necessary. That was covered with the first thing I said about something that you want or need.

Right, but if you need to get rid of something in yourself —

No, don't focus on what you want to get rid of; focus on what you want.

Okay, so forward for yourself, backward for other people.

That's right. Put the front of your foot down while holding on to the image or a thought, but only if it's a thought that fills you with a feeling you would like to have. Otherwise, like I say, if you start thinking about the person as self-destructive or harming others, you'll draw that to either the person or you. This is why these kinds of shamanic things are generally not taught to people who are not familiar with such practices.

Strive for What You Want

Can you say anything about yourself or how you live?

A little bit. I'll be general because I don't want people to say, "Oh, you said that in that book!" I will say that I live simply. I do not crave or desire material things. I use material things, as they are necessary to survive — yes? — such as food and shelter. Sometimes I go around to other people's homes or towns and teach those who are interested in these things. Sometimes I dress very casually. Other times I dress smartly.

In modern-day clothes?

Of course! I am alive in your time. You are on the planet, and I am on the planet. What else?

Were you taught shamanism from the time you were a child?

No. I was fortunate to meet my teacher when I was twelve years old. I didn't have any exposure to this until then. My father thought I needed to learn something that could help others because, well, I was always bringing home cats and dogs or other children who needed help, and he could see that I wanted to help but didn't have a direction for it. He also felt that because I had a strong belief in God, in Creator, and was very religious, I could do this and help in the church sometimes. And so I have.

Wonderful. Your father sounds like a beautiful being.

Yes, he is a good man, and he helps others. He also works to make a living and helps my family — my mother, of course, and my brothers and sisters. When possible, especially during holiday times, he shares things with cousins and aunts and uncles and so on.

That's beautiful. That's what we need to know — how we can achieve what we want to be happy without hurting ourselves or anyone else.

It's important to know that you need to work for what you want. You strive for it. Do the things in your world that will help to bring that about, but as a shamanic student, also do things that are, in this way, asking Creator for help in energy. It's like asking for a blessing, and this is done by concentrating (focusing) and by doing physical things because Creator created our bodies. Since Creator did this, we know that when something is desired in our physical world, we must ask for what we want and need physically as well as use our imaginations to have pictures because the imagination is the part of our thoughts that can help create things. Very often, you can think, "Oh, I wish I could do 'this'" or "I wish I could do 'that,'" and then you imagine doing it. So you combine that with physical actions — going out and trying to do it, build something, say — then ask for a physical blessing. I'm giving you the means to do so. In being spiritual, you can still be religious. I have found it to be a comfort, religion. I am a Christian.

Do you act as shaman to a particular group or to people who ask you for help?

When people come to the church — I'm going to be a little vague here — to speak to the religious people in the church and they have done what they can do and urge others to do what they can do but someone is still suffering from something, then sometimes they ask me to help. Sometimes that's the way I find out. Other times, just being in life and walking about, I see people who need help. Sometimes I can tell they welcome help. Other times I can tell they don't want help at all, so I keep away from them. Life brings it to my attention.

So you have learned also to assist people in their own healings?

Yes, because if you have a disease or discomfort — what you call a discomfort, something that's not really horrible but nagging, always there; that's a discomfort — you do what you can. You try to live better so that it doesn't come up very much. Maybe you avoid some things and seek out other things. You talk to your doctor or nurse to get some help, but it's still there sometimes. Then I offer what I can. Sometimes it's a long path to be healed, and you have to go many places. I am one of those places, you might say.

Children and Physical Need

You sound as if you know you're talking through a channel, and you sound young and full of energy. Are you?

I'm full of energy, but I'm not very young anymore! That doesn't mean I am an old man.

Do you have a family?

Yes, I do.

Children?

Yes, I do. There's nothing like it. When you have children, you find out what the world needs right now. When they are hungry, they need to eat. When they are sleepy, they need to sleep. There is never any doubt about what children need, and it helps people because they're surrounded by other human beings, eh? You can know what others need because whether they're small and young or grown up or old, they are just like you or just like your children. They have the same needs. It is not complicated. In these times, people are distracted by complications. You have these electronic things, you know, your electronic phone or your electronic tablets. And while they seem to be helping you, very often they just take time away from what is more important. How often have you been studying your phone when you could have reached down and talked to your little girl who is saying, "Daddy!" and you say, "Just a minute"?

"Daddy!"

"Just a minute."

After a while, she realizes she's not important, and the phone is the thing you're playing with in your hand. It's not complicated. I'm not saying you have to throw your phone away. I'm saying to keep it simple because no matter how many things you have to do with electronics, you're still going to need to help your little girl or your son or your grandmother or your auntie or your uncle or your brother or your sister or your friends or others. They're going to need help, and you can't say, "Just a minute," forever. People learn they're not important, and they get angry. They get upset, and maybe it's just one more step on the path to being harmful or being self-harmful. Don't contribute to that step.

Yes, especially now. Everyone is so tired and confused, and things are moving so fast that I guess we all need more attention.

Everybody needs more attention. People need to be reminded that they do, and when you're around children, you're constantly reminded. They want and need. And when you grow up, you're exactly the same, but sometimes you develop habits. You think, "Oh, I can't have 'this,'" and then you get sad and go drink a beer or something else. And then sometimes you are lost.

I assume you're in a modern city and not out in a jungle some place, right?

I'm not in a jungle.

Do you have apprentices now?

Only one at this time. My son has shown an interest.

That's wonderful.

It's wonderful when the apprentice is somebody I know well. Although I teach things to my son, I also take him to somebody else I know who is not part of my family — my blood family, you know — because it's good for him to get teachings on things I can do from somebody else so that he isn't always thinking, "Yes, Dad" or "No, Dad." [Chuckles.] Otherwise, it's not balanced. I take him to somebody else too. And sometimes he says, "I want you to tell me, Dad!" And I say, "Oh, well, I'll tell you a little bit, but then ask your teacher." [Chuckles.] It keeps it in balance.

Shamanic Work Takes Dedication

Let's say someone reading this is interested and feels he or she could do this. How would you recommend that person try to find someone to learn with? I mean shamans aren't on every corner.

Maybe not, but I think in this day and age, there are some people trying to teach these things. First off, if you can read and have books or can obtain material or can go to the library, you can read about it. Know that sometimes people will be critical of shamanic things, and that's because they don't understand them. They don't understand that it is of God, just like other things. Sometimes people do things they say are shamanic things, but those things aren't of God. Trust your feelings. If it doesn't feel good to you, even if it's good, then you know it's not the right time for you, it's not the right person for you teacher-wise, or it's not right, period. Don't make a judgment on it. Don't say, "Oh, this is bad," or "Oh, she is evil," or "Oh, he is evil." Just say, "Oh well, that person is not the right teacher for me," and go on. That's it. Go on. Go find another. That's the beginning. Also, it might be that you're just interested in some other thing.

You'll have to decide whether or not you want to dedicate your life to this. I dedicated my life to this, and this is what I do, all right? When you do this, you have to focus on it all the time. It's not something you do forty hours a week or forty-eight hours a week or fifty-six hours a week. You do this all the time for everyone. Of course, you rest. You sleep. You go out with your husband or wife or your girlfriend or your boyfriend. You have a life, but when something that is needed comes up and you have something you can do for it, then you do it seven days a week. I do this seven days a week even though I go to church on Sunday.

How do you make a living from this to support your family? Do people make donations or something?

I don't make a living. I don't charge for it. I just do what I can for people, and very often, people invite me to dinner. I do what I can. I always have a place to sleep because I can sleep many places. I don't require a lot. People do things for me, but it is not like a trade. It is not like, "Oh,

I will help your child survive, and then you take care of me for the rest of my life." It's not like that. If you help somebody's child survive (and others help him or her too, of course), if you contribute that help, then fine. That's something you do. Eventually others see you around; word gets around. They feel good about you, and people help. I don't charge for what I do, and other people don't charge me for what they do for me.

But you still have to buy groceries and pay for your kids and pay rent and all that, don't you? How do you do that?

I don't. Other people do that. You are living in a world where you are used to doing that, but there was a time, eh?

Barter, yes.

People traded. In my case, it's not a direct thing. I do things for others, and various people do things. When my children need something, people provide it. We have what we need. We don't try to accumulate more in case we need it someday.

You already live in the direction in which we're moving, which is where we'll end up, I guess.

It's where you came from. Why would you not end up where you came from? You've taken a long road, and on that road, you learn things. You acquired knowledge, wisdom, and sometimes experiences that you wish you hadn't acquired. But someday, you will come back to where you began, and you'll have a new appreciation for it, and then life will be good.

Recognize You Have Unique Gifts

If you feel as if I'm prying, just tell me and we'll go in another direction. Did you go through school? Or do you get your information internally from inner guidance?

Are you talking about the lessons I had with my teacher?

No. I mean about the world in general.

Did I attend school and learn about geography and mathematics? Yes, of course.

Okay. In addition to that, are you a channel? Do you connect with angels or ancestors or beings or anything?

No, but at times I get inspirations, so my instinct is strong. And sometimes I have dreams. I know by the feelings I have in my body when I wake up whether my dream is something I am intended to find out how to do or something I am intended to do and I might have a feeling of how to do it. Perhaps I have to seek somebody out and find out how to do it, or I have to seek somebody out who is doing it and let that person know it is needed. Sometimes people can do things that are truly amazing, but they don't realize other people cannot do them and need them. So sometimes it's a matter of just finding someone who can do something. You would be surprised at the people can do this. It's very often just simple people, uncomplicated people. At different times, I have met three people who were living on the street who could do amazing things and didn't know that other people needed those things. They thought other people could do them too.

I will give one example. I met a boy. He was a teenager, and he was different. He walked with a limp. The people he lived with were proud people, and nobody in the family ever had anything like that. Nobody ever limped. But he was born with one leg quite a bit shorter than the other, so he looked different, and the people who he lived with weren't comfortable with that. When they would see him on the street, they would give him money, but then they would run away. This is why he was on the street.

He was not a criminal; he was just living as best he could on the street. Very often, he would beg for food. I came across him, and I took him somewhere to eat. We had a meal and a long talk, and it turned out that he knew how to do this (I saw him do it): There was a man at the restaurant who had acid indigestion, and the boy went over to him. The man was feeling bad. He forgot his medicine, and he was sitting there. He had a big belly, and the boy put his hand over it — not quite touching it, a few inches away — and immediately the man felt fine. The man said, "Thank you so much!" and offered the boy money, but the boy didn't want to take money for that. The man was very grateful, and he left.

I asked the boy, "How did you learn that?"

He said, "Learn this? Everybody does this, right?"

I said, "No, not that many people know how to do this."

So you see, I let him know that other people needed this. They needed that kind of curing, and maybe it could cure other things too. He didn't know he was a healer. I took him to my church and said, "Here we have a healer, and he can help." They were happy. They are always looking for healers. He is not living at the church, but somebody took him in, and now he has a roof over his head and gets to take a bath every day and has all the food that he needs. He does his healing, and he tries to show people how to do it, but perhaps he was just born with it. He didn't know. He thought everybody knew how.

So what does he do? He puts energy into the body and takes discomfort out or whatever is needed?

I see. You want to have an idea of how it is done. This is a God-given thing. He puts his hand there. He doesn't think about it. He puts his hand near the discomfort, and the discomfort goes away. Or in one case I heard about (I didn't see it), somebody was having a heart attack, and he was very close by. He went over and put his hand over the person's heart, and the heart was okay.

That's incredible!

Not everybody could do it, see. He doesn't know how to teach it; he's tried! He doesn't know how to teach it because people ask questions like you did. You know, "Well, how does he do it? Does he do 'this'? Does he do 'that'?" It's not thought; he just does it naturally.

He must have so much love that it just comes out or something.

You don't need to define it. Remember, definition, while being interesting to the mind, often makes segments. It separates. Accept the simple and bountiful, and appreciate it. Be thankful to God, whatever you call God.

CHAPTER NINE

Help Each Other to Help Earth

A Modern-Day Shaman

November 3, 2014

Good evening.

Good evening! Welcome!

I am living in an area that is very sparsely populated, and because it is so sparsely populated, I'm going to have to be a little vague about where it is. It's an area known for snow and cold. Is that sufficient?

That is sufficient.

Now, the work I do is largely associated with the stars, and what I primarily focus on is balancing our planet, Mother Earth, in its magnetic center. As you know, there have been a lot of phenomena on Earth, but that's only recently. In terms of Earth being a living planet, one expects any living being to have a personality. Because of that, one expects a demonstration of that personality. Because most people cannot hear her speak in our languages, we feel her similar to how you might feel a friend or even a good animal friend. You're used to the idea that your dog — or your cat or your horse or whatever — is not going to talk to you in your words, yet there is a desire (isn't there?) that your dog be able to talk it over with you or say, "Greetings, I missed you," even though he or she says it pretty well without words. Many times, there's the hope that Earth would do the same. Many people, especially children, would like that.

So what Earth does, to the best of her ability, is to exude different feelings. This is separate from her weather and her earthquakes and all of that. This is something separate. At times, especially considering all the children on the planet (when she considers children, she does not consider only human children; she considers all children of all species at the same time and in the same way, and in this way, you can see how important balance is), she will exude her experience of love. From what I can tell, her experience of love is a profound feeling of welcome. You can see how that feeling would be very comforting to children. Children of the human variety, as you know, do not always feel welcome, and this is understandable. Human beings cannot radiate that feeling every waking moment. Even the best of mothers and fathers cannot do that. They have different feelings at different times.

Just so you know, Mother Earth is constantly radiating a physical feeling. She doesn't have emotions; she has feelings. I think it's that way for human beings and other beings as well, but I recognize that "emotions" is a mental word for feelings. So Mother Earth constantly radiates this feeling of welcome, and while she aims it at or does it primarily for all children, it is also felt — though not necessarily understood — by grownups of all types. When nonhumans grow up, they recognize the feeling and know it's the feeling of welcome. But human beings, being on Earth (and I am one of those in case you were doubting that), come here to forget. That might seem strange, but that is why the phenomenon of forgetting is so frequently found on this planet. It's not just because we forget who we are in the larger spiritual sense so that we can live a life here that is independent (to the extent that's possible) and be who we are on Earth in the conditions in which we find ourselves but also because the overwhelming aspect of having to forget who we are causes us to be forgetful.

Use the Energy of the Stars to Help Mother Earth

Throughout our lives, we are forgetful, especially as we get older. We become profoundly forgetful. This is intentional. It's not intentional in our minds. It is frequently distracting to be forgetful as we get older, but the reason we are so forgetful when we get older is this: When we start getting well on and perhaps, you might say, coming in on the glide path of our transformation from physical life to spirit again, the forgetfulness is actually comforting because we're not able to put a strong grip on who and what we were in the physical life. We are, rather, reaching for something that we can't quite get our hands on. And it is that desire, that reaching for —"Who am I?" or "Who is this person sitting across from me?" — that vagueness that allows us to transition more easefully into our natural selves.

Now, I'm bringing these things up because my focus is in balance. That's why I'm conscious of the way human beings are on Earth and the way I believe human beings are in spirit. We're spirit before we come here, and we're spirit after we're here, and I assume that we go on and have lives elsewhere either in spirit or in some other physical form. I feel that to maintain our comfort level in our physical bodies here — which are not actually natural for us since our natural form is immortal and thus has to be light and spirit — and to have balance, we must not only forgive ourselves for making the decision to come here and live in this really challenging world but also do something that is difficult to the extreme.

We have to be our spirit selves and our physical selves *at the same time*. And there is naturally a contradiction in terms there. While we are our spirit selves during sleep, and deep sleep at that (even in a light nap, our bodies rest deeply, but we go on; we're conscious), we live in another way in our spirit lives. Sometimes there are recalled dreams and other times not. So balance is critically important because there is the constant ongoing, on a day-to-day basis, of being both.

My feeling is this: To help Earth remain balanced, we have to help human beings remain balanced. And when we help human beings remain balanced, it naturally reflects on Earth. Human bodies, as you know, are made up of Mother Earth, yet our spirits — our souls, our immortal personalities, our lights — are associated with the ongoing existence of our being. So our being is undoubtedly associated with Creator, and our physical form is associated with another being that can create, and that's that Mother Earth not only allows her form to become part of our physical body, but she welcomes it as she welcomes children.

My focus in this life, then, is to connect through myself, since I am representative of the human race, with all the stars in the sky at any given time. My focus is to get as close to the magnetic center of Earth as I can (which is, of course, on the surface of the planet) to act as a lens — which

I believe is probably in a greater degree than we have (since I believe the whole forgetfulness thing doesn't exist that much in other places) — to run the energy of the stars through myself (I believe human beings are the only beings on Earth who forget) into the magnetic area of Mother Earth, which I feel in different places at different times. One would assume that the magnetic area would be in the center of the planet along its axis, but I don't feel that it's only that. Sometimes it is in the center in the planet; other times I feel it in completely different places. Perhaps that energy moves around. Anyway, that's what I do.

Welcome the Light

You first said you work with the stars to do this balance, this magnetic balance. How do you work with the stars?

Around the stars, we can be pretty sure there are planets. Of course, I don't want to interfere with other beings' lives, so I work with the light from the stars because that's what I can see. This is something that we have around us as well, you know, our lightbodies. So that's what I work with.

Do you work by asking them to help you do the balancing?

No, I look at the light. I reach up toward it, and I welcome it. I'm standing on Earth, and I remember it. I remember the feeling of being a child, and I remember the physical feeling of feeling welcome even when there were no other human beings around from time to time. I still felt welcome. I remember that feeling even though I'm now an adult. I raise up my eyes, and I welcome the light. I am my physical human self, made up of Mother Earth, yes? So standing on the planet that is welcoming children, being a human being and feeling welcome, and focusing into the energy of welcome, I raise my hands up and welcome the light. I let it pass through me, down through the bottoms of my feet and into the area of the planet where the magnetic area is associated, and I believe this helps to sustain Mother Earth's magnetic energy because I believe her feelings radiate from her magnetic center just as I believe our feelings do.

How interesting. Do you feel this balance helps her survive during this time?

It helps us survive during this time as well. It is not possible to help Mother Earth without helping human beings or all other beings on the planet because we are all made up of Mother Earth. You cannot just help Mother Earth. If you help Mother Earth, you help all beings on the planet too. You cannot separate them.

The Magnetic Center Is Not Fixed

Do you feel that the center of the magnetic field is in the center of Earth?

No. As I said, it moves around. I said you might think that it would be in the axis, but it moves around. I find that it moves around all the time. So sometimes the energy will go straight down into the center, and other times I feel it just moves in some other direction. I know that it has found that magnetic center, though, because I feel more complete. I feel the energy flow through me. But until it goes through the bottom of my feet, it just flows into me. It has to flow through me because it would be too much. It flows through the bottoms of my feet, and then it just migrates toward that place where Mother Earth's magnetic center is at that moment, and that moves around. Therefore, I think our magnetic center as human beings also moves around. That might have something to do with how we express feelings, but I'm not sure about that.

I feel that we are very similar, if not identical, in physical makeup to Mother Earth. We look different, but we are made up of her, so even though we have our light and our souls and our personalities and all this, we are still made up physically of Mother Earth. So I have reason to believe that we are like that too.

Where do you think our magnetic center is in the physical body?

I think it moves around. It does in Mother Earth, so I have every reason to believe it moves around in us. And my thought — I cannot tell you any more. This is what I believe: I believe that what we express on the feeling level comes from our strong magnetic center in our bodies at any given moment, and I believe that different feelings have to do with different places in our bodies. I don't think it's something we consciously do. I think this happens naturally without thinking.

We have chakras, and each one of them relates to different parts of our personalities. Do you think the magnetic center moves up and down from one chakra to the other as we change our feelings?

No. It's not that limited. I feel it moves all over the body. It could be in your big toe, it could be in your spleen, or it could be in your eye. I think it moves all over the body because we have all kinds of different feelings. We don't just feel happy or sad. There are lots of different shadings of those things, so it moves around. I don't know. I can't prove it, but this is what I think. So if somebody's interested, you can try to find out, but that's not my job.

Are you in such a sparsely settled area that you don't have access to computers?

Why would I do that? That's not my work. I don't use a computer.

Okay. I meant to Google the question of magnetic energy in the human body.

Why would I want to do that? See, you would want to do that. I think you use those things. It's up to you or others to do that. I'm not asking people to do it. I'm telling you what I think, but I'm not assigning anybody to do it. I'm not going to do it. I believe this is so based on my physical feelings when the energy goes through me. It wanders around until it finds the place. It doesn't "wander" around. I am moving the hands, but you can't see them. It goes through my feet and immediately goes to the magnetic center of Earth at that moment. It's very rarely straight down.

Do you feel it coming through you, through your magnetic center?

I don't pay attention to that. It's not about me. It's about Earth.

I see. You're interested in where it goes after it leaves you.

No, I'm not interested; you're interested in that. I'm just bringing it up to you because I thought you would be interested in it. My job is to get it to the magnetic center, but it's not my job to think about it.

Is this something you came up with, or were you taught? Where did this start?

My father taught me, and his father taught him. We've been doing this for many generations, and we feel it helps. This is what I do.

Have you connected with anyone else on Earth who also does this other than your family?

No. Why should I? It is my job. If other people do it, that's fine. I say welcome, thank you, and I'm glad we're doing this together, but it is not my job to connect with others. It is my job to do what I do.

Let the Night Sky Tell You Where to Reach

You do this by standing on the land, and you do it every day?

Every day. Many, many times a day for hours and hours. It's a calling.

Do you point toward different stars, or do you focus on different starlight at different times?

I look in the sky, and wherever feels right to me, that's what I reach for. I know if it feels right to me, Earth or some portion of Earth probably needs that, even when it's people. People are part of Earth. We are all part of Earth. Even though we live other lives and have souls and spirits that are beyond Earth. We are now part of Earth. Now is what's important in my work and (I feel) in others' as well.

So that's what you do. You don't work as a shaman with the people in your group or your community?

What I said is what I do.

Are there other shamans around who work with the people of your group, then?

I assume all over the world is like that.

Is it just your family, or do you live with a group of other people?

I'll have to ask my father whether this is all right to say. There are a few people living nearby, but not too many.

Of those people, are there more traditional shamans who do healing work with people?

I am a traditional shaman. This is a tradition. It goes back — just a moment. I will ask my father. My father says it goes back hundreds of years, so it's traditional.

Aha. How old are you? Can you say?

Yes, I am allowed to say. I am thirty-five.

Do you have a family?

Yes.

Do you have children?

Of course.

Is one of your children your apprentice?

Yes, my daughter.

Great! I've never heard of this, so tell me more about Earth's magnetic energy. What part of Earth do you feel it is: her feeling energy or her strength?

It has to do with that welcoming. To me, the children are everything. We do not go on as a species without welcoming. I feel her magnetic energy has something to do with her feelings because when I feel the welcoming, I feel her magnetic energy. I call it magnetic because I think of magnetic as something that attracts, and I think of attracting as welcoming. It's not necessarily physically magnetic. Looking toward Earth right now, I have to close my eyes to do that, to see, because it's not with my eyes, and of course, it's below Earth. How could I see with my eyes what's below Earth? It is like a gold light, but it's not enclosed; it's in motion. So the light itself is in motion all the time. Of course, so is the planet. That's not surprising.

[Laughs.] Yes. This is out of the way a little bit, but we did a book of conversations with planets in the solar system, and Neptune has — you can't see it, but you might be able to focus on it — a powerful feeling of welcome that just exudes from it. If you connect with Neptune, would that contribute to your work or anything?

I go to the stars. That's what I'm supposed to do, but thank you for your comment. Some of you might think, "Well, how can this help me?" or "That's interesting, but so what?" Some of you feel as if your life is dull or boring or there are things going on that you don't feel good about. Some of you are looking for something. Some of you know what you're looking for, and others don't. It's just a restless feeling. This is what I recommend: When you can, even if it is cold out (it's cold where I am all the time!), go out sometime at night. Go with friends if you like, but only friends who want to do this so that nobody's drinking and laughing and joking; it's more important than that. This is not to ask for something for yourself; it's a way to contribute (if you're looking to contribute). It's also, in my experience, profoundly calming, and I feel many of you are restless. It may not bring to you what you want, but it will calm your restless spirits.

Look up at the stars in the sky. If you live in a big city, you may not be able to see many, but you'll be able to see some when it's not too cloudy. If you live in the country, you'll be able to see many. Look toward the place where you feel the happiest or where you feel joy or where you get a good feeling, and reach up — not to try to touch it, but in a welcoming gesture.

You know what it looks like when you reach for somebody to give him or her a hug. Your arms are wide, and you're ready for that hug. Do the same thing, but reach toward the stars, welcome that light, and let it just flow through you. You don't have to think about where it's going. It will automatically flow through you, and after a while, you will feel calmer.

If you can't stand like that for too long (perhaps you are not as young as you once were or you simply can't stand too much), then take a chair out. Sit in the chair, but still reach up with your arms. If your arms get tired, you can lower them, but connect with that feeling of reaching up, maybe from your solar plexus or your chest. If you can't get that feeling, then you'll have to reach up with your arms. It is possible, when you're very tired, to just reach up with your hands, resting your wrists somewhere. Most of you will have to reach up with your arms. Make sure if you are resting your wrists and your elbows and so on that you aim toward that place with your fingers.

I recommend you do this reaching method whenever you feel restless and you can't figure out why. In my experience, it is very calming.

You don't have to worry about where the energy will go. It won't make you feel more restless; it will be calming. When you look at the stars where you feel best, feel good. Don't look for where you're excited. You're already restless. Look for a place in the sky where you just feel good looking at it. Some of you, especially if you're in the city and can't see that many stars, might find that the place that feels best is between stars. Of course, there are stars there; you just can't see them because the city lights make that difficult. So don't worry when it's between stars. Just try it. I recommend it. I think you'll feel better.

Wonderful! Thank you. Do you find that you are drawn toward certain places, or does the feeling of welcome that you get from the starlight occur all over the sky?

I feel it all over the sky in different places at different times. It's never something you can predict. You can't be attached to, "Oh, it's February. I'm going to reach for this place," nothing like that. You go entirely on feeling. It's all about feeling. You use your feeling to know where it feels best to reach for. Of course, when it feels best, you can be pretty sure that the energy is available. If it feels good to you, there's every reason to believe it feels good to them. It feels good to them, so they're reaching back. We're reaching to each other. What could be more welcoming than that?

Do you ever feel an acknowledgment from Earth that she is grateful for this? Do you get some sort of feedback from her?

I don't do this for pay. It's not about that. I do it for the love of the experience of doing it. I do it because it is meant to be done. That's how my father puts it.

Okay, I wasn't talking about praise but just acknowledgment. A connection. You feel a connection with that light.

I feel that, and I feel Earth. The simple answer to your question of whether I feel a separate acknowledgment is no, nor do I need it. When you pet your dog — do you have a dog?

No, I have a cat.

When you pet your cat, does it look at you and say thank you?

No, but it sort of wants to cuddle. I always get a feeling that the cat likes to be petted.

Then enjoy that.

Sustain What Already Makes You Happy

Are you out on the edge of a populated area? Is there a city to go to if you want to?

I cannot say where I am.

Can you say whether you went to school?

Yes. I went to school. I have been to a supermarket. I have not been to the movies.

Never?

I have never seen television, and this has been to my great advantage, my father assures me, because I can stay focused on what I am doing. I do not feel as if I am missing something. I do not have a phone.

But you know about these things.

Yes, I know about these things. I do not think there's something wrong with those things, but they are not things I need. I have my family. I am happy with them, and as far as I know, they are happy with me. We have things that we do. I am not working every second, and we have a good life.

Oh, it sounds wonderful. What a feeling of satisfaction you must have by doing something so important.

Yes.

I have never heard of it before, so I'm really glad you brought it up

I understand. I did not expect you to say, "Oh yeah, I know about that."

Is there anything else in your life that you can share?

I'm very happy with my family and my wife and my dog. Consider this in your lives. I think that many of you work hard to enjoy comforts: a comfortable home, perhaps a comfortable chair or bed, or something like that. Don't look for things to make you comfortable. Find good friends or a mate. Especially try to find a mate, yes. Have children, yes. If you are beyond the years of having children, find friends. Keep it simple.

Don't assume things will make you happy. I believe that the way to happiness is to look toward the core of your happiness: a healthy body, a clear mind, good feelings, happiness, family, and land that feels good to you. You don't have to own it. Ultimately, we are owned by the land, if anything, but ownership is not a factor to happiness. Look at what makes you happy, not just what you can't live without. You must have shelter; you must have food. You know these things.

Look at what makes you happy and what makes those people in your group — your family, your friends — happy. Decide what's really important, and work to sustain those things rather than trying to acquire more of something that substitutes for them.

Everyone may not find the perfect mate in this life, and that is sad. I wish you could. Until you can, find good friends or a good dog or cat who is happy to see you, and make them your family. Good night.

Thank you very much. Thank you.

CHAPTER TEN

Tap into Benevolent Energy

A Shaman in Finland

November 14, 2014

Greetings.

Greetings. Welcome.

I thought you would like to know how this works. It doesn't go directly from me to Robert. It goes through an energy. Usually it goes through a benevolent energy. Sometimes it has to do with a benevolent energy that you know. In this case, it's going through Zoosh, but other times it goes through some other energy that is familiar to Robert so that he is comfortable. In this way, there is nothing passed through. Since this is a person-to-person communication, there is nothing passed that can in any way cause harm or distraction. Even if it were direct, I think the channel has the capacity to filter that out, but it is a way to make it easier to communicate and not so much of a strain, and of course, then it can go on longer.

Now, I am currently in Finland. I am not from there, but I have been there for a time. That's all I am going to say about my location, except that I travel around a bit to places that welcome the sort of person who might visit Finland.

So you're going to ask about my work. I can tell you what I know. You'll have to reiterate your question for the recording though. Why don't you do that?

Shamanic Abilities Then and Now

I was thinking that just as we can now build space shuttles and jet planes and solar powered planes when we were building rail engines a couple hundred years ago, I'm sure that the energies available to and the abilities of the shaman today are far different from what they were before we moved into this new energy, this new awakening.

From what I know, most of what is done today was done in other ways in the past. Sometimes it was more localized, and other times the shaman or the person — you use another word, but we'll say "shaman" — would get a feeling that something was happening somewhere on Earth and could therefore acquire the many skills that are available today. They wouldn't necessarily say words because they wouldn't know what was going on. They would simply know that people or beings (nonhumans) somewhere on the planet were in need. So sometimes by making hand gestures and other times simply by allowing the energy to come through (usually by doing both), the shaman would sit or stand until the energy faded quite a bit. Then the shaman would have known that he or she had done what could be done. If that same feeling that people still needed help came up again, the shaman wouldn't do anything else. Normally after something like that is addressed (it's not unlike a long-distance call), the shaman doesn't get that feeling again. That's what I know about how things were done in the past.

But we have so much more available now. The lightbeings are eager to help in whatever way they can. Humans can hold more energy, and they have more capacity for benevolence. A lot of things have changed in the past twenty-five to fifty years.

But capacity does not necessarily mean application. Think about it. You are different. You are totally immersed in this work, but while the average person has those capabilities, does he or she use them? See, that's the issue. It's not just getting the word out about this; it's motivation. Ultimately, if people are not motivated to do something in this time when life is so full of complications and distractions, it's much more likely that they'll address something that, you might say, speaks louder to them or that they feel stronger about or want more of. They're more likely going to use their capabilities that way rather than for something they do not know what to do or how to do it. I don't want to sound like I am criticizing; I'm not. This is a long, slow process because you can only reach so many people, not because you don't have the capacity to get your message out, but because people are doing other things. What will happen is that people will be up against something because Mother Earth is going through changes, and science or technology or well-meaning people or emergency personnel will not be able to get to them. Hopefully, they will know something about benevolent magic or something like it or some other form of connecting with their angels and guides that can bring about benevolent transformation for them and their loved ones. There are other people doing other things, but this is the issue now. So what you said is true, but the trick, you might say, is getting people to use it.

Actually, that's a very good point that I hadn't even considered. I was just comparing people who were shamans in this moment with those from the past and asking whether the present-day shaman has access to more power, more influence, more energy, and more ability to change things that need change and to be made benevolent. It seems there's more stuff to work with now.

I think it's just that you're more aware of it now. You're in the now. You're living in the now, and you of all people are more likely to know about these things because this is your business. This is your work, and to a great extent, this is what you love. Knowing about it doesn't necessarily mean that you personally have the time to do it, you might say. At times, even you — I'm singling you out because you're a very busy person — are quite representative of many people on the planet now.

Even people who are very advanced on their spiritual paths have doubts about things they identify with — it's either fictional or beyond their capability. It's not surprising to have doubts.

Are you saying that those who consider themselves to be on a professional or vocational life path as shamans don't have access to more aid and benevolent health than they did 100 years ago?

Yes, I am saying that, and there's one really good reason you probably haven't thought about: Aid and comfort and assistance from ETs was much more readily available 100 to 200 years ago when nobody felt threatened by their presence! That's something you're not necessarily thinking about. The ETs who visited Earth were benevolent, and they might very well have set the ship down and come close to shamanic people and said, "You know, here's something you can do," or "Have you tried this?" Or maybe simply compared things that were done.

It wasn't at all unusual for people in those days on the ships to have people on the ships who were shamanic, who could do shamanic things. They wouldn't have given the people on Earth electronic devices or any of that stuff. They would have simply said, "How do you do things?" and "This is how I do things." And the people would learn. You see, it was a sharing process that went on between people, and it is not really done that way these days. So while your question is valid and relevant, it's not exactly in the picture of what I know to be true. If you speak to people from the past (I think it might be good to speak to some more people from the past), you can ask them that question. You can say it the other way, but you don't have to. You can say the same thing. You can say, "People in our now time ..." and "What about people in your time?"

Help Spirits to Move On

Okay. So tell me about your practice, your path.

One thing I do is to help people to move to the other side, as it's said gently, or to move on after death. Very often when people die, there are loved ones, or conversely, others who really hate and despise them who will not get over them. Death is not enough for them to get over that feeling, and there may be perfectly relevant reasons for them to get over it. There also might be perfectly relevant reasons for them not to get over it. You might see loved ones who are very sad about the one who died, and they bring up memories and wish that person could still be on the planet and so on.

That holds the dead one to the planet, right?

It doesn't hold the body, of course. The body returns to Earth, but the spirit might linger because it feels loved or might feel stuck. Generally speaking, hate will not hold a person on its own. For one thing, you shed all that was hateable, you say. Essentially people hate a residual of your life. But the people who love you don't realize that sometimes the loving and hanging on will cause the soul to linger. Sometimes people will even say, as in the case of a long relationship, "Oh, I'll wait for you," but something comes up, and they don't. Very often, this happens with spiritual people. Sometimes (more often), it happens with longtime lovers or people devoted to each other: "I'll wait for you." It's not good to do that, but sometimes people do it. It's not good to linger.

So what I very often do is walk around. I go places. If I feel a slight discomfort, it might just be an old energy in the land, but if I feel someone is lingering, then I'll help that spirit through. It involves light and energy. The spirit just moves on with its guide, and that's that. Invariably, I feel the land and people's lives lighten up, even those who were missing the loved one. Sometimes in missing that loved one, people don't realize they became stuck in the past. They can't move on with their lives very well, and it just doesn't work well.

Do you focus on an individual, or do you go where there were great battles or other unpleasant events?

I don't do that. Other people do that. I just work where people who heard about me call me up and let me know that there's an uncomfortable energy. They noticed an uncomfortable energy, and if I happen to be in town, they ask whether I could come over and feel that out and so on. I do it in the presence. I know some people can do it from a distance, but I haven't found that I can do that the way I like. I like it to be very clean and complete, so I go to the actual place, and when I feel the energy, then I make a request. Sometimes I make a request that has to do directly with the life or that the forbearers of that person — you know, the grandfather, grandmother, great grandmother, and so on — come and bring a guide. Other times I might ask for angels or guides and so on. I help by bringing in an energy that is compatible, comfortable, and safe for the lingering soul, and then it moves on. It takes as long as it takes. Usually it doesn't take more than a few minutes.

How do you know whether to ask for forbearers or angels?

I just know instinctively, but it took time to learn that. A lot of time is involved in learning how to trust that intuition and making mistakes. Sometimes it just doesn't work very well. When I started, I had a few of those, but my teacher was with me, and she would complete the process. My teacher didn't encourage me to go out and do this myself. She'd say, "Okay, this is how you learn." I learned to recognize the energy that was completely compatible with the particular soul I was working with. The energy always feels very similar. It feels very good. "Benevolent energy," you would say. Sometimes it's a little bit different for "this" soul or "that" soul because of the life lived. However, the underpinning is that benevolent energy, so the challenge to me was to first connect to that underpinning energy, that benevolent energy, and then to tune into the recently deceased. Until I learned to do that, my teacher kept reminding me. I had the tendency to tune into the energy of the recently deceased before I connected with the benevolent energy, and then I'd just get muddled. When I finally learned that (and it takes discipline and time), it worked well.

How old were you when you found your teacher, or she found you?

Seventeen. She was giving a talk about spiritual things. It wasn't in

Finland, but I will say it was a place where tourists go. They were speaking my native language (which is not English), and I was a tourist at that time. I went to the talk. I was traveling with friends not too far from home, and I thought it was interesting. I went to hear her talk about reincarnation and life after death and so on. I was fascinated. Afterward, I went up to talk to her, and one thing led to another. I couldn't start studying with her until I had finished my basic education, but then I did. I had planned to go to college, but we didn't have much money. I told my parents I found somebody I could study with, and they met the lady and felt good about her, so they said okay.

Do you make a living from this, or do you have another job?

It's not that I charge money for it; it's that when I travel around, people invite me to stay with them. Quite a few people in different places invite me to stay with them. They give me a meal and a place to sleep, and I go on to the next place. I don't feel good charging for it. I'm not saying others shouldn't do that. I just wasn't raised to do that, so I don't.

Do you just support yourself? You don't have a family to support?

I don't want to say too much, if you don't mind.

Yes, I understand.

I could be found. It wouldn't be a real problem if I were found, but I think it could cause embarrassment to you, and I don't want to do that.

Spirits Need Time to Adjust

Okay, help the readers understand: Someone passes away, and there is a great, great grief from the surviving spouse and maybe children. Does the spirit, then, have the ability to turn away from the guide that wants to lead it into the light?

The spirits don't turn away from the guides. Very often, before they really get connected to the guides (souls need to be able to be with the guides for a few seconds, but it's not time) once they've passed over (you know, out of their physical bodies and are in light, in spirit form), it takes a moment to adjust. If people are crying and wailing and saying, "Come back!" or other things that are completely understandable (especially if the person doesn't want to die), then the spirit wants to stay with its loved ones, which is usually the case, and there's a tendency to linger, to not even look for a guide or acknowledge the guide even though the guide will make itself known from time to time. Sometimes I have to inform the soul that the light coming around is its guide because if the spirit is lingering on Earth, it won't trust its natural wisdom. It will still try to think. It will still try to live in a linear world, but it is spirit, so it can't do that.

If it knows nothing about what happens after death, it might not know it has a guide.

Very possibly. But people who are religious, from certain religions, will look for an angel or something like that. If the guide knows that the person is religious or at least has a background in that, the guide will look like the conventional idea of what an angel looks like — not necessarily with wings, but sometimes, and especially when it's a child. Then often the guide will look that way if the child is from a particular religion or has been raised with exposure to those ideas and might be comforted by it. Children usually do not linger. They go immediately. They feel the love, and they follow the love. That is their guide.

Do you work with any people in the hospice organizations to teach how to let people die and what to do afterward?

No. People in hospice know what to do. If you're asking whether I educate people about this, I have shared with some people about how to do it, but I don't approach people about it. When people are interested in it beyond just thought, beyond simple curiosity, then I might. If there's a certain energy about them, then maybe I tell them a few things. Maybe I suggest they try "this" or "that," and the next time I come through town, I'll let them know. If they look me up, I'll work with them a little more. I don't look them up; they have to show that they're interested.

Other than that, do you have students that you teach what you do?

Not at this time.

So you travel, and there are certain places you go back to more than once?

Yes, but not all over the place, since I walk. I do not use a car. I have found that to feel energies, I need to be very open to feeling. If you're in a car, you're automatically insulated.

What about between countries? Do you fly between countries?

I don't fly. If I need to travel across borders like that for an urgent situation, then somebody will give me a ride, and I am okay with that. But only if it's urgent. If it isn't urgent, then I just work my way along in the area where I work. At this time, I am in Finland. I don't go all over the place. One can only walk so much. [Laughs.] It has an advantage. Theoretically, if I was on a horse, that would work. I could do that. But I don't do that because, you know, horses need a lot of care.

Yes. So how many people would you estimate at this moment you have helped be unstuck or move on?

Hundreds, I'd say. No more than hundreds — not in the thousands yet. I'm not that old.

Well, that is wonderful because they all have to go to the light before we move to the next level. Everybody has to leave here at once, right? They all have to go. We can't leave anybody stuck.

Well, that's the intention, I think. But I can't cover every place. I know there are other people doing work like this, so I'm not worried.

Have you met or been in contact with some of them?

No, but I read about it several times. I can tell by what people say in an article or what they say on the Internet whether they're doing it.

Do you ever think you will write a book or an article about what you do?

No. What I do takes all my time. Furthermore, when I travel and I walk, I like to look at the rainbows and the sunsets and the beauty. I'd rather experience life through my senses than through my thoughts. I'm not saying that's for everybody, but it is for me.

That allows you to be more sensitive. It allows you to be more in tune with the energies of the land and of the beings, right?

It does. It keeps me sharp. Sometimes I just walk along and find a situation that needs to be addressed in the way that I know how to do it. That happens. about 7 or 8 percent of the time, and I'll just stop and do it. That happens because I am in touch with it. If I were driving in a car, would I notice? I don't think so. Sometimes, you know, roads have been paved over the old dirt roads, but other times, the old dirt roads are there because they were always there when somebody first made a road out of it with a wagon wheel, or maybe it was even where the animals walked. So I like to walk on dirt roads because it's not unusual to find a place where somebody died but, for some reason, hasn't moved on. Then I help them move on. It's very gratifying work. Everyone is grateful, and it's nice to work with beings who are happy and enjoy what's being done. Others who have felt the uncomfortable energy are happy that the uncomfortable energy is gone. Everybody wins. It's a win-win situation. That's what you say.

Experience Your Grief

Sometimes survivors or sometimes people who feel discomforting energy contact you?

Yes. Sometimes, if they can't contact me, they'll contact friends I have, people I know in various towns. They'll say, "You know, so-and-so is going to be in town again. Will you ask him to come over and do thus-and-such?" Sometimes they don't call me directly — not that many people call me directly.

Well, if you're on the road all the time, that'd be a little difficult unless you have a cell phone, wouldn't it?

I have a cell phone. It's something somebody provided for me, and I try not to cause that person to have too much expense.

But it's nice to have one in case of an emergency. Would you have an emergency? You'd probably be able to take care of it, right?

Well, you know I could have one. I am a human being. I do some things. Let's just say I don't take unnecessary chances.

Okay. Do you work with any other energies, such as with the weather or wind or lightning or anything like that?

No, just with people.

What would you say to the reader? How could they begin to help?

Well, when you lose a loved one, by all means, go into your grief. Don't push it away. Don't feel as if you have to "be a man" and you can't show it. Don't feel as if you have to be strong no matter what. That's not just for men; that can be for women too. And there can be a lot of reasons you might do that: "I have to be strong for the children," "I have to be strong for the others," and so on. But when you have the time, go into your grief, and feel it totally. The more you go into your grief, the sooner you'll get through it, and it will transform your life. If you cry, you cry. Let it be. Don't judge it. It's a natural thing, and you'll go through it.

Sometimes you'll just shudder. You might not cry, but go through your grief as soon as you can. Otherwise, you might find you're putting out a lingering attachment of a lack of resolution. Sometimes when people die, you wish you had said "this," or you "that," or you wish you could have resolved something, so you hang on. So when someone dies, just know that's it. It's final; they're gone. "I'll see them in the spirit world," you can say, which is certainly true. You'll see them when you cross over. Or maybe you'll visit them at the deep dream level. That's possible. You can even ask that that happen, that you want to do that for a loving purpose. But go through your grief. That's what I recommend.

Have you ever talked through another human like this?

Not in this exact way.

What did you respond to when you began to talk through Robert?

Oh, I see. I didn't respond to Robert; I responded to an energy, a benevolent energy that felt good to me. I connected with that energy and felt connected to Robert. There weren't words; it wasn't a thought.

But you knew it was Zoosh?

Well, I don't call him that, but I know you do.

What else can we say here that will be helpful to people? What is it that I haven't asked about that I should have?

I think you've asked all you can. If I did a great many things, you could have asked about all those, but I really only do one thing. So I think you've asked what you can ask.

You do that well, and it's a great service. That's wonderful.

It really helps. It changes the energy in the land or in a house. Sometimes I go into a house someone has died in, and there's an energy that brings people down. It might be the grief that people are feeling, or it might be that lingering attachment to that self. So I do my work, and the energy feels more buoyant. The children become happy. It's not something they think about. "Okay, now it's okay to do this." It's not that; it's just that energy disappears and life can go on — happiness, sadness, whatever life is for the people. It goes in cycles. You want to be happy all the time, but life sometimes has surprises for us, doesn't it? That's true for me as well. Sometimes I'm happy about things, and sometimes I'm not. There are ups and downs, but we can look forward to the ups, eh?

Yes, and learn from the downs.

Well, at least try to outlast them, eh?

Yes, survive. [Laughs.] Have you noticed that you personally can do something more or quicker or deeper or anything in the past few years? It just seems that we're in a different space or a different reality now.

Well, I can't say that I have. I'm now thirty-five years old, and I've been doing this for a while now. This is my life. Perhaps if I were doing other things and driving a car and watching TV, I don't know. But I don't do that. No, I haven't noticed any difference. The simple answer is no.

In my ordinary, mass-consciousness life, it just seems that there is more energy and more ability and a deeper perception now.

Is your life different now than it was?

Not externally, but with regard to my feelings and perceptions, it is.

So feeling and perception is more vital for you now?

Yes.

Excellent!

Yes. It seems to be changing for a lot of people now, so it's possible that you already had those abilities and those sensitivities before. You know that we needed a kick or something, activation or something. What would you like to tell people who read this?

Live your lives as well as possible, and do good things for people if you are able. Enjoy life, laugh when you get the opportunity, and sing even if you can't carry a tune. Once a day, see whether you can make someone happy. That's what I try to do, and I find that I'm the happier for it. Good night.

Good life, and thank you so much.

Move with the Earth

An Ancient Islander

March 11, 2015

I will speak to you from my time.

Who is this?

I do not use a name. Our people are few, so there is no need for names. I'm speaking to you from my time, which is, as close as I can tell, about 3,000 years ago from your time. We number only nine people, so names are not necessary. My work is to attune my body to the temperament and expression of Earth. There are many Earth motions where we live. It is very frightening for the young ones, so the woman sings to them in an attuned way for the children's bodies. Children's physical bodies are not attuned to the same sounds as adults. Some sounds are calming for adults, different sounds for children. But Earth stands in your time nowadays. I have been alive in my time for about thirty years of your time. And this is considered not an elder but mature.

When I was born, my grandfather almost immediately recognized in me the ability to listen and make sounds and move with Earth — not just with the plants and animals but actually Earth: the water coming up on the shore, the slight motions of the land. After one or two earthquakes, Grandfather realized that my giggling not only warned them of an earthquake to come but also seemed to make the earthquake smooth out so that it wouldn't be sudden and jerking. I don't know whether you've seen this one, but they can be sudden, and move suddenly, regularly, for some time. That is more frightening than moving in waves that feel like a slow wave at sea. Once Grandfather recognized that, he started to train me because even though he did not know how to do that, his father had known, and he had been looking for it in a child. He was relieved that I came along and could do these things.

Mother Earth Speaks through Motion

One thing I do is I walk around on the island, and when I feel even the slightest motion underground, I start to move with it with my legs and feet and sometimes my body and head and even my arms. I move with it throughout the motion. Even though it might be very small, I am attuned to it now, and I can tell. When the motion stops, I very gradually stop my motions — not right away, just very gradually. If the motion is firmer, I might lift my feet up and slightly move them around from place to place. I believe that in many years and perhaps by people of other places, this is recognized as dancing. But for those who know about connecting and attuning to Earth, it is not dancing; it is moving with Earth, it is joining with Earth, and it is being Earth.

Now, there is more. I speak to you about these things from this day because this day is the time of a great tragedy in your time.[1] Perhaps you know. It happened a few years ago. If you do not know, you can look it up. At that time, the earth moved very strongly and had even moved quite a bit before. Unfortunately, no one knew how to move with the earth in that place. It is my gift to you to speak of these things. And at some point, I will demonstrate through this human being how it can be done. Now I will describe it for those who can visualize.

The motion is less important than feeling the earth under your feet. I recommend you always go without anything on your feet. I know that there are some places you cannot do that, but we lived on an island, and underneath our feet very often was sand. Further inland, leaves had rotted and formed a comfortable soil to walk on. So it was all right.

---

1. A magnitude 9.0 earthquake struck Japan on March 11, 2011, creating devastating tsunamis and killing nearly 16,000 people. See http://www.theatlantic.com/photo/2016/03/5-years-since-the-2011-great-east-japan-earthquake/473211/.

The way to learn to move with the earth is to find a place where there is a lot of motion in your time. When you feel the motion (as long as you are safe), just feel them through your body. Let the vibrations happen in your feet, of course, but try to allow your body (keeping your feet on the ground, barefoot) to move naturally. Some of you will want to pick your feet up, but if your body does not want you to do that, don't. Just move around.

It is not meant to be a dance of entertainment. You are learning Earth's language. Earth's language is motion and sound. That is all any language is on Earth. Most importantly, it is a means to create an intimacy between you and Earth, you see. And after a while, Earth trusts you and will make these slight vibrations that perhaps only you can feel because you know what it feels like under your feet. Then move with it.

As I said, sometimes you'll want to lift your feet, especially if you have danced as entertainment. But unless your body wants to do it and seems to do it on its own (like with instinct, you know?), then don't. Leave your feet on the ground. If your body wants to, you'll know because your toes might start to lift or you might start bending at the knees. But those things can all be part of learning Mother Earth's communication, yes? Mothers teach their children. They teach them how to eat. They teach them how to love. Eventually, the children learn how to make sounds because mothers sing to them. This is Earth Mother, Mother Earth, singing to you. Many times when she makes these (you say) vibrations, she is trying to say something to you to teach you. When you become good at feeling these things, you might have inspirations. You'll know the inspirations are clear if they have to do with the land you walk on, not so much the people you are with or who happen to be near. If you are very advanced in the walk, you might get some greater inspiration at other times about the people you are with and care about — perhaps family or possibly your friends — but it will not coincide with the motions of Earth. These things, as I say, have been lost in your time. That's why I come through to speak about them.

There are places even now that I see in our time. I will give you a place so that you will know. I am looking at your time. These islands are in the chain near the Solomon Islands, and there are many islands there. That's just good enough to know where. The peoples there — it did not get cold there, so bare feet would be natural.

Earth's Messages Can Differ from Person to Person

I want to speak to you about another thing. When I did this work, Earth would tell me she needed to make a big move by providing three or four very evenly spaced subtle movements. It may not be the same for you, but if you want to learn how to do this, you can save a lot of people — who knows, maybe yourself. Learn the space of the motions because then she's trying to tell you something, and in case it turns out to be a big earthquake, you will know. So keep track of the space. It doesn't matter whether you use a watch. You can guess the time. If you want to make a record of the time, that's okay, but this is not about science. This is an art. It's entirely about your physical feelings. Also, while the general practice is something you can teach others, if they want to do something their way, don't say they have to do it your way. They must learn in their own time and in their own way. The message from Earth might be different from person to person.

When I was growing up, Grandfather told me that I was doing it different from his father, and he wasn't sure if I was doing it right. In time I learned that the way I was doing it was the way I was meant to do it. And Grandfather then nodded. I knew by that nod that Grandfather understood that it was my way — not just a way I decided to do it, but the way I could hear, feel, and be Earth. We are made up of Earth-body that is inspired — yes, inspired — by our everlasting spirit. And we are all different personally, though we can usually be compatible. I am compatible with the woman, and she with me. We have children from time to time, but there are only nine of us now. Grandfather is no longer with us. If all goes well, I will be a grandfather someday and perhaps train someone.

Sometimes, when I receive a message from Earth that there is going to be a bigger motion, my woman will come with me. (Sometimes she carries one of the children, sometimes not. But they're nearby. There's an older sister and older brother, so they are all safe.) We go to the place where I hear the message from Mother Earth most often, and I prepare for the motion even though that may not happen. When the motion starts, the big one, I start to move and the woman starts to sing. She sings the same way she sings to the children to soothe them when, say, they are growing teeth. You know that's painful. So she sings to Earth two times when there is a big one.

Between my motion and the woman singing, the motion started out with that sudden jerk, and while it stayed big, it became more like a wave. No more sudden motion. And the wave is actually kind of comfortable; it's enjoyable. It reminds you of swimming, and the wave swells up underneath you. Some of you may have experienced that. It's a nice feeling. That's how we feel. If you could see us, you would actually be able to see ripples underneath our feet. It is a wave-like motion. I have looked at the ground afterward, and even though I could see the ripples happening while it was going on, and the woman said she saw them too, there were no ripples afterward. The ground was just like it was before. I have experienced, before I learned how to communicate with Earth, the sudden jerking, and often afterward, the land looked different. Sometimes part of it is up high, sometimes lower. Perhaps that happens in your time too. But since I have learned this, the land never changes. Thus, Earth has taught me.

You said Earth has taught you?

Yes.

Do you have any idea how you got to that island where you came from? Do you know where your people came from?

We were always there. I asked Grandfather that, and he said that he could not remember being any place else, so I feel we were always there. I understand that in your time, people move about. The island is not small. It is big, and toward the center — not quite at the center — there is some higher ground. We have not had the waves come up to that higher ground yet. Still, to be careful, we sleep on higher ground, not at the highest part, so that I can still get to the place where Earth speaks to me.

Animals and Birds

What do you eat? Do you fish? Do you grow crops? Do you gather berries and leaves?

There are some foods here. There are tree nuts. I do not know what you call them, but they fall sometimes, and we can eat them. Sometimes the woman will go out into the water and ask a water being to jump into her arms if it is all right for us to eat one. They always do that. Once she did not go, and I tried instead. It did not work for me. This is something only a woman is meant to do because it is required that you have love in your heart at all times. Sometimes I am focused on other things, but the woman always has love, so whatever water being jumps into her arms, it knows its blood won't be cooked, and with as little pain as possible, she will do that in her way. She knows the place to press on the body so that it first becomes like sleep. Then after a short time, it is no longer alive, and right after that, we can consume it. We start with the shells to cut it up and consume it. In your time, you make fire. We do not do that. We just consume it — not all parts. Some parts we don't, and we place those parts on the land near the water (but not in it) because there are other beings who move about on the shore with many legs. This is our offering to them so that they will leave us alone. [Chuckles.] The woman has spoken to them in her way, and they honor her, and she them. So she puts the parts there, and says, "This is my gift for you," in her way (no words). We do not use words, so I am adapting to your needs.

Have you ever seen any other people on the island or coming on a boat or passing through?

I have been everywhere on the island. I have never seen another person. I have seen other life forms, and we communicate in our way with no words. We are very compatible. We do not eat their food, and they do not eat our food except when the woman makes her gift, and then they are happy to receive. We have not seen vessels — water vessels like a human might make? We have not seen anything like that.

Can you describe the animals on the island?

You have them in your time. They have shells, and they have more legs than we have. They can move sideways. You have seen this?

I think they're called crabs.

Perhaps.

There are no mammals? No large animals?

Not that I have seen. There are small beings. Sometimes there are seabirds, and they do not communicate much, I think. This is because they don't live here. They live on some other island, and they come over sometimes to visit or to seek, I'm sure you know that birds tell what's going on here and there. They're like …

Like gossips? [Chuckles.]

You can tell when a bird lands near you and looks at you that it has news for you. For those who can feel that instinct or get inspiration, it would be good to ask for inspiration of what the bird is trying to say since you are in a worded time. If you do not need words so much, then notice how you feel as the bird looks at you, but do not stare at the bird.

That would make it uncomfortable. Just take note that it is looking at you, and nod gently toward it — just your head — and then you will have a feeling. Pay attention to the feeling. This could help those who do not need words because they will have some idea, some understanding, of what the feeling means.

You can look around. Perhaps someone else will have something to say to you that maybe you listened to before, but it could be something else. I'm bringing that up as an example. Birds in your time — I'm looking a little bit, and I can see them a little bit — are some of the same birds we see. They seem to be exactly the same. I am sure they will give you messages if you pay attention. If you don't pay attention, they will not. Sometimes they will try many times if they feel you have the ability. You will always know when a message is from a bird because when it gives the message to a different species, like to humans, it will always be good news. It will never be a warning. The only exception is when the bird looks at you and even though it stays where it is, it moves its wings, as in a flapping motion; the wings move up and down. That is a warning, so be alert.

Appreciate the Talents You Have

You certainly live in cooperation with the land. What are your greatest joys living there?

We enjoy the sun coming up and the sun going to sleep. It's very beautiful; every day we watch it. The woman sings to us — everyone — before we sleep. She knows the sleep song, and she is an expert at the pain song, like I said before about the babies. She sings the pain song when she gives birth. She is training her daughter now to learn these songs, but she tells her daughter in her way. We don't give words; you know that. That daughter will do it her way, the way that feels right for her and her children for her pain or for her happiness and other things. The woman knows how to make the sounds for every feeling, and it's always love. Are women the same in your time?

No, not always.

It can be; you can be. You do not have to use words. You have song. You can make tunes or sounds that do not make words that have an effect on people. That is a good thing. You want the effects to be a good thing, for them to feel better — always better. If you make a sound and people do not feel good, then stop immediately and make a soothing sound as you would do with a baby. You will know what to do if you've ever been around a baby for a few minutes. You will know.

How do you get fresh water? Is there a spring on the island?

There is an underground spring that comes up. It is like a pool. There is a small pool that forms, but we feel that the pool is for the others, the birds and the beings that have many legs and a few others. There is another place where the water trickles over some stones, and we cup our hands and drink from there. There is no — what you say? — disease. It is a comfortable place to be.

Is it just you and the woman in a relationship, or are there other adults there?

There are nine of us. The oldest son and daughter are what you call adults. The others are children. Grandfather is not with us anymore.

But they're all your family? Yours and the woman's children?

Yes. We know not to have too many. The woman knows how much food there is, how much to ask for. She knows by going out in the water and communing with the water beings, not with words. She knows how often that can be done, and it would not be polite to do more than that. She knows when there is concern about too many people, and she says no. [Laughs.] you understand?

Yes. Can you look into our time? Are there still people on that island who trace back to you?

I cannot do that. The glimpses of what I can see in your time can only be for important things. I do not wish to make that feeling on you, but perhaps that's not as important as the Earth motion. You are not feeling bad, I hope.

[Laughs.] No, I agree with you. I was just curious. Do you wear clothes?

No, there does not seem to be a need. The other beings on the island and the birds do not, so we do not.

So it's warm enough that you don't need to be covered when you sleep at night.

Where we sleep, there are leaves that have fallen. You say "leaves" or fronds — whatever you say — and they are soft and comfortable. It gets a little cool, but we all bunch together. We sleep together closely, and then we are warm. There is not any problem with that.

It sounds like paradise.

It is comfortable. Are most people as comfortable sleeping in your time? Perhaps you do not know, but in places like this where it is warm during the day and it is still warm enough at night, perhaps people still live like that. I do not know, but it can be a good life. With higher ground, it could be a good life

You feel that if you did not talk to Earth and smooth out the earthquakes ... it sounds as if it's in an earthquake zone. Am I right?

Many earthquakes, you say, yes, many. But I do not take any credit for smoothing out the earthquakes. It is my body that does that without my thinking — no thinking. My body does that, and my body is Earth, yes? So my body knows what to do. I do not try to say, "Oh, I know better because this is what I think." My thinking is all right for imagining and other things, but when it comes to moving with Mother Earth, my body is Earth, so my body knows what to do. It is not me; it is my body. I know my body is me, but I'm not trying to take myself there. Do you understand?

Yes, I do. It's more of a nonthinking process where your body uses its instinct and its inspiration.

Yes. Very good.

Have you always had someone do this? You had your great-grandfather do this. Has there always been someone in the family in the past who could do this?

There was a time when Grandfather said that there wasn't anybody. That's why Grandfather, who was getting old then, was concerned. But when I came along (he told me later in life in his way, in a funny way), he beat his chest and smiled, and made like, you know, an "I'm so happy you got here" type of sound. Then, I think, he was maybe concerned. But he had faith that the family would not be there without someone who could do these things. When I came along, the dance resumed, but there was a time when no one could do it. So when there would be earth motion, because there was no one who could do it, they slept very high on the high parts just to be safe. But once I was trained, we could sleep lower — still above the water, but not as high as Grandfather, not as high as those days.

Do you have one of your children trained to do this after you leave?

Not yet. I think my daughter shows signs of interest, but to have the responsibilities of woman and to do this seems a lot to me. But if it is to be her, I won't hold back. I have shared a few things with her, and she is still interested. I will continue to share with her as long as she stays interested in what I have to teach her.

How old is she now?

I do not know. A moment. You would say she's not yet three years.

I see. Well, I can't think of any more questions. You have been wonderful.

I'm hopeful that the knowledge will get out. Perhaps you can share a little bit about the earthquake. My feeling is that in your time this is very serious. No one is doing this in your time, so Earth is trying to say something. I do not know what because I am not in your time, but with these big motions, the waters can be especially dangerous for those living in lowlands. For mountain people, certainly not as much changes. I can see mountains. I can see a big one from where I am. It must be big because it's way higher. And a bird has told me, in a bird's way, that it is very big, much bigger than our high place. I am concerned for you all who don't know how to do the things that calm Earth.

I am grateful, and I am hopeful that there will be people in your time who say, "I want to do that," especially people who live where they can walk with their feet directly all the time. Tell them, and perhaps they'll be able to share with you, and then people all over will know how to do this. That will be good.

Can you look ahead, like with long vision, do you feel that there's nobody on Earth doing this now?

I do not know. I am hopeful that there are people doing this, but I do not know. I am concerned. What little I have been able to see, I have seen a bad thing happen a few years ago during your time on this date. And if a thing like that is happening, then it is urgent to learn how to do these things.

Oh, thank you! Thank you for coming in and sharing. Have you ever done this before, talk through a human, when you don't usually even talk?

I have not done this before. Earth's noise allows my words to come through as I'm thinking about today's state and what it means and what's sad about it. I was concerned that such a thing could happen again, not really seeing, but just — what do you call that concern?

Compassion?

Yes. I felt and started sending pictures and then energy, and throughout the day, he felt it and knew that I would be here now. So it is a good thing.

Excellent. All right, well, thank you very, very much. Thank your wonderful woman and your children, and I wish you a blessed life.

I am very grateful for your blessing. And for my own, I say live with each other with as much love and heart from person to person at all times in ways that you would welcome to receive if so.

Beautiful. Good life.

CHAPTER TWELVE

Connect with Otherplanetary Shamans

Beings Who Assist Those Who Are Shifting Their Existence

April 6, 2015

We function to coordinate connections between shamanic people, so as spirit, we work with one individual who lives in what you call Montana. That individual links with one of the outer planets in your solar system beyond Pluto and then links to our energy. Doing that, he is able to see the future not only for his people but also for all people.

Our function is to help him differentiate between his people's future and all of the futures there are for everyone. This is how we do it. Since the color blue is very significant to his people, we tint the pictures he receives with a very light blue, regardless of what he sees, so that he knows that is their future. This individual interacts with his small tribe, but they are trying to join the people who they stem from in the past. They are not comfortable in their time, which is, depending on how you measure it, about 400 to 700 years ago in your time.

They are trying to connect with the beings who are referred to as the Anasazi [ancestral Pueblos]. They feel they were left behind — not intentionally, but it just happened that they were away when the migration took place. At this moment, they are starting to move through time to be with those ancient people, and soon they will, with those ancient people, move temporarily to that outer planet, within it, in a little different dimension from yours. From there, they will move to their home planet, which is in the Vega star system. Do you know that one?

Yes.

Then they will experience a shift in their existence and move into a different time sequence. It is comparatively measurable in your time now, which would be about three and one half years in your future. Keep in mind that these are human beings.

This knowledge is being shared with you so that you know it is possible with the aid of benevolent spirits and others (some ETs, yes) for the human body to undergo such transformations and still function as a human being. It is also important for you to know that human beings existed three and one-half million years in the future. The human body is not something archaic as you know it.

In Search of the Lost Place

Insofar as the forms of bodies of physical beings, moving physical beings, I am taking out the mineral world and the plant world. The human body is not an ancient form, but it has certain versatilities that some forms do not have. One of them is the capacity to transmigrate through time (with the proper measures of caution), and in that transformable condition, be transported into a very different form of life. When they arrive in that future time, they will not look exactly human anymore. Some of them have chosen to remain human, but most of them will look humanoid. They will not look human. They will have heads that are shaped a little differently and bodies that are a little stronger, but they will be about the same height.

I bring this to your attention because the nature of the being who was the shaman for the group is an interesting being in his own right. He is what is considered in your time deformed. The way he is deformed is that his head is shaped a little differently. His people did not reject him because of his different appearance. The elders felt that he was meant for something, so he was allowed to pursue his own interests as a child. As a child, he would sit on a particular rock, and sometimes he would turn "this" way and sometimes he would turn "that" way. The most unusual thing that would be observed was that sometimes he was translucent and sometimes he was transparent, but he was always visible. He was transparent, but you could tell he was there. So if there was something beyond him, you wouldn't see it.

The elders realized that he had the capacity to transform and that he was learning more about it. The people were not talkative; they didn't have a spoken language, but they had strong feelings and made certain gestures. Mostly they were able to transmit pictures — not demands, not requests, just general pictures. The elders would sometimes communicate with the young person, and the young person would communicate that it was possible to go to that lost place. The elders had educated everyone about the lost place, so of course they were excited. Although if you were to see them, you wouldn't think they were excited, but for them it was excitement.

When this person, the shaman, became a mystical shaman of his people, he was about thirteen years of age. That's when this thing takes place. He was old enough then to be able to do the connection, meaning work with the spirit who had taught him how to be translucent and transparent. In other words, the spirit taught him how to change form.

The shaman told all of the people to line up behind him, directly behind him. He wanted them not to be touching, but some of them were children who needed to be touching, especially babes in arms. He asked for spirit to help and for any others who could help. So some ETs helped from their vehicle a short distance away, about 1,500 miles. And then it was possible to move them. As I said, it is happening right now, depending on the way you time it, but I am going to speak about it as if it had already happened. So they joined the others and moved to Vega. That is really all there is to it, but you can ask questions if you like.

What is the planet beyond Pluto — by name or number?

It is the next one beyond Pluto. Planets don't actually have names. I am referring to Pluto because that is what you people call it, but of course it doesn't really have a name. Cultures refer to planets as names, but I don't think your people have named that one, the one beyond Pluto, have you?

I don't know, but I will look it up. This is not clear to me. There is a small group of people in Montana at this moment. Are they descendants of the lost ones?

Not at this moment. It is not that they exist at this moment, but as you said, you are not clear. They existed from 400 to 700 years ago your time, depending how you measure time. I am allowing for the measurement of time from where you were in the third dimension to where you are now between the third and the fourth dimensions. So time is not the same.

So this thirteen-year-old is in — what time is he in?

The people existed 400 to 700 years ago, all of them.

But it sounded like the lost tribe were his ancestors? But he, they, were the lost tribe?

No. You have heard of the Anasazi? These beings, the ones who moved, felt that they had originally been part of the Anasazi. They felt that they had originally been part of that. They managed to keep their bloodline pure.

So they are home now with the original group of Anasazi?

Yes, I thought you might be interested because when you move between dimensions, your physical bodies will change. They will not be the same. You cannot go from the third dimension to what you call the fourth dimension without a transformation in your bodies, and it's happening to you all now in your neural pathways. That is why some of you are forgetful; it does not mean that you are losing mental capability. It means that you are letting go of your capacity to remember sorrow, hate, anger — all of that — because to make the shift from the third to the fourth dimension while in the same body (this is a very spiritual thing to do, you understand), you cannot bring along hate and anger and all of that. So you actually undergo a neurological change.

The main way you can tell the change is taking place is that the electrical impulses in your brain speed up. For those of you who can measure these things, you will notice that at times when people are relaxed or in a spiritual frame of being — especially if they are attempting meditation or even some kind of spiritual act that goes beyond the norm, but it is a benevolent thing — that you will be able to measure (if everyone has volunteered for it) the transformation in the processes of the electrical impulses. Scientists, do not interfere with the process. Don't experiment: "Oh, how can we make it faster? How can we make it slower?" Don't do it. If you do that, it will just corrupt you.

You Do Not Need Help to Ascend

You are a spirit who is working with this child in the past. Are you working with our bodies also in the present?

No, we felt that it was important for you to know that such transformation is possible, but we do not see that it is necessary for you to go through that much transformation. You will have to go through some things that are happening for you right now and cannot be stopped. The reason it cannot be stopped (for those who would like to stop it, you see, which is a very small group, and some of you are a little frightened by it, so you want to stop or slow it down) is that you are essentially, on an immortal basis, your spirit self. Only temporarily are you your physical self. So the overall abundance of you is in spirit form, and this is not some vagary. It is the means by which you would recognize your personality, your love, your happiness, and your sense of goodness. So all of that lives beyond you, and it is that that you are made up of primarily. It just means that you are becoming more of your natural self.

It also does not mean that you are unable to be physical again. Of course you will. And those of you in physical existence during the shift from third to fourth dimension, even though it just feels like a slight alteration, it will alter your experience of life a bit. It will just make your life more pleasant and more comfortable and much safer.

Wonderful. Is there anything that we can do to flow with it and to not interfere with the process?

Yes, try to get as much sleep as you can. I recommend eight to ten hours of sleep a night if you can do that. It is in the deep REM sleep that you can identify with your emotions, your feelings of nervousness. It's that sort of nervous feeling of being rushed. You know you have all been rushed before, and you don't like it, usually. Those feelings are calmed so that you do not feel rushed. The conscious way you would experience that when you are awake is that you would feel a little nervous for no particular reason. That nervousness stems from a feeling of being rushed. You would prefer to take it slowly.

So what other things have you done besides work with this Anasazi group?

This is what we do. We have done this with others on your planet and occasionally on other planets. We work to help beings who are moving from one state of existence to another while remaining alive in those lives to make the motion in a safe way. That's what we do.

But you're not working with us. Why?

I do not understand. Why would we? You are doing this. You have the capacity to do this yourselves. Why should we work with you? You are doing it — with the Creator's blessing, of course. You do not need our help. This group of nine (that's how many people there were) needed our help because of the tremendous distance involved and the huge difference in the so-called dimensions involved. But for you, there is no distance at all, and there is just a slight shift in dimension. You don't need our help at all.

You say "we." Are there many of you?

Well, there are a few, not a lot.

This is what you have always done?

This is what we are available to do. We don't do it all the time because we are not always needed to do that. When we are not needed, we just simply exist, much as you do when you are not doing something.

We're almost always doing something. What are some other examples of the work you do?

There is only one example that would be relevant to you, but it is very far back in your time. You have seen these pictures on the stone walls in Egypt of these peoples. You have seen pictures of their faces and how they look and so on?

Ancient Egyptians? Yes.

Some, not all of them, transmigrated also — not a lot, but three of them did. We supported it because they had worked with Earth people a lot, trying to teach them how to do things in benevolent ways, but they had to work in secret. Then they were found out. They had the knowledge of how to be unseen, but it took effort. In order to be supported, since they were being pursued, they had the knowledge of what came before the Egyptian culture, and they could see what was coming in the future, which is not unusual in your cultures on Earth with conflict and so on. They requested help to get home, and we supported them with the request of another.

Home, for them, was on an outer planet in the Pleiades, and on this outer Pleiadian planet, there was a lot of knowledge. There are libraries all over, and that is where those people were from, yet they were human beings. There are many human civilizations around the universe, so with the assistance of several ships from that place and our assistance, they were able to become not only unseen but also completely invisible (like the young thirteen-year-old shaman). Thus, they were able to travel in the light spectrum with our assistance and the assistance of the Pleiadian ships that have a capacity for travel in the light spectrum also.

Why would these beings be pursued when they were helping Earth people?

They were teaching Earth people how to do the things Earth people can do, but at the time, there were many struggles, many different factions, a power struggle you would say. And in power struggles, there is always the idea of the enemy. Sometimes people who are simply different get classified as the enemy, even though these people were not political at all. So their problem was not themselves but rather being in the wrong place at the wrong time.

Was this in a time in Egypt prior to what we know of Egyptian history?

The reason I mentioned the stone paintings is that they looked like the stone carvings; that's your term. They looked like that. They looked like the people living there now.

So these three beings you helped had come to Earth from the Pleiades?

No. They hadn't, but there is a limit to what I can say. All I can say is they were not born and raised on that planet. But they were from the Pleiades.

Can you say when this happened, what time?

All I can say is that they existed before the Great Pyramid. That is the best I can do.

Wow, that is really a very long time ago. Are you beings from this universe, or did someone ask you to come here and help?

We have existed before this universe, but as is typical for many spirit beings, universes are not boundaries. You in spirit form are not bound by this universe, either. But perhaps you know this.

I do. Did the Creator ask you to come here because he knew what your skills were?

Yes, we were asked to come, so somebody must have known. We will have to say goodbye now. Be well. Good life.

Okay, thank you very much for coming. Good life.

CHAPTER THIRTEEN

Remember Your Dream Soul Journeys

Beings Who Assist Those Who Are Shifting Their Existence

April 8, 2015

You know how people have been talking for some time about Earth changes? Now we are going to talk about human changes. For a long time, your bodies have been able to function in worlds other than your own. This means that at the deep-sleep level when your body rests, you are still involved with other forms of life. You call it dreaming, but in fact, it simply means that you are able to migrate about in your soul personality and talk to teachers and explore and have fun, essentially. It is not so much for teaching although it has come to be believed to be that way, or the thought is that is the way you communicate with other parts of yourself. And that is true to a point.

I bring it up only because in that form, your personality can go anywhere and be other forms. It can travel at light speed and beyond as you become your natural self. So more and more now, you — everyone — are going to have experiences. Granted, people who are more spiritually aware might be able to understand and be more comfortable with the experiences. But you are going to have experiences that will be, in many cases, otherworldly.

Notice Otherworldly Experiences

While you are awake, you may very well have experiences that transcend your normal conscious day-to-day thoughts. For example, you will be, say, walking along, doing something that does not require a great deal of attention. You won't be driving or in traffic or operating machinery or anything like that. You will just be walking along — or just sitting in a chair reading a book or a magazine or watching TV — and you will get a flash of something. I say a "flash" because it will be very much like the amount of time that it takes for a camera to flash and illuminate its subject, that much time, just briefly. And you will experience, but you won't realize it, another locale, another place, another time. It somehow looks like Earth, but it is a little different. The biggest difference for many of you will be that there is a lot of space, a lot of room. Nothing looks crowded. Even if you have been raised in an uncrowded condition and have known only that all your life, it won't look crowded. It will look very roomy.

Initially, you will just notice it after the fact. If you pay attention to it, you will realize that you have actual sensory experience of it. You might remember the warmth: You will feel the warmth of the sun, the warmth of the day there. You might have a sensation of having been in a breeze or even a light rain shower with possibly a rainbow. You might remember a sensation of fragrance, such as the fragrance of flowers, something attractive. Some of you might even remember something that sounds vaguely like singing, a melody that is in the background, like the sound of people singing but at a distance. In short, you will have an experiential moment when you look at it more closely. Granted, most of you will think nothing of it and just go on with your lives.

It will happen again. It may not be the same place, but it will be similar, a place with lots of room; you might see trees. You might even see something that looks like green grass. You might see people moving about. Sometimes your perception will be from overhead, so you will see it from above. Other times you might be very close up to trees or vines, and occasionally you will see things moving around that will remind you of beings you might see from time to time on Earth, often birds, for example.

So I am going to tell you what this is about. These are not unlike things you see at the deep-sleep level when you are "dreaming," yet you do not generally remember that when you wake up. If you remember a dream, you don't see that. But that is a place almost all of you actually experience, or variations of it, when you are out of your body. Your body rests asleep.

You are dreaming, but really your consciousness, your soul, travels. Most of it stays in your body, but your soul wanders. It doesn't have to sleep, you understand. You see that area, and you go through that area.

Your sensible mind wants to tell you this is the higher level of Earth. This is some place that we are all migrating to as we change dimensions. But that's not the case. This is a place that all you human beings in this universe experience as your home port, you might say, your place of belonging. I wouldn't call it the human planet because it is more than a planet. If you were able to move back quite a distance from it, it wouldn't look like a planet at all. It would look rather like an array, in a sense, meaning that it has an arc shape and is hard to describe. It has an oval shape, a long oval that is turned down on the sides — not frowning. It just happens to be an arc-like shape. So this is a place that is home to the human beings of this universe. It is a place where the essence of humanity exists. This is why you all go through this place and have not remembered it until now. You will have these experiences as a conscious thing, but as I say, initially it will just be a flash. It will last just a second.

Over time, if you want to experience it more, you can try to remember what it looks like, and then you can try to memorize what it looks like. You will have the experience more often as you will be able to be comfortable with that place. What will happen is that you will gradually begin to remember more of what you do and where you go at the deep-sleep level. So even though your body will be in deep sleep and you are getting complete rest, when you wake up, you will remember everywhere your soul went. I can assure you that your soul only goes to places that are benevolent, beautiful, and loving. Your soul only goes where you experience love and kindness and all kinds of things like that, never anything unpleasant.

I might add, for those of you who experience nightmares, you don't and you won't experience anything different from what I am talking about for everyone else. So don't worry; you are not going to have to go through some excruciating nightmare, experiencing it in greater detail. No, that won't happen. This is all an element of your waking-up process. You have to gradually remember who and what you are, and in order to do that, you have to be able to be on a greater intimate level with what you experience every single day. You sleep every single day, so you experience this every single day. You just don't remember.

Can you say a little more about that place?

I don't want to say too much because I want you to remember it as you experience it. I don't want to say it's "this" or it's "that." Then you will be stuck seeing that, and if you don't see that, you might be disappointed. So the reason I am giving you a general description is that most of you will see something like that, so I am not to say much beyond what it looks like now. I want you to be able to discover it because, as you discover it yourself, it will be very personal — something you saw. Don't expect everybody to see what you see.

There might be a few people who see some of what you see in your sleep, and you might see some of what others see, but generally speaking, it will be personal. People will see different things, and it will be fun to compare notes about these things with your friends and perhaps even some family members. This is all part of your process of waking up, and you need to have processes like this so that it not only feels personal but also real. Some of you are already having these awarenesses, and initially there will be times when you wonder whether you are just a little crazy. Some of you will even talk about it to a counselor. However, speaking to psychiatrists and counselors now, this is *real*, and you will have the experience too, so just treat it as a gentle reminder of the overall goodness of life (a note for therapists).

Physical Changes

What about other human changes — the body itself? How is the physical body changing?

The only real changes are certain activations in your nervous system. You all know you don't use that much of your brain, but you will now. It won't happen all the time. What happens in your brain so that it will remember these things is as if something moves out of the way. You all know, if you have been reading this material for a while, that there are what we have called veils between who you are and how you experience yourself on Earth. It is as if a veil is being removed from your brain, and your brain is allowed to function more in its natural state. I can assure you that human beings who are not on Earth have these experiences all of the time because they do not need these veils, as they are living in benevolent surroundings. When they see something like that, it is just part of their lives, something to enjoy. They expect to have that when they sleep.

"Waking up" simply means you are becoming more of your natural self, and the more you do that, the less Earth will have to help you stay in balance when you are really too far out of balance to function and you live in a place of polarity such as Earth as you have been experiencing her. This experience will excuse Earth from having to maintain that for you. Since she needs to take care of herself right now, she is happy to step aside.

The being who spoke on April 6 said we need more sleep. Do you feel we need more sleep?

No, I do not feel you need more than eight hours of sleep at night. If you get more, that's fine. If you get less, it is not good on an ongoing basis, but it will happen from time to time. The reason the being might have said that is so that you would honor the need for deep sleep, for it is when deep sleep happens that you experience the complete release of your soul to travel in such ways as I have described.

How else is the physical body changing? At what point can we grow new body parts, for instance?

I do not feel that is something that human beings can do. So if you lose a finger or a leg, that's it. It is gone.

Should we change our diets to accommodate this higher frequency?

Absolutely not — and I am not calling it a higher frequency. You are. This is something natural for you. You don't have to change a thing. Of course, if you are, say, an alcoholic, it will be a little difficult, but you will still see it. The reason it might be difficult for alcoholics, for example (and I am bringing this up because many people are alcoholics in your time), is because alcoholics might think they are having experiences associated with alcoholism, like the DTs. So it might frighten them because they might think they are experiencing something associated with the disease of alcoholism.

When and how will we notice that we are using more of our brains? Will we think more clearly or have the ability to get more innovative solutions? How does that work?

No, it is exactly as I said. You are not going to suddenly have an IQ that goes off the charts. It is not going to interfere with your life. It is not going to be something that changes your personality. You are going to be who you are. In short, it is not going to be threatening. You might think that suddenly having greater capacity to think or to innovate is a good thing, but that would alarm many people. They would find that it interferes with their personalities and even their relationships. No, it is not intended to interfere with your life. It is intended to allow you to experience more of your natural self. It will be gentle like that. But these are all good questions that you are asking because other people want to know these things too.

Levels of Conflict Will Decrease

As we continue to awaken, we will have more empathy, more compassion, because this awakening to the self is the road to unity, right?

In time, you will — especially as you compare notes on these experiences with others — have a greater feeling of brotherhood and sisterhood with other people, regardless of who they are. So, yes, it is another step on the path toward unity. It is not going to be as if a bolt of lightning suddenly strikes and everyone is going to wake up. It is not about that but rather one step at a time. Do you understand why it goes as slowly as it does? Some people will be ready and raring to go, but other people won't. So the process of awakening needs to go only as quickly as the slowest members can adapt to and become comfortable with and can live with. And that is an element of love. Never forget that.

Who is talking?

We will get there. You think that Zoosh says that (never forget that), and no one else says it. But this is not Zoosh.

Yes, I know that. So if we want to experience this more deeply and quickly, that is not an option?

Absolutely not. You want to leave others behind? I am not picking on you. Remember, you are a representative of the people who read this.

So how quickly will this awareness and awakening change and stop some of the violence on the planet? Shouldn't the feelings of closeness mitigate some of that?

Slowly, one step at a time. I will give you an example. In the past, two people might have been edgy or upset about something, and they had fights. But as time goes on with this experience, they will be less likely to punch each other. They might just move away from each other and yell at each other instead. Now, that might not sound like much improvement, but for people who would normally start punching each other, it is a big improvement. At the other end, people who are normally good friends and only occasionally have disagreements, their disagreements will be further apart.

Good. So we can assume that same process will work on a country level and a religion level?

Yes, absolutely. Although, keep in mind that countries and religions are represented by their leaders, and very often in the past, leaders had disagreements. All the people in all the countries suffer even though it is just a couple of leaders who had disagreements. This is really quite silly. It has to change.

Now can you say who you are?

You remember the person you spoke to on April 6 referred to himself as "we"? I am one of the others.

Good, thank you. Will we start remembering our past lives not to get distracted but to remember and be able to use talents and abilities that we learned in past lives? Will that surface now?

Only if you are in circumstances where it is necessary. But even in emergency circumstances, it may not happen because past lives are sort of an iffy thing. I don't want to insult anybody, but my feeling about past lives is that (this much I can say to you) they are not exactly real though they feel real. So I will simply say that there will be times when you can do things that you didn't know you could do, but it has nothing to do with past lives.

Don't Let the Wave of Culture Take You Along in Its Flow

How do we understand this expansion? Do we take little steps and assimilate, constantly taking little steps? Can we plan for the estimated changes in our lives in two years, three years?

No, it is probably better for most of you to do less planning and less in general. You are overly distracted by and complicating your lives with many things now. To be aware of your senses and your experiences is very important, so don't overly stimulate yourselves. I personally feel that having earphones in your ears is not a good idea. It affects your balance, generally speaking. I am not saying you should revert to playing loud music for others just because you want to hear it, but I think it would be better if you learned how to play an instrument or how to sing and then do that with others. That would be good for you.

I also think it would be good if you used an instrument that was not electrical or electronic. Make time for things like that, because to do things like that, you have to do more than think. Good musicians or even poor musicians have to be aware of their inner and outer feelings in order to enjoy the experience. For example, if you are singing in the shower or in the bath, you experience it internally and externally as well, and it is fun. You need to have simpler and benign fun in your lives. To do that, you need to let some things go that you don't need to do.

So simplify our lives?

I recommend it. You can be aware of your feelings and your instincts so that you recognize the thing I started talking about at the beginning of this talk. Experiencing that is going to require perception, but playing loud music in your ears or watching loud television or being in the movie theater that's loud — do you notice that everything is loud? What are you afraid of? Why do you have to overwhelm yourselves with loudness? If you go to the movies, it will be loud, so keep that in mind. If you watch a movie at home, let it be something that is not violent. When you watch violent things, it tends to make you, especially if you are a youngster, very tolerant of violence in life. This is not good. Don't let the wave of culture — and that is a form of culture, loud music, loud movies, loud everything — take you along in its flow. Don't be afraid to be quiet and feel. Good night.

Thank you very much.

CHAPTER FOURTEEN

To Get Along with Others, You Must Be Present

Energy Stream

June 8, 2015

Can you tell me who you are or what you are or where you are or when you are?

I am a stream of energy that runs from the foundation of this star system you are in. I reside in the swirling effect of some star systems. Some star systems have beings who like to grow, migrate, or travel, which is why some star systems have the swirl and others do not. The ones that do not have it are in the formative stage, or the beings who reside there — on planets, of course — are happy to be where they are and as they are. I don't know whether you know that.

No! I never heard of it.

It is helpful to know (for you as a people) when you begin your migration and explorations beyond your own star system or have communications with different star systems to try to focus on those systems that have the swirl. There you are likely to find people with common interests. Other star systems have people so different that communicating will be like climbing an impossible mountain. You can never quite get to the top, so you'll never know whether your communications, even though the languages might be almost identical, are actually achieved through communion.

That's great. Thank you.

Get Along by Finding Common Ground

Like other beings, I need to have a question and the purpose of it, which is about not only getting permission to speak but also opening the door. As a representative of Earth's human race, it is up to you to ask about what you feel others might be interested in. It is not easy for you, perhaps, even if you are in the mainstream of your culture to imagine what other people might need, but you are able to have some knowledge.

For instance, one obvious question is: "How can we influence people to get along with each other?" To some extent, this has been approached in your material about how business functions and how one person does not have to agree with someone else's way of being in order to do business. That is a good beginning in your economic times and has taken root even in cultures that feel business, in its own right, has harmful aspects, and they would not choose to participate unless they truly wished to create communication, such as some civilizations that are influential in your now times.

To get along with people, you must be absolutely dedicated to being in the present moment. If you allow yourself to think even for a moment about the past or worry about the future, it is not possible. This does not mean that one is not careful. I am speaking to diplomats here for first contact, all right? First contact does not have anything to do with extraterrestrials in this situation. It just has to do with people who live on the other block, people who live across town, or people who live on that farm that no one ever goes to. In short, it doesn't have to be far away, but it could be.

You must first look for common ground. Some common ground is absolute: water, food, and shelter. You all need these things, but beyond that, there is a desire for peace, happiness, fulfillment, and similar things. So only speak about subjects that you can be sure the other people have in common with you. This is why the old wisdom says that when somebody calls on you or you are in the position of having to call on others, always be polite, share your food, and speak as little as possible except to be thankful, grateful, and humble. That's the old wisdom, and it still holds up pretty well today in your now time.

It is something, if you think about it, that is very uncomplicated. However, in your society in which you now live, many of you find that these steps are often skipped because you don't have the time or you've done it before with others and you feel you don't always have to do it. But to make a friend is not the same as maintaining a friendship. Maintaining a friendship very often requires certain basics to get along, so I recommend not straying too far from what I've already recommended. Then even if you are old friends, you can go on from there — sharing food and being humble.

"Humble" does not mean that you are subservient. "Humble" simply means that you do not, in any way, place yourself above anyone else. Obviously a parent would be taller than a child, but I mean in terms of your past or your manner of being in the world or your appearance. You do not act as if you are better or treat others as if they are. That's what I mean by humble, not subservient. I think in your time that has become confused, the idea of humbleness being subservient. It is not that, just so you know. That's why I'm stressing the point.

Conflict Caused Humans to Lose Wisdom

Okay. So we're going to start with getting along.

You understand that the reason to start with that is very simple. If you look at the history of your people, say in the past 5,000 to 10,000 years, the reason wisdom was lost is that people could not get along. Great amounts of wisdom that your people would love to have in these times have come and gone because people didn't get along.

Right — wars, colonization, religion, all of that.

Sometimes Earth as a planet itself has become upset with its residents, its resident human population. So if necessary (such as when Earth functions are damaged in some way by that population), Earth would simply use its waters and its wind to make it unlikely that such behaviors would perpetuate while still welcoming a human population that knows how to get along. That's the first thing — to get along, of course. You must survive.

There have been civilizations on your planet that have survived for a long, long time, maintaining their knowledge and wisdom ultimately in secret ways so that those who don't get along do not ever find out. Sometimes these civilizations have nothing to do with race or nationality but rather more to do with common ground. Even in your now time, there are a few civilizations that exist like that. Their numbers are small, and they do not all know about each other, but they do exist.

I will not say much more about them. I will only say that if you can fulfill the basic precepts of getting along as I've mentioned, then you might find life is easier in some ways. It all has to do with living better in a comfortable way, not necessarily anything to do with possessions, or sometimes perhaps it does.

Can you give me an overview? How many civilizations have existed on Earth that are lost, gone before our own?

Thousands. I'm not going to give you an exact number. Do you mind? It's just thousands. It's all you need to know, and of those that have been lost, the number that would have at least a significant value in their wisdom (not their knowledge but their wisdom, all right) in these times you are living is in the hundreds. Some of that wisdom, I have already begun to teach you, and some of it, you already know, but if we don't begin at the beginning, then how will we ever get to the end?

[Laughs.] The beginning is a very good place to start. Do you want to discuss things by topic, civilization, or area of the world? What's a good way to start?

By topic because certain topics are more pressing than others.

Well, you choose the topics.

No. No. You are a human being. You are learning in your times. I chose a topic that we could start with, and that topic could go on for a while, but ultimately, if I choose the topics, then the readers will feel as if this is something that they are being told, not something they are requesting. As a human being, you must accept your responsibility. Ask about what others need to know, and also ask about what you need to know. Quite obviously, you as an elder might be interested to know what you can do about pain. That could be a good topic, as that is not always but often something people experience as they get older.

To function smoothly in a society, you must learn how to get along with your brothers and sisters. You start off in the family, and regardless of who you are or what you have been in previous lives or even what concurrent energies exist with you, you must learn how to get along in the life in which you find yourself focused in that moment. Very often, even though you might have been born with very important knowledge or wisdom that could help the people to whom you were born, you have to set that aside as a baby, the young child. You have to set that aside and learn how to get along in your environment. Then the challenge later in life is how to retrieve that knowledge and wisdom you were born with. That is another important subject we will pursue.

Everyone on your planet in the past thousand years — every human — has been born with special knowledge and wisdom. The wisdom is the foundation, and the knowledge is the way of achieving the wisdom. So you do not necessarily have to go the same route every time to achieve the wisdom. The wisdom is not something you need to achieve because you already have it. Rather, it's how you pursue it on a path of knowledge, influencing as many people as possible with the wisdom you have to offer. If you know this or if you can find this or if the path you are on is because you've had to learn how to get along in your family or group, then that can be helpful.

But if you are on some path that is so far afield from your knowledge and wisdom, it is possible that you might not be motivated to find the wisdom. It is even more possible in your now society (with its many distractions) that you will not even know you were born with the wisdom needed during your lifetime — meaning from the moment you were born to the moment of your natural death, and by "natural," I mean how you were expected to die or whether you have an unexpected death (meaning before your time) — up until that point. Once you know you were born with it, it is possible to have this as a thought or a reminder, something you carry with you, such as a statement in your own language:

"I have wisdom in me now. I will find it in the most benevolent way for me."

Or you could have a statement such as,

"I ask to dream of this wisdom, to have pictures I remember, and to notice in my life where I go and what I do when there is something familiar or similar to the picture I see that is an example of my wisdom. In this way, I will know that I have found some portion of my wisdom and can put a toe there or have a touch there," so to speak, "and with that contact, I can find my wisdom. It will always be something that is easy for me to do but might not be easy for everyone. So it will be something that I believe that others can do easily, but in fact, very often, it will be something others cannot do easily or otherwise."

All others will have this same experience. If you know that your wisdom experiences and the pathways of your wisdom found, felt, and sought have this in common — what you feel is available to others and what isn't — then you will have a foundation for understanding that wisdom has a feeling as well as an interpretation. That is all for today.

Will you continue this book? I'd love to talk to you.

I will contribute as much as possible, but there are others in my swirl, and you might hear from them as well.

Wonderful. I'm glad to meet you.

May you have a most benevolent life.

Yes, you too.

CHAPTER FIFTEEN

Your Experience Becomes Your Wisdom

Ioniss

June 25, 2015

In times past, there was never any singular planet information and wisdom. It was always the combined total of wisdom from any universe so that people instructing their children or, in some cases, children sharing wisdom with parents and others could access whatever would be helpful to know in any circumstance or simply just for pleasure. Stories that entertain and nourish and, yes, nurture came out of this type of dialogue. Information is useful when it can be applied in some beneficial and benevolent way in any circumstance. But there are times when people are well fed and well clothed and comfortable and they would simply like to hear a story, so it was always possible to simply relax.

Sometimes it would be the father or mother or grandfather or grandmother or aunty or uncle, like that, and at other times, it would be a child. It was not at all unusual and sometimes considered to be an advantage to have a child tell the stories. These would always be stories that had value, wisdom, and fun. The reason it was considered an advantage to have a child speak these stories is that the child would not have a lifetime's exposure to the stories, wisdom, and information of the culture he or she was living in then. So it was thought at the time that even if your own children could not do this, people would gather — not big groups, maybe twenty or thirty at the most — and the child in that group (or the child from other parents, all right) might be better at this. It was not a competition because all children were known to have talents and abilities. Some were very artistic or musical.

The Magical Tales of Children

So, what would the children talk about? They would always talk about something that was fun and amusing. In other words, they were not that different from children today. This is important to know because even today, with all the entertainment and distractions, when children are not around that much — not being taught or instructed for "this" or "that" reason or sponsored by "this" or "that" business, no agendas like that — they are often imaginative, people say, or they can speak great truths. As people say, "Out of the mouths of babes," yeah? That's where that came from because children, even today, have an innate ability to speak the wisdom, stories, knowledge, and ultimate joy of all cultures everywhere — not only on this planet, but also on other planets that have knowledge, wisdom, information, and joy that are compatible with this planet.

Some wisdom, of course, is not that compatible. It's not that it would harm, but it just doesn't relate in any way to life on Earth, so there is no value nor any sense of familiarity and comfort that a child would need to speak this kind of wisdom.

I'll give you an example of a story told in the past that has echoes of your now time. Children would sit, usually in whatever architecture they dwelled in — not usually anything built up out of the materials used these days or even in old (what are termed) ruins. Usually it would be some naturally occurring situation. Other beings would be around too; you say animals. The story would be told in a comforting voice, sometimes musical. Sometimes the child would stop in the middle of the words of the story and sing a song. Keep in mind that the psalms were originally songs. Then you would have the experience of being able to relax into the magic — the happiness, the joy, and the capacity to feel transformed from the child speaking this story. If the child relaxed into the story first, the child could change his or her feelings (like a mood, all right) and become this story. The child literally speaks the parts of the story, so here goes.

Imagine a child speaking, and the child says, "Down the lane came the mommy and the daddy and the children, and they were whistling and singing a happy song." And the child — I really cannot reproduce it because it's such a high voice of a child — sings this happy song in its own language, whatever it was. That goes on for about thirty or forty-five seconds, and it puts everyone in a happy and cheerful mood.

"Picture people walking down from a hill, and it's an easy road. They get to the bottom of the hill, they look around, and as far as they can see, the land is alight with a golden energy. There are groups of color moving around and — oh! They must be fairies because everyone knows that everything has its own protective fairies," says the child.

"The people walk around and notice that when they get closer to one of the fairies, they get a sweet taste in their mouths. They feel as if they can float, and they do float. They float up off the ground, just like the fairies. To experience the life of these beautiful beings, the mother and the father stay nearby, and they experience it too," says the child. "And my brothers and sisters run around and float sometimes, and sometimes they're on the ground. They all do this for as long as it feels good.

"Then one of the fairies says, 'Let me remind you that you can do anything. You can fly without wings. You can be whoever you need to be. You can go wherever you need to go in your imagination and in your physical being as long as there's love without attachments and happiness without greed. Then you feel that there is enough for everyone, and everyone is providing as well as receiving.'" Thus is the wisdom of the story.

People begin to imagine themselves meeting the fairies and being around them, and the fairies just look like musical color. "When you get closer to the fairies, you hear music. And when you get very close to them, you float up off the ground, and you feel as if you are a fairy yourself." There is laughter, and there is happiness. That is all you feel during this time. Then you wake up, and in your life, you feel as if you can be this and do this any time you need to.

That's a story that was not unusual in those times. I bring it up to you because in your times, even if children do not have all the entertainment we'll talk about and all the instructions and everyone telling them "this" and "that," it is in their nature to be imaginative. It is also in their nature to feel as if they can fly and to feel some kind of music as well as to experience something that sometimes children call angels or fairies. All these things are real.

So, parents, if your children want to tell you a story, try to listen. Put down what you are doing, and listen as long as it makes you feel the following things: If the children stop speaking every once in a while and sing a song (it may not have words; it's all just "tra la la," what have you), then it is perfectly all right. But pay attention to your feelings. Don't worry about being frightened because this is strange. It is perfectly natural for children to be imaginative. Always remember that and that they won't be questioned. They won't be thought to be weird or strange. So as long as you feel the happiness of the story, no matter how it goes, and you feel relaxed and comfortable — remember that it's perfectly all right if the child is talking about human beings flying around on their own — and you love your child and you feel the love, then everything will be fine.

If you feel that the child is going into things that are unhappy — by "unhappy," I mean not just things that conflict with your beliefs and your life experience, no, but the dramas of the day or movies or scary stuff — then just withdraw yourself a bit. You know your child is being affected by life experience in some sad situations or, more likely, by something seen on television or the Internet.

TV is not a good thing, regardless of how you think it is the wonderful electronic babysitter. It is largely not a good thing to have children exposed to television and the Internet for the first seven years of their lives. It is also not a good thing for children to be read to out of any book that proclaims to tell them that "this" is what life is about and only "this." It is important that children be able to interact with the birds and the flowers and the trees and the grass around them (hopefully there are those things) and to simply be imaginative.

You won't be able to prevent them from being exposed to TV and the Internet completely because they're not always at home, but you can encourage them and support them in being imaginative and, in short, a child, which doesn't always mean getting up to mischief. It means that they are allowed to be imaginative and to believe in things that you don't quite believe in but that you can remember from a story. It might have been, could have been, and maybe it could happen like it felt when you were a child yourself.

This is what it means when it says in various philosophies and wisdoms that only a child can lead you or (what the original statement was) that only the pure, childlike self can easily find the path to the benevolent ways of all being that are of the absolute and total expression of almost everywhere in this universe. One finds that by always being connected with happiness, joy, and love. When you see — those of you who can (as you know sometimes your cat can do and as your dog does when he or she is dreaming and as you do when you are dreaming a happy dream) — beings moving from one dimension to another, then you will know that you are constantly being reinforced that it is your natural ability to find your way to the benevolent world right here. But you can only get there with those feelings.

Life on the Sea

Who's speaking?

Ioniss. You spell it I-O-N-I-S-S.

Well, welcome. What part of the universe is home to you?

I am a child. I am an ancient. I am asleep. I am awake. I am of feelings. I am of quiet. I am a thought. I am a journey. I am of peace. I am alone. I am the multitude. I can be what I need to be to communicate or to sleep or to dream to all those who ask. You asked to have the lost knowledge and wisdom, and I refined that to be what would be the most helpful for you and for the people of your planet now. That is who I am.

That is very beautiful. Can you tell me in what civilization or when you had a life on Earth?

You mean a life in your times or any time on Earth?

Any time on Earth.

There is no measurement of time, but if your people were to measure it, it would be about 100,000 years ago. This does not mean it was 100,000 of your years ago. It means that that's how your people, your scientists, would measure it.

Can you give me a little context for the life you lived, something about where on Earth and how long you lived and what the other people were like?

A little bit. I lived on a boat at sea with my parents, brothers, and sisters. Also there were uncles and aunties. The boat sailed about, always on the water, but sometimes we would come to a sandy shore. I never saw any mountains. The water was clear and blue, and at night there was always light from the stars and from the Moon. I do not remember there ever being a sky, a night, when there was no light. Of course, it was like moonlight, but sometimes the stars would be enough light. And always during the night was story time. My brothers or sisters would tell a story, or sometimes my grandfather or grandmother would tell one of the old stories, and everyone would laugh and sing. It was a pleasurable time.

We were able to eat certain beings, but we did not wish to do that because it made us sad. For a while, fish would jump in the boat, and we would include them in our stories. But they would be struggling to breathe, so we found that they were just enjoying the happiness and the love of the moment. We put them back in the water and then leaned over the sides of the boat to tell the stories. The fish would gather and listen.

After a while, we realized that the fish were trying to tell us to eat them, and my grandparents said we mustn't because they are the laurels (and that word does not exactly refer to plants but to the continuity of life). After time, we ate one, but there was such a feeling of grief for the loss of this life that we didn't do that anymore. So we put the remains on (it was like) a shelf, and we used that to cry when we needed to. Sometimes someone would feel overwhelmed with feeling, not necessarily only sad feelings. Sometimes the person was overwhelmed with happiness, and maybe the person had a hard time crying because of also laughing. So the person would go over and look at the shelf with the bones of the fish and would then be able to cry. We didn't stand around grieving, but we found a use for it.

When we told them of our use, the other fish nodded. (Fish can nod; I don't know if you know that. They do that in your time too.) They nodded, and we could tell that they knew what it meant and how it would serve us. We could tell from their feeling that they knew what a self-sacrificing gift that life was that it provided a means for us to weep when we could not do so on our own.

Natural Light Leads the Way Home

We lived mostly on the light. During the day when the sun was present, we would close our eyes and cover ourselves with thin garments. Under the garments, we could open our eyes and feel the warmth of the Sun. We wouldn't look at it, but we would just feel the warmth. Then we would just breathe in and out. I cannot tell you how long that took, but I would guess if you were to do it now, it would take you from ten to forty-five minutes to feel refreshed — as if you had eaten a meal of some food that easily digested perhaps an hour before. It would be comforting, and you would not need any more.

At night, since the starlight and moonlight were so bright, we could do something similar. We did not need to cover ourselves with the garments because the light was not as bright. We lay down on the deck of the ship, and we breathed in and out with the starlight, sometimes looking at it, oftentimes with our eyes closed. Sometimes we slept. Many times we stayed awake. Again, if it were measured in your time with the starlight, it would be about twenty-five to twenty-seven minutes to get that feeling of having eaten, and with the moonlight, it would be around forty-five minutes. So this tells you something interesting, doesn't it? It's possible to live on the light.

I'm not saying that you should do that in your time instead of consuming what you consume, but it is something worth trying. Remember, don't look directly at the Sun. But if you're going to find a garment, a piece of cloth to cover yourself up with, I recommend, in your time, to use linen. That fabric is just perfect. If you cannot get pure linen, then a combination of either linen and a little bit of silk or linen and cotton would work. It needs to be a loose weave — not so loose that you can stick a finger through it, but loose enough so that you can very easily and comfortably breathe without getting too warm.

It might work for situations in which you wish to be enriched by different aspects of light, but don't make it a discipline. Don't insist on looking at "this" star system or "that" star system. All the stars have something to offer. And remember that the Sun, the Moon, and the stars are your natural light. They are meant to enrich, stimulate, and support you in your imagination, love, and happiness, for these things can bring about your natural state of wisdom and your ability to use your instinct to find your way Home. And by "Home," I mean that place of complete benevolence and love.

Your Many Threads of Life

Did you spend all your time on the boat, or did you dock to barter or trade, like for cloth or something? What was your mode of subsistence?

I can see that you are naturally relating this to your times. I can only tell you my response. You asked how I lived my life. That is how I lived my life. We pulled up to places occasionally (in your times) about once every three years or so, never any shorter of a time than that. If we pulled up to a sandy beach, it was always of white sand or sometimes had beautifully colored rocks. There were never any other people around, so we didn't trade for things. The cloth we had never wore out. If you were to look at it today, you would say that our ship is a wooden boat. But we didn't think of it as being made of trees because none of us had ever seen a tree. We were people of the sea, and our life was always and only on the boat. We did not trade with anyone. We were all born and raised on the boat, and that's what we knew.

Can you say whether you are related to any people existing on Earth now?

We are related. I'm not sure whether it's good to say, given the cultures of competition. The environments are extreme, and so are people's tendencies — not everyone, of course, and not even all the time for people who are like this, but for the underlying and most-damaging aspect of your culture — of being self-destructive. You tend to harm yourself or harm others for whatever rationale that you have. Sometimes it is just for excitement, and other times it is for competition or the lust of having more, even if you don't need it. So, yes, we are related to some people still living in the Northern and Southern Hemispheres, but that's all I will say. Given your environment, even though there is still much beauty and love and happiness, it would not be safe for these people to be mentioned.

Have you ever had a life on Earth since then, an embodied life?

No, but you have not asked how long our lives were on the boat.

[Laughs.] Okay, pretend I asked.

Normally, we expect you to ask that, only because we have knowledge of you as children. So our lifetime as children on the boat in your measured time was about 10,000 years, and then we evolved rapidly into adults and even more rapidly into elders. Then — and this is how our feelings came about — as elders, we felt the time of transformation coming. The elders would go toward the bow of the boat, not the absolute bow but toward the bow, and they would go to the side of the bow (starboard, you say). It felt right to them, and they would step over the side and go into the water.

When they'd go into the water, they'd gradually transform until they became one of the fish. That was our way of moving from one life to another. If you were to see us today, you would say that we were human beings, and yes, we were. You have all been like this. This is why people will sometimes, out of nowhere, get the feeling to be a vegetarian because there is something in their deepest memories. Memory is not only associated with your own life. It's associated with all lives lived on Earth — to know that the fish and, I believe, the animals are all beings that you have transformed into at the end of a life that you know.

You have these threads of life in you now. I am not saying you should all become vegetarians. I am not here to tell you what to do. I am only here to respond to your desire to know about lost wisdom. Lost wisdom is often an experience or experiences of many types that make up the wisdom of all beings because, as you know, experience is the way that life works for you. Experience becomes your wisdom because you can repeat that experience and know it will work.

The Visitors of Transformation

In your times of competition and other aspects of life that are self-destructive (people are not that way all the time, but it happens), the transformations you experience are not always the best. The reason you have so much self-destructiveness is that you know, at the deepest levels of your existence, that you're supposed to transform in some way into some other type of life. Your religions have understood that, those who compile religions and who bring about beliefs and experiences into something that can be followed as an example of a good way to live.

The transformation over time was turned into angels and similar things like that. Then it was turned into moving from one type of place into another with angels as guides and so on. You can look that up for yourself in your own times. I just wanted you to know where it came from as far as my life goes, and it probably came from times before that because in the distant past before my life — well before my life — the beings who came to Earth could be all things to all beings at all times. They showed themselves in different ways to those who witnessed their showings. Sometimes they would be people, and sometimes they would be (I'm going to say) animal people (because you use the term "people" to define someone who is an equal). Sometimes they would be the fishes. Sometimes they would be the birds. Sometimes they would be the hoofed animals. Sometimes they would be the animals who were on many legs and everything else. They would show all the forms of life to those who witnessed them. Perhaps someone else will talk about them, about the visitors of transformation.

I'm very grateful. Thank you. Thank you very much.

Very well. And I will say, given that this is becoming popular now, good life.

[Laughs.] Good life to you too, yes.

CHAPTER SIXTEEN

Consume Nutrition Energetically

Meda

June 28, 2015

This is Meda [mee-dah]. About 200,000 of your years ago, there were people living on an island well out in the Atlantic Ocean. These people were not very tall, and they were broad. It was not typical of them to grow any taller than three feet two inches, and they were not slim. They were what you might call squat, well-muscled, and perhaps easily taken, if you were to see a picture of them. They looked as if they were from the Stone Age. Since the island was very warm, they did not have to wear much.

These people could do wondrous things. Because they had to eat, one of the things they could do was (to survive, of course) walk into the sea and then transform. If you were to see them, they would look like people standing in the water, up to no more than their abdomens at any given time. They would stand completely still other than for breathing, which would come slow and shallow, maybe once or twice every minute. During that time, portions of them would go out into the water and become water beings, not unlike other water beings, that would find food. Those parts would also be able to absorb water.

You don't necessarily think about it, but all beings need water to survive. Those who live in the water are able to live on that water as well as what they consume. So the type of being they became was able not only to consume in the sea but also be refreshed with water. They would do this twice a day, once not long after they would awaken from their sleep cycle and one other time later in the afternoon, maybe two hours or perhaps three hours, depending on how they felt, before the light faded.

This went on for many years in this capacity. Even though you were able to see the process, there also seemed to be a spiritual process, and their bodies were well fed from this experience. Now, you might reasonably ask how Earth people could do this because they were Earth people. If you could see them, well, you'd say they were just short Earth people. I will tell you how they learned.

A Visitor Brings Knowledge of a New Way to Live

In the early part of this people's history, they hunted, but this island was not very big, and even though their numbers were small, never being more than forty and oftentimes much fewer, they began to run out of what they could eat. There was a spring on the island, so they had plenty of fresh water.

One day, a being came to visit, and they had never had a visitor before — ever — so they didn't know what to think of it. They were not violent people, other than hunting. When the visitor came, they were very surprised that it could speak their language and knew their gestures as well as the nuances of their language. By that, I mean that in your time, sometimes people say things to good friends or family that just involves a word or two even though they represent a whole thought or sentence. This works to communicate because they know each other so well. That would be an example of a nuance.

The being looked like them — the being did not dress like them but looked like them — and the people were confused. They asked, "Are you one of us?"

The being said, "I am not, but I am here to help you survive and thrive."

The people responded, "We are in trouble because we are almost out of our food source here."

The visitor said, "I am actually here because that which you are eating cried out for help because they need to survive, and they have only just barely enough of their own kind to survive and be able to thrive once again."

The people said, "We welcome that, as they are beautiful beings, and we have felt bad about having to hunt them and consume them."

The visitor said, "There is a better way for you to live, and I will show you now." The visitor took off his garments (he had no clothes on underneath) so that he could transform easily.

Then he said, "Watch this while you sit and rest a moment."

The being transformed gradually into different life forms. First, he transformed into the other life form on the island, which was a type of miniature deer. The people gasped when they saw that, of course, never having seen anything like this. Then the being transformed back into how he first looked, slowly transforming into about seventeen or eighteen different life forms, all of which existed on Earth at that time but none of which the people had ever seen.

He finished by transforming into a tree, which if you were to see the tree today, you would say, "Oh, that's a palm tree." The people laughed, and the children smiled. Then the being transformed back into presenting itself as one of the people.

The visitor said, "Come with me." They walked down to the sea but not into it. The visitor asked, "Now, who among you is the strongest?" One of the men stepped forward. "And who among you is the weakest?" One of the children stepped forward. "And who among you has the most love for all beings?" Another one stepped forward, a woman. Then he asked the three of them to line up. The child was almost full height, but was about, at that point, two-foot-seven.

The being said, "Come with me out into the water, and everyone else, watch closely, for we will not go out far."

Keep in mind, 200,000 years ago the oceans were completely clear, so you could stand there and look at what was in the water out for a ways. Of course, the people had perfect vision, meaning, you'd say, like 20/20, but actually it was more like 10/10, better than 20/20. That was actually the case many years ago for everyone, and it could be the case for your people now. But I don't want you to get distracted.

The visitor walked out, and the three followed him and went into the water at a depth just slightly above the knees. This way it would not be a problem for the child, as the surf was shallow when it came in. So at any given point, the water was never above the child's abdomen.

"Now turn and face the sea," said the visitor, "and I will instruct you on what to do." The visitor then instructed them to feel the water as part of their beings, and they did that. "Feel the sand under your feet as part of your being." Then they did that. "Now follow me, but let your bodies stay exactly where they are. Remain focused on the water and sand." The sand, I might add, was white sand, though if you were to look at it under a microscope, there would be other colors too.

The being also stood in front of them, and then the process I described earlier happened in which the being transformed into a water being and went into the water. The people's eyes were closed because they were focusing on being the water and the sand. Only the people on the shore had their eyes open, so they saw the visitor transform and, from their point of view, not quite disappear. There was a hue out where the being had been. Then they saw that hue or color appear around the three people, the ones standing in the water, yet their bodies remained standing there.

To get a better point of view, some of the people on the shore got up and slowly walked toward them. There was a strong energy, so they could not walk too quickly. Then they stopped. Some sat down, and some remained standing. They could see that underwater, the visitor was swimming and eating some smaller fish. They could see lights moving with the visitor, three lights. They were gold-colored and sometimes white and sometimes green and occasionally blue or purple. They moved with the visitor.

When they got closer to the little fish, the lights absorbed the fish. They could see that behind the visitor, who was a water being — you would say a fish — there gradually appeared to be other fish, three others. But they had a glow of color around them, and the people on the shore looked as their three friends stood there in the water glowing.

The being in the water swam around for a while. You would say, if you had to put a time on it, that they were swimming around for maybe seventeen, eighteen, or nineteen minutes, like that. Gradually the hue, the color around them, faded from the three beings, and the other being, the visitor, became more visible. Over the next five to six minutes, they all reappeared in the form they were in when they went down to the water.

The visitor came over and touched the three people very lightly. If you were to look at him, it looked as if he held his finger up, on his right hand, the first finger, and almost touched the forehead of the three without actually touching the skin of their foreheads. But for those receiving the touch, it felt as if they had been touched because their own auric field, you see, was very strong at that point. When that occurs, you actually feel as if you're being touched.

Then the three relaxed and began to move around a bit in the water, and the visitor said, "Now you can be in your bodies only. Release the water, and release the sand." The people standing there relaxed, and they moved their toes around in the sand, something they always liked to do anyway. Then the being stood off to the left side and said, "Now let us return to the shore," and they all walked back to the shore.

The being said, "I want to show you how to do this." At that time, there were about eighteen people, and he took all of them in groups of three out to do what the first three had done. He did not show them how to turn into other types of beings or the palm tree, for that matter, just fish, you see. So they learned how to do that transformation. It was not just an appearance, you understand. It was a way to actually be fed and nourished and to function in a way that allowed life.

The beings learned how to live in that fashion, and they lived there for a long time. After he showed the people how to transform, the visitor said, "I will visit you one more time."

The people said, "Thank you," of course, and the visitor became light and was no longer present.

The people were grateful. They came together and touched each other in a way that you would call a hug. You have seen people stand shoulder-to-shoulder, sort of reach out, and lightly hug each other. It was something like that. So the people learned this new way to live, and they lived that way with their population growing to no more than forty, occasionally from that point on, generally no less than thirty-seven, because they were well-fed and nourished, better than they had been before, and they still had the spring.

Safe Transit to Another World

Twenty-three years later, the visitor returned. Most people who had been alive during the first visit were still alive, but there were a couple of people who had passed over, and there were a couple of young ones. So when the visitor appeared, it was explained to the young ones. "This is the visitor we told you about." The people were happy to see the visitor and welcomed him.

After the welcoming, the visitor said, "Now, this time that is coming on your planet is going to be a water time. I have prepared you to be able to live in the water, and you will be able to go down and stand in the shore waters and be sea beings. But it is not like before, as it has been for you. The waters will rise very much, and they will not go back down for a long time."

The people asked, "Well, what can we do?"

The being said, "The reason I am here is that you are people we consider our relatives. A long time ago, there were just a few of you here — two, sometimes three. My people came to visit, and we were strongly attracted. My people stayed for some time, and there was a coming together and then children. But then my people had to leave. So the way we see it is that you are like us. So we have come to make an offer. There is another world, very much like this one, only a little smaller, not quite as big as this world. But if you were there, you would say, 'This looks like home.' We can take you there." The people sort of shifted around. They weren't comfortable with that because the island had been their only home.

The visitor asked, "I don't want to upset you, but who among you is the seer or the elder?" There wasn't an elder at that time, but the seer stepped forward.

The visitor said, "Let's sit over by that big tree." There was a big tree there. "I will show you a little bit of what will happen so that you understand." The visitor showed the seer that the water would rise so high that it would be almost above the tallest tree, which was about sixty feet tall. They talked while the seer was seeing this.

The seer asked, "How long will this last?"

The visitor said, "It will last for half of one of your life cycles." A life cycle for them would be when the Sun comes up in the morning to the following day when the Sun comes up, so essentially he referred to one day. The seer said, "We cannot survive that."

The visitor said, "There is a way you can, by staying here, and I will show you now." The visitor showed the seer what was essentially a boat, but it was more like something of light, and the people could all be in it until the water receded. "But then the island will not look the same. The other beings on the island would not survive, and instead of the sand being there, a big storm would be involved at certain points in that transformation. There would be no sand, and it would be very rocky, and most of the trees would be gone."

The seer said, "I understand." Then the seer walked back to the people and explained what was going to happen.

The people said, "What is this world, and how far away is it?"

Then the seer said, "It is not far at all. It just exists right where you are but in a different way." In your time, you would call this the fifth dimension. So the people said, "You mean, we don't have to go on a boat or anything?"

The visitor said, "No, you can stay right here. But there will be no water rise, and everything will remain the same."

The people said, "Yes, this will be fine." Of course, the other beings on the island, since they had originally invited the visitor, were very happy as well.

The visitor began to bring that about with the people, and it was possible to do in a very short amount of time. If you were to measure it, you would say, "Oh, this was years," but it felt like (to the people who were there) a couple of seconds.

All the people felt a little sleepy for a moment, but they didn't go to sleep, and they didn't pass out. They just felt slightly, not dizzy, disoriented, you would say. Then all was well. The visitor smiled, and the people smiled, of course. They asked, "So, when are we going to go?"

The visitor responded, "Oh, you have already gone!" Now, I know you are going to ask a question here: What dimension is this? This is a dimension you would call five. But it's different. It's not the same version of Earth as has been mentioned to you. At different dimensions, it is possible to have more than one expression of any given person, place, or thing. So on this planet, dimension five was where they lived, and they are still there.

So I'm bringing this to your attention today. This is why you are always reminded of the needs of the people of these times. For some of you who are very sensitive and feel drawn to the water, as if the water is welcoming — especially clear water — it might be possible to visit some springs that are clear or even go to some place in the ocean where the water is still fairly clear. We do not suggest that you try to swim like a fish, but it would be good to imagine the experience. Try to imagine it in a way that is very benevolent, very good, very loving, you understand? Like that. You can even make a meditation out of it, or what you call a vision, so that you can feel the experience.

For those of you who are sensitive and can do these things, don't stop eating your food. Notice — just notice — whether you are as hungry as you were before. It is possible that you will feel not only well fed — satiated, as you say — but you will not be hungry.

For those of you who want to lose weight, this will bring that about with the greatest of comfort. For those of you who don't want to lose weight, you will not lose weight. I'm not promoting this to you as if it is a weight-loss system. I want you to notice how you feel. If the vision is very clear for you — not just briefly, not only in your imagination, but remember what the visitor said to the people: "Feel the water as if it is part of you. You are the water. Feel it physically, and feel the sand as if it is part of you. Feel it physically," and you can do that, maintain that. You might very well have an experience similar to the people who were instructed in this way.

In this way, now, as the sensitives learn how to do this, your people in your time (all different kinds of people) will learn the old way, the ancient way, of being fed in this benevolent method that will feed a physical body all that you really need to eat, and it will be absorbed entirely. There is no waste matter. It will completely be absorbed and be totally fulfilling.

A Method to Thrive

Now, if you try this method, you sensitives might also notice that you are not as thirsty. If that is the case, don't avoid the water that you normally drink. Just notice whether you feel less thirsty. If possible, remember how it was for the ancient people. There was no soda pop, there was no beer, there was no coffee, and there was no tea. There was just pure water and foods. Try to cut back a little bit on anything you drink but water for the maximum experience. If there are some things that you have to drink, then good. You have to do that.

Try to create for yourself, as much as possible, the way it was for those ancient people of 200,000 years ago, yes, in your now time. However, they are still alive, still an example of what you can be in your now physical bodies, even though your physical bodies are different from theirs. The only real difference is that you are taller. That's all. Other than that, your bodies are the same. No matter what your skin color is or how you look, it's the same.

We feel that this is something you can do, but don't turn it into a sacrifice. Don't starve. Don't go without water. Remember, the whole point of it is to discover whether you can, in a similar way, experience what these people experienced and discover a way that people can live on Earth as it is now and need less food.

There are people coming up now; there are way too many people on Earth — but maybe not. Maybe it's just that you need something to eat that is different, or you need something to drink that is different, and it needs to be much more comforting to your body. Much of the food you eat now passes out of you as waste matter because your body cannot absorb it, cannot take it in. Your body is not fed by it. By these old ways, your body will be fed. So don't sacrifice anything. Don't starve. Drink what you need to drink, and eat what you need to eat, but in that experience, notice how you feel. These are instructions to those of you who are sensitives and can try this.

Some of you might be able to succeed and not just brag to your friends and say, "Oh yes, I did it!" You will thrive because you will find that consuming in this way actually feeds your body — providing everything your body needs to be able to live in your body now for hundreds of years. That's what was originally meant for you to live on this planet. The first dwellers who looked as you do now — Earth people, humans — lived to be 700, 800, sometimes close to 900 years old. They lived because that's how they ate. That's how they drank, and they drank spring water as well, and sometimes they ate foods, especially fruits, like that, and vegetables. But the "fishing" method is primarily how they survived and thrived.

Sometimes, for some of you in your times, you find yourselves eating even when you are not hungry. You know you're not hungry, and you might think to yourself, "Why am I eating?" It is because your body is searching for the food it needs to not only survive but also to thrive. The food I'm talking about here and instructed you on using these examples is the food you're looking for, and you can have it. You don't have to be in dimension five; you don't have to live 200,000 years ago. You can have it now — not everyone. It will take the sensitives to learn how.

The reason it will take them is that people of different cultures and different places on your planet learn according to their own culture, and you will be able to teach it in your own way and in the ways you understand and can share it with others. The sensitives will know how. Some of them will be able to teach it, and some will not. It is important that you be reminded of this so that you can begin.

The Original Earth People

Can you say anything about yourself?

I am, you might say, a friend or associate to the being who spoke previously [chapter 15]. But it was difficult for the channel to handle the energy afterward. It was a little too intense. But my energy will be fine for him. Now, I won't say too much. I will just say that I am a being of light like all of you — of love energy like all of you — and immortal such as all of life.

Know this: It is your nature to be as those people were taught. But when you are embodied, learning something so that you will be able to pass it on to others as good teachers in spirit someday, you are on Earth the way it is now. You learn to adapt and to be able to teach in all circumstances. None of those circumstances will ever be violent. That is something that is being transformed now.

Soon violence will cease to exist as people learn how to be fed with their bodies. I will say something else about when your bodies are fully fed. There are some people who always want more and more and more even when they don't need it — not just food, but things and experiences. Those needs will also fade once your bodies are completely fed in this benevolent way I have spoken of.

That's wonderful! Will you speak to us again?

Perhaps. But it was today that was the easiest day to come to speak. So I thank you for allowing that.

Of course. Were the people on this Earth at that time?

Yes. They were always on Earth — on an island in the Atlantic. They were Earth people. They were some of the original Earth people. This material is intended to save the people on Earth and allow them to transform themselves and Earth, which needs a lot of transformation to be a place that welcomes all life once again, as Earth once was. Good life. Good night.

Thank you very much. Thank you.

CHAPTER SEVENTEEN

Transform Violence by Rooting In

A Spirit Being

August 20, 2015

Is this someone who can talk about ancient wisdom that we lost or future wisdom, or are you interested in something else?

All right now. The transformation of violence into calm, peace, quiet, and a gentle attitude is very difficult when done mentally because the mind has almost nothing to do with it. This is why the psychological approach is not working. If you asked a psychologist, he or she would say, "It is working, but it takes as long as it takes," but that doesn't help in the immediate circumstances. There are a few things that can be done, and we can share one for when you are in a position in which you are not involved in the violence (perhaps people are fighting or the violence has been something unintentional, such as a car crash, for instance) but you are a witness and wonder what you can do about it and wonder whether it is even possible to re-create the sequence. For example, there is a car crash, a particularly violent one, causing injury or death.

If you are someone who can make contact with other planets or star systems (not to channel like this but just to reach out and touch, as a few have been trained) it is possible to reach into the center of this galaxy or the center of any nearby galaxy. It would be easiest and perhaps best to reach into the center of this galaxy. It is within this galaxy that your planet resides with all of its unusual polarizations, so you don't have to look toward a direction. It doesn't have to be astronomically correct. You just need to have the intention. You can use your right hand or your left hand if you have that capability to feel the energy change as you reach toward the center of the galaxy, and you don't have to actually point your arm there.

Use the system you know. Then it would be good to point a couple of fingers (if you want to be unseen and unnoticed, you probably will be because people will be looking at the scene and trying to help) toward the vehicles and ask for re-creation of the events that led up to this intersection of automobiles so that there is a potential that no harm was done. You can say it in a different way, such as that there is a potential that life goes on unimpeded. You might wish to say that instead.

This may have up to a 40 percent chance of success because the center of any galaxy, including (quite obviously) the one in which you reside, has the capability to create and re-create, and it does so all the time. Even planets, solar systems, and so on, that have been filed out of the center, still the center is in effect. Right now, your own planet is, in effect, of the center of this galaxy, and the center of the galaxy can transform your planet at any time. So that leads to the obvious question: What can you do about the transformation of violence for your entire planet? Granted, one individual might not be able to do too much, but more than one individual — say eight or nine or more, and it doesn't have to be simultaneous — might be very effective.

Transform Violence on Earth

To transform violence on Earth, you will have to make an exception, and that is the planet's personality. The planet's personality is one of action, activity, and motion. Those three words are the core description in your language of the personality of Earth, and to even ask that personality to stand down for a few years is not acceptable. So you would have to do something else. You would have to superimpose, which would involve creating an option — not control, but a means by which people can choose to transform their lives, knowing that it will be easy.

What you would superimpose is not unlike a veil or a drape. You would reach into the center of this galaxy, and then you would reach into the center of a galaxy of beings who have also frequented and sometimes even resided on or in your planet for a time. That would be the Pleiades or Virgo. Granted, in Virgo there is more than one galaxy, but it is up to you. Virgo has a particularly comfortable aspect with this planet, having many compatible aspects of personality.

Now, there is something you do in this case. You would probably be alone or in a small group of people, so you can feel free to use your arms. If you are missing an arm, just reach from the center of your chest or the center of your solar plexus. If you have arms, reach with whichever arm feels best (you may have to experiment) toward the center of this galaxy, and with your other arm, reach toward the center of Virgo. Again, you do not need to be astronomically correct; you just need to have the intention. You will be reaching toward the center of something, and there is one thing in the center that is completely different, so you will have to make sure that your arms are very comfortable doing this. This might take a little while, so lying down might be the way to go because then you can have your arms propped up. If you are lying on something, make sure it feels comfortable so that it is not distracting you. And don't lie where you might be distracted or disturbed as you do this, at least the first time. It is very important for you to stay focused.

While you reach into these places, simply relax to feel as calm and comfortable as you possibly can. If you fall asleep, you will just have to do it over. Wait until you get to that point — say, you can relax like that — and then you can say two words, or you don't have to. Be aware that you are a resident of this planet. In a way, you are anchoring what you are reaching for, and your mood is that calm and relaxation. So if you have thoughts, try to keep them quiet. You are going for a physical feeling in your body. Then you say two words so that it is clear. Say, "Rooting in." (Now that is "root," like a plant's root.) That's all.

You just say it once. Some of you will barely say it; you will just whisper it because you don't want to disturb the feeling you have, and that's good. Others of you might say it more boldly. But remember, you are not saying this on the basis of a command; you are making it clear to your mind that something is happening so that your mind does not look about to see how it could be thinking or how your body could do other things. It's an instruction to your mind. Make an effort to not think. If you catch yourself thinking, don't give yourself a hard time. I think you have been told that before. Just stop, and if you need to focus on something, focus on feeling calm. If you have difficulty with that, imagine physically easing yourself into all that is around you. If you are on a bed, that's fine, become the bed. If you are lying on the beach, become the sand — although you don't really want people traipsing through there [laughs]. It has to be calm, maybe in a group with a few people out at the edges to keep other people from walking through there. (If it is a public beach, you know, that will happen.) I am picking a beach because sand can be very cooperative in such cases, and it is probably the best thing to do this with.

In case you are wondering, yes, white sand has the advantage because it very often contains crystal along with other bits and pieces of what is found in sand, but any form of sand is fine, especially if it is naturally occurring in the place where you are, not just shoveled in there (that's not naturally occurring). Dirt is almost as good, but it is not the same. It is up to you what to lie on. Do that for up to two or three minutes without thinking.

Your Differences Create Harmony

There is much to do. That's why I feel that those who are more spiritually trained or trained as sensitives (sensitives are born to the role) pretty much know early on that they are sensitive or become aware of it later in life when people criticize them for it. But you are that way, so you can do these things. You can contribute toward the potential for the human population on Earth to transform in that way as desired. People desire to be calm and peaceful and to live in calm and peaceful surroundings. This doesn't mean you can't have fun and laugh and do things together; you can do that. It means that when people might disagree, they can just disagree about those things and then go on with life.

One person does not have to convince another that he or she is right. People will always have different points of view; that's what makes up a whole picture, a whole environment, a whole planet. The different points of view make it possible for things to create a harmonic course. So that's what you can do in this case.

You might ask, reasonably, "Where does this knowledge come from?" This knowledge is very ancient on Earth, and it has come from a species that is still found in various places on Earth. They are found at the very bottom of the deepest sea trenches. If you have vehicles that go down there, don't touch them. Don't even come within twenty feet of them. Just because you don't know what they are doing down there doesn't mean they are not doing anything. So scientists, I am pointing a finger at you here. I know that you want to investigate. It is fine to investigate without causing harm. Always remember that. That's what I have to say.

Embrace the Wisdom of Nonhuman Teachers
That's magnificent! Can you say anything about yourself?

It was felt that I would be of interest because you have not yet, in your societies for the most part — individually, yes — embraced in a major way the knowledge and wisdom available to you from beings on the planet, which is almost unbelievable to me. Here you are, surrounded by teachers — not of your own kind, granted — who cannot speak to you in your languages, and you ignore them. Just because they cannot speak in your languages does not mean you cannot know what they know if it would be of benefit your species. There is no need to know what they know for themselves, but if it would benefit your species, it would be wonderful to know that.

Your dogs, your cats — you call them animals. I think it is just a way of making yourselves better, which of course you are not. They are another species, but you are the only species on the planet who does that, who ignores that. All the other species on the planet are open to having that shared knowledge if it would benefit their type of species or other beings to have that.

I want to tell you something else that I feel is important for you to know since many of your people are attempting to be nonviolent or, more specifically, peaceful and calm, happy, yes. It sometimes upsets them to see films or videos or make-believe or fiction of animals attacking and eating other animals.

On your planet, when human beings are around nonhuman beings (I'm not talking about pets) who attempt to be open and to welcome you, you might find, for example, birds seem to fuss with each other — argue and carry on. Okay. You might find that so-called animals fight or attack or eat each other, but this is not necessarily their way. Granted, on this planet, animals (so-called animals, but really human beings also) find themselves eating other beings to survive because that is something of the planet, and we gave you something before to help calm that in human beings.

All these films of animals eating other animals or being violent and your experiences of not necessarily walking up to birds that were calm and suddenly jump into battle with each other but seeing it unexpectedly. These birds may not have any difficulty with each other at all. It is sometimes — not always, but at least one-third of the time — because they are trying to demonstrate something that they recognize as a quality in the human being. If you come across that, you can make the effort to relax, be calm, and be peaceful. Don't radiate it toward them. They don't need that. That's their normal state of being. Just be it for yourself. If they don't calm down, then they are fussed up like that (you might say) for somebody else, and you may or may not have influence with them, so don't run around everybody and say, "Be calm! Be peaceful!" [Laughs.] Just know that it's not you. I thought that might interest you.

Don't Engage the Past You Want to Change

There are things you can do then, as with the rooting in, to help your planet and things you can do to perhaps transform time sequences. You can request that the cars didn't crash or that the train didn't hit the truck or whatever. It doesn't mean that it will transform, but it might. When you do that, don't linger, all right? Don't linger around the scene of the crash unless you are in a position to directly help or you know the people in the vehicle. If you are going some place, if you are doing something else, continue on; do that, and completely let it go. Once you have done what you can do there, walk on with your life, as I think somebody else used to say to you. Go on with your life. Let it go. You've done what you can do. Go on. If you linger, you'll get into the drama of the moment and tend to reduce the work that you've already done because you will (how can we say?), by engaging with it, insist that it is so, all right.

I'm not trying to talk you into the idea that people in need of assistance do not need that assistance; I'm trying to say that if you can give them that immediate assistance — if you're a doctor, for instance, or a nurse, obviously go forward and try to help. But if you're not or you can't be of any help, walk on with your life. In this way, your last experience with that scene would have been your attempt to transform it into something that is calmer and is more peaceful and essentially never happened. Then go on with your life. It may or may not be effective. It may be effective for one or more of the people involved, or there might even be animals involved. Perhaps the truck was carrying horses. It could be effective for them. It could be effective in a number of ways.

However, I'm going to tell you something you're not going to like: Don't make an effort to ever find out. If you make the effort, then you are attached to the outcome, yes, but you are also getting involved in the past that you were attempting to change. If it so happens in life that you find out about it, that's all right, but don't seek it. Even if you're walking along and you hear people talking about it — there's a bit or a snatch of the conversation, and you know they're talking about exactly what you'd love to know — and they turn off, don't turn off with them. Again, that engages you with the past you were attempting to change for the better. Just a little instruction that a lot of you don't know.

What about helping in other situations, for instance in an area of town that has a lot of domestic violence or shootings or a war area or something? Do you do the same thing?

No, I think that's something else. I'm not conversant on that. Is that the term? That's something else. What I've been giving here is — no. No, I understand you want to transform a specific area that you feel is under siege or one situation or another that is harmful. I don't think that this would necessarily be a case for that. However, the *rooting in* would help overall. Remember, when you provide something that is available for people to use if they want it, I assume (perhaps I'm mistaken) that there are some people living in or visiting or simply passing through those dangerous areas. They would prefer that those areas be calm, happy, and peaceful, yes? So you've already done what you can do.

Encourage Children to Have a Reverence for Life

Okay, you were going to say something about yourself.

No, you asked me something about myself. I just didn't respond. That's what actually happened. You asked me about myself. It is not really important who I am, but if you would like to know who I identify with in my spirit, I would say I identify with those beings living at the bottom of the sea who seem to be doing little dances or are otherwise engaged in solitude. They're not really that way because, of course, they came from somewhere. But they like to wander around without much distraction. I am not one of them, but we are similar in personality.

I am not embodied. I am a being like you but not embodied like you. Of course, you are embodied only at this time. Your natural state of being is spirit only, as it's called. "Spirit" is simply a term, isn't it, for a personality that is not physically engaged with life. Spirit can often be physically engaged; it's just not in the type of physical body that you would say, "Oh, this is a physical being." But spirits move about. They may have an effect by needing something, or they're more likely to have an effect by providing something. And they are very often in motion. So they're physical; they're just not physical in the way you are.

Okay. I just love stories about people, places, beings, events.

It would be good to be more focused on human beings because the variety of life and life experience that one lives through as a human being is much vaster than the variety of life one might find as any other being in this universe. If you have been doing this kind of work for a while, perhaps you've noticed a great deal of similarity in the beings you hear from through channels, whereas on Earth, the variables of exposure — the experience for human beings and nonhuman beings alike is much vaster in terms of variables and thus in terms of the outcomes on a daily basis. But it's up to you.

You have a wonderful, calm, loving way of speaking. Is there anything else that you can talk to us about in the future, or do you prefer not to?

It's perfectly all right

Okay. Do you want to make a closing statement to the people who read this?

Pay attention to your surroundings, and when you see children looking at ants walking across the sidewalk, the only piece of instruction to ever give them is, "Don't hurt them." Recognize that these little beings may have vast knowledge that someday when you learn it will cause you to feel very grateful. Say it in words that your children can understand. Involve them in a reverence for life, and prepare them for the times some forms of life won't be kind to them because of the planet you're living on — mosquitoes, for example [laughs], or fleas or such things — but encourage them to have a reverence for life and to know that the being who made them and their parents and grandparents and people they love is the being who made the ants, the birds, the fish, and so on. May you have a most benevolent life.

Thank you very much! Thank you.

CHAPTER EIGHTEEN

Your Drum Is Your Ally

Drum Maker

October 19, 2015

Many people in your time like to gather in small groups and drum. This is not strictly a tribal phenomenon, but such events often attract young people. I want to give them some support, and then we can talk about other things. First, in drumming, I assume you know how to make the drum become your friend. For those of you who are unsure what to do, on a day when you are warm or can make yourself warm (so that your forehead sweats a bit), reach up with the first two fingers of your right hand (if you use your left hand, that's not too bad, but I recommend your right hand), and take some sweat off your forehead and rub it on the drum any place that feels right. It doesn't have to be any particular place, but it ought to be on the part of the drum that you strike. That will help make the drum yours, and it will then get used to you. If you do that, though, you'll have to make sure that the drum is yours only. The drum will expect only you to use it. Therefore, it would be best to put it aside somewhere until you use it for such gatherings or for yourself.

Now, there is more. When you strike the drum for the first time of the day, even if you're going to an event where people will drum, don't go until you've struck the drum at least once. You can use your hand to strike it, or you can use something else. Very often, people use something else. Keep in mind that once you have made it your own, the drum will be like some*one*, not some*thing*. Never think of your drum as something; it is an ally. Always remember it is an ally.

I recommend not striking the drum with a stick. Strike the drum your hand, even if it doesn't make much noise. Tap the drum with your hand and with your fingers. Always use an open palm, all right? That is best. In this way, the drum knows it's going to be struck (that's why it's a drum), but it feels more personal, and it's more comfortable with you striking it that way. The advantage of this is that over time, the drum will expect to be tapped in that way or struck in that way, and the more you strike it that way, the more the drum will become your ally.

Now, I intentionally mentioned the drum is your ally. I want you to understand that there will be times in your life (and you know this) when you will need something. I'm not talking about wants; I'm talking about needs. Maybe your need is something urgent — not necessarily an object, but a situation. Perhaps your child is sick. Perhaps you are not well, and you need support to get through what ails you. Keep your drum nearby. At times like this, you do not have to strike the drum. At times like this when you hold it (especially touching the part that you normally strike), the drum will support you. It will help you with your health or to get you through whatever concern you have so that you can heal and feel better.

In the case of a child or someone you love, do not touch the drum to that person. Lay your right hand on the surface of the drum, the part that you strike. Then remove your right hand from the drum and put it on your loved one. You can put it where that person is not feeling well, or you can put it some place else, where it feels like the spot to put it, all right? If the person cannot be touched (occasionally this happens), then hold your hand about 6 to 8 inches away from him or her and just hold your hand there or move it around very slowly. If you're not sure where to hold your hand, you can put it over the chest or over what you say is the solar plexus. I recommend the chest.

Now, as far as what to keep your drum in, I suggest you keep it in something you use only for that. Maybe even wrap it in something. If you wrap it in something, use something natural, like wool or perhaps cotton. Wool is better. That's a good thing to do. I don't want to say too much because many of you who use drums will know what to do and how to do it based on how you've been taught or on your own spiritual insights. I just wanted to give you that advice. Now, to the person I am speaking with here, if you have a question, you may ask it, or I will give more information.

Oh, please continue. It's very good.

Materials Used to Make Drums Are Sacred

You might wonder who, what, and where I am. I am still on Earth in spirit. I am not a wanderer, but as spirit, I no longer have to walk from place to place. I can be in different places. You will recognize the terms for some of the places I go because they are in your usage. I go to Africa, I go to South America, and I go to North America. Only rarely do I go to Australia. At places like that, I try to help people who are involved in the drum world, you might say. They drum or they make drums, but the drums they make are for people to use in a spiritual manner, the way we are talking about, so I usually just lend my presence. I do not instruct or correct because it is not my place to do so.

From time to time, a drum maker will have a question, and if the teacher is no longer present in the drummer's life for whatever reason or is unreachable, then sometimes the drummer will speak to a teacher (whoever that was) and say he or she needs to know something. The person will usually say this out loud. In that situation only, I am allowed to answer for the teacher. I will give the student the answer to the question with as few words or pictures as possible.

Because I am able to do this, to help people who use drums for spiritual purposes or (more often) who make drums, I decided to stay here as long as I am needed in spirit. Understand that when I died, I went where everyone goes after that. But my teachers and my guides said that if I wish to serve the people of Earth, I could return as spirit. That's the process. I didn't just stay on Earth. I returned as a spirit. Initially, I came with two of my teachers, and the teachers were with me because on my passage to return as a spirit, one must go through a process that is not like a trail or a pathway. Of course, it is not being born again. It is a spirit pathway that is of light. So my two teachers came, and one stayed with me for a time while the other returned. And now both of them returned. That's how I got back here.

If you are involved in the drum world and have had communication that you felt was from your teacher but there was another presence there (you briefly saw a light that was either blue or purple, for example), that was probably me. Keep in mind that when you speak to your teachers, you might catch a quick glimpse of purple if they are allowed to be more present with you when they answer questions. [Laughs.] That is not the clearest response, but I am addressing this to maybe two or three people on the planet. Now, I do not really do other things on the planet. I do not look at your society and consider "this" or "that." I am on the planet doing what I do because I am allowed to do it and because, as my teachers told me, it is believed to be a proper use of my devotion to the drum practice.

Honor Animals

The only instances I know of using drumming are soul recovery and, I guess, dancing. What are some other uses?

I brought up drumming not because of the things you mentioned. The reason I brought it up is that people very often come together to do what they call drum circles, and those are the people whom I originally was speaking about. If you want to talk about soul recovery, I did not do that in my life, so I have no personal experience with that. I'm not refusing, you understand. I'm not keeping anything from you. I did not do that. My job, when I was on the planet, was to make drums. That's why I am speaking about that. A drum maker will often visit. In your time, there are still drum makers, you see? And sometimes they visit "this" or "that" drum circle or an event, perhaps, among their people or among certain groups of people they serve. Those are the people I am more familiar with.

When I was on the planet — it was not that long ago in terms of your time, about 150 years ago — I had to assemble the materials (sinews, animal hides, and so on) myself. It took a long time to make a drum, and it was not always a pleasant experience because sometimes one had to kill. The animal would offer itself, but because I had love for animals during my whole life, it was hard to kill one just to use the hide. (Of course, the meat did not go to waste.)

I did not kill the animal myself. A hunter would go with me — one or two. Hunters would do the killing because they were not immune to suffering, and they appreciated and honored animals, as did I. When the killing took place, it was never a deer with a fawn, nothing like that.

Always honor the family. Remember that. Ask for an animal to come forth who would offer its body for such uses. In your time, I recommend that to those of you who hunt for meat. Always ask for an animal to come in the forest where you hunt (or wherever) who is willing to offer itself so that you and your family or your people can eat. In this way, families of animals will not be disturbed. If you just go out and shoot whoever or whatever, families might be disturbed, and the meat will not be healthy even if it seems to be. It is not a curse, you understand. It is just the feeling — the loss of the family that is destroyed or harmed — in the animal that is left in the meat, so if you eat that meat, no matter how it is prepared, the same thing can happen in your family.

Again, it is not a curse; it is just a fact that you need to know. So if you go hunting, always ask for the right animal to come to you. Know how to hunt so that when you shoot an animal, it does not linger and suffer. If it happens that it is suffering when you approach it, immediately kill it so that it does not linger and suffer. Then thank its spirit for giving such a great gift.

Can you tell me a little about drum circles? What is their purpose or function?

Drum circles are very often done for social reasons. I am not talking about a drum circle as if it were a spiritual thing that I have knowledge of. I am speaking about this because people sometimes come together to do this socially and for fun. There are other reasons people come together to do this, but I am not an expert in your cultures, you see. I am talking about people who might go to a drum circle just for fun. That's what they do.

Can you say where you lived on the land when you were in a body?

Canada.

Do you look in on relatives or on descendants?

No. That is not something that would be allowed, actually. No, that would definitely, definitely not be allowed. When you return, it's different. My understanding is that when you have just died, sometimes it is possible to have a quick visit in some way — just appearing in a dream or (more often) in a vision — but this is not something I do. When you return, there are other returnees. When you return, it's completely different. You don't go to where you used to live and all of that. You return for a purpose, and the purpose is to help. Usually you helped with something you did in your life that was of service or was helpful for someone on the planet (because you might be needed). I am not perfect at your language, but perhaps that helps.

The Drum Comes Before Its Keeper

Can you talk a little about the spiritual practices of drumming, or is that something you do not want to get into?

Some people — spiritual people — use drumming to put themselves in an altered state. And certain aspects of drumming can even allow the drummer to share that altered state with one or more people. If the others have drums, they might want to beat them and do that too, but it's always best, in this case of drumming, for the drummer to do something to help you through what you are going through.

Be aware that my job was to make the drum, not to use the drum. I did not make that clear, so your question helps to make that clear. I made the drum, and then I passed it on to the person who would use it. I think I once carried a drum for a year and a half because I had to meet the person who would use it. It was different like that. With my people, there was someone who used the drum. I can tell you this: When I made a drum, it wouldn't be something I would just do over and over again. "Oh, I'm going to make a drum." It's not like that. I lived as well as possible with my people, and then I received a feeling: "It's time to make a drum." I would do everything I already indicated, and then I would get the materials together and put it together very slowly. And usually sometime during that construction or very shortly after, one of the elders approached me and said something like, "The drum keeper will be here soon."

The drum keeper was the person to whom the drum went. At some point, I would know that the drum keeper was coming or perhaps had arrived. You might have an idea what I mean now. This was a situation in which the drum keeper was going to be born. That's why I would get the feeling that the drum needed to be made: so that the drum keeper could grow up with the drum. In that way, the drum keeper would blood the drum, you might say. Is that the term? The baby would be born. The mother and the elders would know that this baby was going to be the drum keeper, so when the baby was born, a little bit of the blood — this happens during the birth, you know — would be touched by the spiritual woman present. There would be other women present to support the mother but usually no men. The spiritual woman would take the first two fingers (not the thumb) of her right hand, and she would touch the blood on the baby. Then she would touch the drum. (I would have the drum there at that point. Before that, no one would have touched that drum, including the mother.) So the spiritual woman present (you might say medicine woman, but we didn't say that) would touch the drum just a little bit. She would touch baby just a little bit, picking up some of the blood, and then she would touch the drum some place, wherever it felt right to her. She would move her fingers counterclockwise very gently with a little bit of the blood, okay? Then it would leave a little smudge on there and soak in to the skin a bit. Of course, from that point on, the baby would be cleaned, and the rest of the birth process would happen the way the women did it.

Growing up, the child would always have the drum nearby, even when he or she could walk around comfortably, not just toddle around. When the child was young, three to four years old, the drum would be very big compared to the little one, but when the child got older, the drum would be a comfortable size. In the beginning, the drum would be big because the baby was small, so it couldn't carry the drum. However, only that child would touch the drum. It would never be touched by anyone else: not the mother, not the father, not the brother, not the sister, no one. It would usually be kept in a special place, and the baby would know. The young child would know that the drum is a companion, you see? The drum is a companion, and someone would never think of a drum as some*thing*. A drum is some*one*. The child would learn from a drum teacher, meaning usually the drum keeper would come along after drum teacher was a few years passed on. Sometimes, there would be more than one drummer in a group, a "tribe," you would say. That would be good because the other drum keeper could instruct the baby, and the child (I'm going to call it a child) would also be allowed to know how the drum wanted to be used and what the drum was for.

Sometimes a drum is for healing ceremonies, and sometimes it is to pass on stories. Sometimes drums have stories in their energy, and the child might beat the drum and tell stories. This is not a story that anyone would have told the child. The child would beat the drum and sometimes tell the story while beating the drum. Other times the child might just beat on the drum and then tell the story. When that would happen, the child might just be young but old enough to be able to communicate. You see? It could be any age. Let's see, in your time it could be three to six years old — something like that. When that would happen, many people could be there, but the hunting party might be out. They wouldn't hear it then, but they would hear it from somebody when they got back. That is how a lot of wisdom would come to the tribe. The drum is someone, but the drum, in a way, grew up with the child, so the drum keeper (the child, you see) and the drum would be one. And given that, the drum would be very special.

Now, you might ask, "What happens to the drum when the drum keeper dies?" The drum is not buried with the drum keeper. There is nothing like that with our people, anyway. The drum would be kept in a special place, usually with the family. If it was a big extended family and sometimes was less of a tribe than an extended family, the drum would be kept some place in case somebody who was a direct relation, such as a cousin, might felt attracted to the drum. If that were the case, the person would approach the drum and usually would take a year or two to be able to get up to the point of touching it. The person would know he or she couldn't touch the drum because walking toward it, he or she feel a sense of resistance, all right? The person wouldn't feel it in his or her body usually. Instead, he or she would feel it from the drum because the drum grew up with somebody else, you might say. However, if the drum allows the person to touch it, then they might be allowed to accompany another drum keeper after some instruction, the other drum keeper in the tribe who grew up with the drum. They might be allowed to participate in some way.

I could talk for hours on this, but I don't want to do that because of what we are doing here, you understand. I am adding those things in because I am taking into account the spiritual people in your time who use drums. I want to pass that on not to say this is how it should be done but to say this is how we did it. You might have your own customs. I can only speak about how we did things.

The Drum Maker's Journey

How did you come to be the drum maker? How did that start?

Not unlike other tasks. The way the hunters became hunters and the way the drum maker became known was always by birth. The elders always knew before a baby was born who that baby would be, in that sense, and what that baby would do. So the elders knew I would be a drum maker.

The drum maker was not allowed to be too close to expecting mothers because he was a man, you see, the drum maker at that time. (The drum maker sometimes was a woman). At that time, the drum maker was a man, and he was not allowed to be very close. "Very close" — I'll use your measurements — meant he would not be allowed to approach a mother when she was with child very early on or later on when being with child didn't make any difference. The mother would always know when she was with child. If not, the woman elder would know. The drum maker was not allowed to approach closer than 20 feet, so we'd have to keep our distance. Generally speaking, when a woman was with child, all men kept their distances with the possible exception of the husband. The husband could be near his wife until about, you would say, two and a half months before the baby was born. Then the husband was not allowed near the mother, either. That's how we did things.

When I was born, there was no drum maker, and there hadn't been one for a while. The previous drum maker had been a woman. In that case, they knew that when the drum maker died, there was no new drum maker. That was about three years before I was born. They kept items of hers, personal items. They kept a garment made of animal skin in a special place. And that garment was not touched by anyone until I was born. Then without altering the garment (even though it was made for a full-sized person), it was wrapped around me when I was a child, and that's how I learned. I was told by the elders that I was the drum maker, but that's how I learned how to make drums. Plus, I had a little advice from elders who had seen drums being made and from hunters who had hunted animals and seen things. But the spiritual nature of making the drums, as well as many other aspects, couldn't be taught because drum-making always took place, once the materials were assembled, when the drum maker (myself) was alone.

As far as I know, it was always this way with my people so that only the energies that needed to be present in that drum would be understood because no one else was there. I made it, and the animal was there because the animal had contributed all the aspects that were there, and the tree would be present. All aspects of everything that was used (sometimes no tree, but branches) were present: those spirits and my spirit and the spirit that would be in the drum for the drum keeper. All this was present. If somebody else were there, it could disturb that, so the drum maker was always alone when making a drum. I came to understand many of the techniques of how to do it because the previous drum maker's garment infused me with her knowledge and wisdom of these things.

How beautiful. What did you make the rest of the drum out of? The part that you hit with your hand was deerskin, but what was the rest of it made from?

Usually, it was made from branches that were woven together, but I cannot tell all. I won't say how it was woven together. How's that? Branches had to be young saplings, flexible, and they had to be woven in such a way that when they dried, they would be tight so that it made a rim, you see. When it was strong and tight like that, it was possible to attach the animal hide and use the sinew to tie it on in the way we did.

There was significance, then, in how it was woven, you're saying?

The wood part, yes. It had a certain pattern. But I cannot say that. My people are still present in Canada, and it wouldn't be right.

Can you say how big your tribe was, how many people?

It was fewer than 500 and more than 10. [Laughs.] That would range over some time. It never got to be more than a few hundred. I don't want to say too much. I must protect them.

The Drum Knows Its Person

Did you make drums only for your tribe, or did you travel? Did every tribe have its own drum maker?

Not every group. I know you say "tribe," but not every group of people had its own drum maker. The only time I wandered away to go to other places was when I had a drum that wasn't for our people. I could tell, so I would go and stand some place, holding the drum that I had made, and I would very slowly turn until I felt the direction to go in order to take the drum to whomever was supposed to have it. If it was winter, of course, I had to wait out the winter. See, I think with that drum, I had to wait out a winter, that part of the time.

It took a while to find the people, but I found them. They were a very small group. When I found them, I didn't know what to expect. I thought perhaps they would be a large group like ours, but when I found them, there were only nine people, and they saw me coming a long way off. In those days, you didn't necessarily assume. Plus, there were some dangerous animals, so somebody was always watching. They saw me coming, and they could see the drum. When I was looking for the person the drum was supposed to be for, I carried the drum in front of me — fully exposed, not hidden. I held it in such a way from the sides. I tried not to touch the part that is beat on. I held it from the sides and in front of me. They saw that, and they knew it was something for them, so they allowed me to come in.

We did not have the same way of speaking, but the elder approached me and did not touch the drum. He pointed to it and then pointed to his people, and I nodded my head. Then the elder used his left hand in addressing me, and his gestures ended up with the back of his hand facing the ground. (I'm making the gesture but you cannot see it.) He gestured toward me and then toward the people. There were nine people: There were adults, there were young children, and there was a baby. I knew immediately the drum was for the baby, so I walked with the elder. I didn't touch their people. It was polite, you see. I pointed not with a finger; you don't point with a finger, but you indicate. He had his hand up when he addressed me, so I had my hand down. I pointed with my palm down but my fingers curled toward baby. The mother had a twinkle in her eye. She knew the drum was for her child.

I left the drum with the elder. The elder was very respectful of the drum. I had something wrapped around the drum before, so I showed the elder the way I carried it, but he knew anyway. I put it in the hide, and I was going to give it to the elder, but he indicated no. So I gave it to the mother, and she took the drum for the baby.

They asked me whether I wanted to stay and eat with them. They had some dried meat, and they were kind enough to share it with me. I slept in their camp that night, and then they were very kind and shared more of their dried meat with me for my walk home. We said our goodbyes, and I went back.

How many days' walk was it?

Well, you have to understand that I didn't walk from where I lived in a straight line to where they were. Not only was there terrain — you know, up and down — but also it was like feeling the way. But I wasn't feeling the way, you see? It wasn't for me. The drum had to feel the way, and I would get the feeling from drum. The drum would instruct me on which way to go. So it was sort of roundabout. It took about three months to get there, but the way back was not as long. It took about half that time to get back.

Two Grieving Mothers

That's a fascinating story. Did you marry and have children?

Yes, I did. Unfortunately, my children did not outlast my woman and me. There was a bear. I don't want to talk about it — not that I am traumatized by it. My children and my family, we did not blame the bear. It was meant to be. The bear was forgiven, and some years later, a young bear came. I will tell just a little bit of this.

Some years after the loss of my children and mother, my woman was still grieving, as you might understand. But one day, watchers said a bear was approaching, bringing a cub — one cub only. (Normally, a mother bear would have more than one cub.) This bear approached very slowly and stopped every once in a while to hold the cub and pick up the cub. It stood up, you understand? Big bears do that sometimes when they are frightened or have to fight, but this was different. The bear took about two and a half days to arrive even though if it had walked at a steady pace, it could have gotten to where we were camped in, you would say, an hour. But the bear took this very slow route. So the elders felt the bear wanted to communicate in some way because this was not natural. The hunters, however, felt it was better to be cautious. They prepared for battle just in case. The elder went out there with the hunters. The hunters were not too far from the people and were not aggressive toward the bear.

The bear reached the hunters and stopped and looked at the elder. The elder looked at the bear and the bear cub, and the elder knew something. He allowed the mother bear and the cub to come to where we were. Of course, most of the people moved away, and the hunters stayed around the bear — not directly behind her and not directly in front of her, but to either side and at quite a distance. If they had needed to, they could have gotten to her in a couple of seconds.

The bear walked very slowly through the people. The bear came to where my woman and I were, and she looked sorrowful for a moment.

This was not the same bear that brought about my children's death. That was a male bear. This was a different bear. She looked very, very sad, and she took her cub and placed it in front of my woman. And then the bear wept. They cry, you know. Perhaps you don't know that bears and other animals cry just like human beings. When they grieve, they cry. The mother bear cried, and the elder hunter put his weapon down and spoke to the elder. The elder approached us and said the hunter believed the mother bear was offering her cub to my woman so that she could kill it since its father, you understand … my woman and I both cried at such an offer, and the mother bear cried with us. So did the elder.

All this time, the bear cub was very quiet and laid on its back. It knew why it was there. It was frightened but laid on its back. My woman went over to it and used the back of her left hand to touch the cub in a couple of places. Then she used the back of her right hand to touch the cub in a couple of places. Then she went over to the mother bear. She wiped her own tears with her fingertips and touched them to the tears of mother bear. She didn't touch the cub again, but she made a gesture so that the mother bear knew she could reclaim her cub. The mother bear nodded to my woman with tears of gratitude and left.

Oh, that's beautiful. Thank you.

Yes. It is important to know that even though human beings do not look like bears or deer, we are all very much alike. Not all animals are like human beings, and not all human beings are like animals, but we have much in common. Of course, love is one of those things we have in common. This is something to always remember, no matter how many steps you make in life (you say "years"), no matter how long and with whom, and no matter where or when, there is always — before life (if you are fortunate), during life, and after life — love between all, with all, and in many ways. And now I say goodbye.

Thank you so much. That was wonderful.

CHAPTER NINETEEN

Hone Your Instincts with Planet Ten's Support

Shaman Spirit

February 15, 2016

I would like to talk to the tenth planet or to a shaman.

Greetings.

Greetings.

I will try to provide you with both.

Both? Okay! [Laughs.]

Now, in days gone by, there have been pictures and stories and knowledge of people using — or apparently using — crystals to help others to feel better. But crystals, especially when used in the hands of one traditionally trained, are really a bit of a disguise. Many people feel the need, when undergoing what is essentially a mystical experience, to see something of beauty that apparently has something to do with why you feel better when it's over. This is not usually necessary for you to feel better, but for many people, it is a comfort, especially if the person doing the healing is an elder. And while photographers and artists like to show the traces of beauty of the wisdom in the faces and bodies of elders, younger people as well as many others do not always see that and might feel nervous, upset, or even frightened.

The crystal, in its beauty, often brings about a soothing relaxation. For the healing to work well, it is very helpful if the person who is receiving the treatment is relaxed, comfortable, and at ease. The crystal is not used to put people into some kind of hypnotic sleep. It is used to give them the feeling that this will be an experience of beauty and that regardless of how nervous they are, they can trust in this beautiful object. So I wanted to say that first.

Humans Imitated the Predominant Species by Eating Meat

You asked to speak to a shaman, but I know what you mean. We'll get back to that, but I want to give you the gift of knowledge about the planet you refer to as the number ten.

We knew about these things in our time, which is about 600 years ago from your time. And we knew that all of the planets circling the Sun where we live (what you call the solar system), which number twelve — but sometimes there is a thirteenth, not always — influence on a feeling-physical level through what you would now call astrological signs.

The purpose of astrological signs is to support people's understanding of their personalities, which directly refers to different families of orientation, whereas the planets refer to physical life, physical feelings, and the means to know, such as instinct. Each planet contributes to the capacity of all beings within that system to have not only the ability to survive in whatever condition they are living but also the opportunity to live well with ease — with neighbors, friends, family — with everyone so that there's cooperation. "Everyone" includes other species of beings — not just the predominant species as they're sometimes called on Earth, which you think of as the human being, but the predominant species (if there is one or even believed to be one) on the other planets.

In the past, the predominant species on Earth was not the human beings, and even today, there are vestiges of those beings on the planet. You see them all the time, but you don't think much about them. You don't realize that they were once the predominant species and that their nature has affected you very much. This predominant species is birds. The way birds that you see now are is very much the way birds were thousands and thousands of years ago.

Before human beings on Earth began to eat other beings, they ate other things. Many years ago on Earth, there were trees and bushes growing everywhere, and on the trees and bushes there were foods — nuts in some cases, fruits in other cases. Sometimes there were even foods growing on trees that you would now call vegetables, but they were either sweet or bland (I think you would say that word) foods. So the human being did not eat meat, but after a while as knowledge spread among different people that it was clear that there were many, many birds, all kinds of birds, some of which you don't see today, or you may have a few leftovers from them — say, feathers — and you can imagine what they might have looked like.

The birds in those days were often *very* colorful, beautiful, so beautiful that it dazzled the eye. By that, I mean that there was one species of birds in particular that on a sunny day with bright light, the light would actually reflect off the feathers. There was a metallic quality, and you could see that. It was considered special for people to see such a thing. This was long ago, but it was still remembered in my time when I was a boy and my grandfather and grandmother told me about it. Everybody, when they saw such a bird, would immediately sing a special song that bird seemed to like. That is how songs of blessings got started as well.

So that was the predominant species, but as I said, human beings noticed what the birds did, and the birds would often eat other beings, not just fruit, all right, not just things from trees and bushes. As it is with human beings, there is a tendency to imitate, especially to imitate life forms that are observed to be special. So there began to be the tendency to want to eat the kind of beings that birds were attracted to. Elders suggested that this was not a good thing to do because it's what the predominant species liked, and we did not want to take away their food.

Then the people started to look around, and even though some species had been friends — literally friends, like deer — they became a species that people decided to eat. Part of the reason was that deer would sometimes be open to sacrificing one of their number so that the people could have meat. For the first years, many, many human beings refused to eat such things because these were considered friends, equals. There was never any belief that other species of beings on Earth were anything but like humans. There was never any "better than this being" or "better than that being," nothing like that. The desire to imitate and the belief that the predominant species' way of life was something worth being like ruled in the acceptance of consuming other beings. But not all families and groups, which you sometimes call tribes, did that. Many did not. So it was slow to catch on from what I understand now.

I bring this up because it's important for you to realize that there are many planets that your machines do not detect (or even though they detect it, people do not believe it), and we knew about these things. Knowing is different from observing, measuring, and quantifying. This is very important. Many of your famous people, though they are no longer with you, have had the ability of knowing. Einstein was such a being. He used the figures on paper (you call it mathematics) to try to prove to others what he knew through knowing, but he was not always successful, or sometimes he was successful and was sorry. He attempted to try to share knowing with a community that did not want to know or thought it already knew, which was worse. So he did his best, and that's all anybody can do.

Planet Ten Supports the Sense of Knowing

This planet ten, you will probably ask, "What does it do? How does it support our physical awareness?" Planet ten supports your physical awareness because it helps you. It is not in charge of this; understand this is all helping. It helps you to know when something is for you or is for others. It is not in charge of that, but it is an element of your instinct. Sometimes you begin to reach for something, say, and for some reason you don't quite continue that reach. Then you pull your hand back. That's part of knowing, and it's part of instinct.

Instinct isn't just "go this way, not that way" or the awareness immediately of what you need to do without having to think about it. It's also subtler things: "Is this color right for me today?" or for a lady looking at her lip colors, "Is it this one, or is it that one?" and the feeling, the knowing, that it's "that one" and not "this one" today. I did not pick that as a silly example. Colors are very important to how people feel and to how they want others to know they feel. So I'm giving you this overview so that you will understand that the nature of healing is all about the nature of knowing.

Now, a little more about knowing: Knowing is not only instinct but also a physical feeling rooted in love. Love is a physical feeling. I'm not talking about passion now. Passion is one demonstration of want, need, and love — not always, but those are the components. Love indicates the knowing is about the basic kindness or friendliness between all groups of beings. If the human being in your time didn't have the reputation with all other species of being dangerous, then you would find that all other species would be very friendly. They'd hop over to you or they'd swim over to you or they'd fly over to you or however they get around, and they'd be very friendly just like any of your friends are with you now. Your reputation has spread to create not a blanket assumption, meaning not *all* species consider *all* humans to be dangerous, but rather; it is part of their knowing that one must approach human beings with caution if at all. Given such knowledge, such knowing, they do approach you with caution.

However, since knowing has a component of love and since all beings are born with love (even though love may not have had everything to do with how you were conceived) while you were in your mother, Spirit comes and goes and brings with it love. A mother very often loves this wonderful being growing inside of her, so you are born in love even though it is difficult and painful for the mother. You don't necessarily know about that because it's all you can do to get down that little tube and get out. Very soon after you are born, you feel the love physically with your mother hugging you and your father perhaps looking on in happiness at your arrival. You are born with love, and all species around you celebrate your arrival.

Knowing, then, is about love, and it is about awareness, meaning awareness of your surroundings with all of your senses, and it is about the nurturance you receive as a young one from your parents, your grandparents, your uncles, you aunties, your brothers, your sisters, everyone, and very often other species. There might be goats or chickens or so on. It depends whether it's a farm. If it's some place else, it might be pets, which are often very good to have around babies — cats, dogs, very good — and sometimes other beings (horses, sometimes, though they don't like to be penned up; you wouldn't like it, either).

Still, I talked to you a little bit about these things so that you will understand that the physicality of these planets all affect your own physicality. Other planets function in other ways. They support that element of the physical you, sometimes in your feelings of, say, bravery or daring do, not in the theatrical sense, but in finding yourself in a risky situation and wondering *what to do*, so knowing whether to jump, whether to run, whether to fight. All these things are supported (not controlled) by the physical planets that are moving around the Sun, including your own.

Remember Who You Are to Strive and Thrive

I mean to cover all things because it is important to give you knowledge and wisdom of more than one thing. The days grow short for the human being on Earth. This does not mean that some terrible calamity will befall you all. It means that in a moment's notice — a split second, I believe you say — you could find yourself in a better place, and that could happen without warning. Some people will be sleeping, some people will be working, some people will be eating, and so on.

People will be doing anything, and it will happen so fast that it will surprise you. So it is not of any great value to accumulate any type of knowledge or wisdom now that you cannot use immediately in your lives, especially if it is that which is involved in your day-to-day survival and well-being. I'm not suggesting that these are times that are more dangerous now than ever before, but there is a tendency by people now who are very involved in very complex lifestyles (not times) to repeat things that you know (at least in the back of your mind) shouldn't be repeated. It's happening on an individual basis, and it's even happening on a country-to-country basis.

This is occurring largely because many people are frightened, and they don't know what to do except for what they've already done. Even if they know it's not a good thing to do, they do it. They understand it, they think, and they're inclined to do it, even though it is ultimately and quite obviously almost immediately self-destructive. This is why some people, not all — some people are just risk-takers and create opportunities for others by taking these risks — are clearly, you say, bent on self-destruction. Sometimes they seem to be that way because this is what they know, this risky act or dangerous act, and it might not even be that dangerous to them. Perhaps it's just dangerous to others, like going out and drinking too much and then driving home as if nothing had happened.

Your times are not as complex as you think because basic human behaviors are based on love (when you are born) and knowing (which you are supported in as you are born). Then you adapt to your societies, which are often artificial, meaning you're told that your knowing isn't real and that it's just your imagination. People set about trying to prove it to you, even if they're taking away your basic wisdom-creating apparatus, you might say. So there is a problem in your times.

People have forgotten how to use their basic abilities. That is why, through this channel for some time, you have not been able to get just interesting information; there is no need to accumulate that. The urgent need is to be reminded who you are, how to use what is natural to you, and how to apply it in the best and most benevolent way for you and all other beings. That is what you were born with, and that you must know and be able to do without question in order to, yes, survive and, what?

Thrive.

Thrive. Thrive. That's right.

The Choice to Remain on Earth

All right. Can you tell us something about yourself? Are you speaking from that life or from spirit?

I am speaking from spirit because clearly it is not 600 years ago, but I remember that life well, and I am on the planet in spirit because I am watching all of my people. You might say, "Well, how can you be watching all of your people?" because it's not 600 years ago, but my people live on in the form of others. There are many people, those who have succeeded (you understand), the young ones who used to live in those times, and sometimes the people who would be considered grandchildren or great-grandchildren and so on, however you would say it. I still watch over them, and I'm concerned for them. So that's why I'm here. When it came to the end of my life, I wanted to be able to help my own children and help their children, and this was the strongest desire I had when I died. I was surprised that after life and after being in spirit and going through all those things, I was given the choice: I could remain in spirit on Earth and watch over my children and my children's children and so on for as long as they were on Earth, or I could simply revolve through spirit, be reborn, and live some place else. I chose to be here, and here I am.

Hmm. Can you tell me what tribe you were part of and what part of the world you are from?

I won't say that because we did not call ourselves by a name. Other people came along later and used names. Sometimes the name they used was simply a description of how they saw themselves, and that word or sound became the name others called them. Or others simply gave them a name, even though they had a name for themselves. So I won't say. I will simply say that I lived in what you now call the Americas.

Okay. Are the people you watch over now still part of that group, or are they beings you knew then who are reincarnated in other bodies?

From my way of looking at it, you understand, they are part of our family. Of course, in the larger sense, we're all part of the same family. I understand that well, but I have a special affection for them because they are literally a portion of our family, and they are all over Earth — everywhere. They live on every landmass. So I get the opportunity to travel around to see how people live elsewhere. Some places are more comfortable, and in some places, I don't feel quite as well because sometimes some of them live or spend a great deal of time in things that are entirely constructed by human beings, and such places do not feel natural.

Supporter of the Birth and Death Cycle

What was your particular specialty in that life? Were you a mystical man, a shaman, a healer, or what?

What I did was support the birth and death cycle of our people. I was present at all births, and I was present at all deaths. Of course, sometimes people died away from our people, so I wasn't present there, but I was present for all births. Oh, you may be confused because this is a male being bringing through these words, but I was a female.

I was just going to ask that. Did you have secret knowledge or just common sense knowledge about how to help women during childbirth? Did you have things you were trained in?

I had been trained by the elder who did these things, but mostly it was about providing a feeling. Our people were very focused in feelings. That's how we survived so well. I would experience a physical feeling of happiness, welcome, and love, and I would stand very close to the mother because it helped her to give birth quickly. There was no struggle in the body. When a baby was ready to be born, birth would happen in a few minutes. There was no long struggle such as mothers have come to experience in your current times in some places. Birth happened quickly, and babies felt welcome.

Of course there were other women there, and they all felt welcome and happiness. Some of them worked strictly with the mother. There would always be somebody near the mother and supporting her to bring the baby out and letting the mother know it was safe for the baby to come out, that it would be loved and protected just as much as she had been doing with the baby inside of her. Of course this is known in the mind, but people need such reassurance — not in words, but in feelings — so that the physical body is reassured that even though the baby has been inside for very long and the physical body grows accustomed to the baby being there and enjoys it, it is time to release the baby so that it can come into the world. It is reassurance for mother's physical body.

How old were you when you died?

In your years as you count them? In my late thirties.

Was that typical for your people?

Oh, I don't know. Some of them lived to be in their early fifties. It just happened. You can see that my body returned to Earth, but I live on. The personality I have now is the same that I had in that life. It will be so with you as well.

How do you interact with these — let me get clear — reincarnations of the souls who were in your people that you watch over now?

No. No, no. No, it's the physical.

Right, the physical people but they're not still in that same group?

No, no, no, you don't understand. It's the physical. I'm not talking about souls. You have terms you use in your world. It is the physical strain; you would say the "genetics." That's your word.

Ah, okay. People in that genetic line even though they're all over the world. Okay. And how do you interact with them? What is it that you do with them?

I just am myself with the same feelings I had during birthing. If that supports life, you see, that puts life all through it. When they're closer to the time of death, then I use the same feeling I used for those who were dying, which was to welcome them into the spirit world. It's never to try to hold and grab. That's not it. It's about the worlds of spirit and physical uniting. It is this way with all species, for the ones you love and that live with you — your pets, you say — or for the ones you admire from a distance, a beautiful bird flying by or something. It is this way for them too. Death is really that Mother Earth welcomes back that which she gave you for a time, but your life goes on and your personality goes on. And the only things that fall away from you are the parts of your life that were sad or that (you would say now in your times) you could never figure out. Your unhappiness falls away from you.

After life, after you've gone through a process with your guides and teachers and if you're lucky, with Creator directly, then you move on. You are born some place else, or as in my case and a few others around, you may be able to remain on Earth if you have a good reason to be here. You will do good things for the time that you are here and not just walk around and look at "this" and "that" [laughs]. You have to do things that are worthwhile for others so that you can stay on Earth in spirit.

Okay, are your people sensitive enough to know that you're there, or are they just feeling the feelings?

Sometimes I can tell that they know, and other times, I don't know that they know. But I do what I'm doing, and I don't need to know, you see? I don't wish to interfere because they might be getting inspiration from their guides or teachers, so I don't interfere with that. But they know that I am there. It's like this: When there are beings in spirit form, sometimes they will tell you, "Oh, I can be at many places at once." It's not that way for me. I can be one place at one time. I see myself in my physical form; only you wouldn't see me. I am one place at a time, never all over the place.

But you can feel from a distance when someone needs help, right?

I don't necessarily go. It depends. If I'm in the middle of something with somebody else, I complete what I have been doing. If I can go, I do. But many times, many have needed help, and what do I do? Well, I go where I can go. But perhaps you think I'm talking about just a few people, eh? There are hundreds — now thousands, really — because, of course, they had children and then each of those had children and each of those had children. So there are many thousands. I do not count that high, perhaps more than thousands. I do not know.

I do what I can do for who I can do it for, but my feeling is this: I have been here for a while, and I feel that things are getting different. It feels as if things are going to change because I don't feel a great sense of (how can we say?) openness all around me. See, with openness all around me, that means that not only can I go where I need to go when I am needed but also that the past, the present, and the future are all welcoming. Now, even though I feel welcome in the future, I can feel it being very different. This can only mean that the future is very different for you all, which means that you must be very close to some change that feels better.

So will you go with us when we change, or will you then go back to your reincarnational cycle? What will you do?

It's not my choice. I will go where I go when that time comes.

How do you get from one place to another on the planet? Can you just will yourself there or fly or what?

[Laughs.] Remember what my people were focused on: physical feelings. So when I feel someone needs me right away, then I am there. But when I feel *many* need me, then I am open to being where I am needed the most, and then I am there.

Planet Ten's Visitors

What is your knowledge about planet ten? How did you know anything about that planet?

We — my people — were about physical feelings, yes? Many of the elders had knowledge about everything that is physical. We paid attention to what was physical around us, and that's how we lived and knew what to eat and what not to eat — the trees, the fruits, and so on — because they still existed, you know? There are things growing on trees in your time too. So we knew what to eat and what not to eat. That's still an issue in your time too. So there's that. We focused on those things, but there were others, you see.

There are sometimes very bright stars in the sky, which I don't know how to explain to you because you want a mental reason. You want a thought, but it is knowing. We could feel the planets going around us. We could feel our planet, Mother Earth, going around the Sun. It was all in physical feelings. We knew how many planets there are, even though planet thirteen is not always present. We cannot explain that. It may not be a planet like the others. Sometimes it goes around the Sun; sometimes it doesn't. We do not know what that means, but all the planets are real.

Is there any history in your people or any oral legends that talk about having seen this planet up close, this planet ten?

You mean, did we try to look at it from a distance?

Okay. Did they?

Of course.

What did they see?

They looked to see whether we had any friends there, meaning people who looked like us or people who looked like our friends around us, even those who were not two-leggeds. We didn't see many, but we saw people who look like us on other planets, not the ones going around the Sun, as we say. We saw some people who sort of looked like us on some other planets. And we didn't feel it was right to communicate with them because they were living their lives, see? This is not something I did, but I heard some of the others talking about it, elders. I was very young when they were talking about it. Still, I remember what they said. They said it wouldn't be polite — using your words for it — to interrupt them and that they, not knowing who we are (I don't know), might not be all right. So we didn't spy on them. We just looked at how they lived and so on.

What did they look like, the ones on planet ten?

Oh, a moment. [Pauses.] Looking at them now, I'd say, I don't think they're from that planet because they're in some kind of building that looks like it's not … I think they're just visiting. They are visitors there. Oh, but they look like human beings — *almost*, not exactly, a little different. Their heads are shaped just a little different, and I think their brains are a little bigger.

Those are the visitors now, not the people who live on the planet?

Those are people visiting. That's who I can see.

What about the people who live on the planet?

I don't see that right now. That is veiled to me, so you will have to ask another, another time.

This is very interesting. So you have the ability even as a spirit. Did you have this ability in the physical, to do this, to look at a planet and see the people on it?

I do not know whether I had the ability. I do not wish to use that, as you call, ability now because it is not why I am on Earth. So I cannot comment on that. If I were to do that now for you, I would not be on Earth for very long.

Well, I certainly do not want to interfere with your life.

Well, you see, I was allowed to be on Earth to do exactly —

What you're doing.

Yes. But only that.

Well, let me phrase it this way: Did just a few of your people when you were alive have this ability to do long touch or commune at a distance or see at a distance (or however you say it), or was that something many people in your group could do?

It is interesting you ask that question because it is so typical of people in your time to want to know about things that are far away and that they will never actually touch. It is an important question because it is very much a representative question that you ask. In my time, I only heard the elders talking about it once. They did not consider it to be very important because they knew they would never be there. It was just something that someone was talking about, and it sounded like, to a child, a story, but my mother said, "Oh, it was real." That's all I remember.

I am glad you asked that question because the desire of your people in your time is to find something better, so I'm going to say that the better thing is coming. Try to live now as well as possible, and be kind to others if you possibly can. And if you can't, then just leave them be and hope — perhaps even say a prayer for them — that kindness and a good life will be theirs as soon as they are ready. Good night and good life.

Thank you very much, and good life to you. Thank you.

CHAPTER TWENTY

Transform Discomfort with Motion and Imagination

A Shaman Woman

March 30, 2016

All right. Now, I am woman; you say "shaman." It's not our word, but then none of these words are our words. Language, you say. Hmm. So the time in which I lived from your time is about 600 years ago. We lived at times in a flat area — not much of a mountain, you'd say, not even a hill — but it depended on the time of year. The flat area was our home during spring and summer, and during the other time of the year, there was a mountain we were near, a beautiful mountain. But below the mountain, there was a warm, steamy cave, very big, and it stayed very warm all through the winter. Plenty of fresh water in the cave, so [we had] no problem drinking, and we could store the food we had saved during the warm time. This area you would now consider — I'll give you a location — Colorado. And I believe that some of this cave (it's possible) is still accessible.

Now, you want to know about knowledge, wisdom. I will share what I did. I was taught by Grandmother. My mother did not do these things, but Grandmother did and knew that her daughter, my mother, was not meant for it. So she was determined [laughs] to stay alive in hopes that a granddaughter would, and I was that person. She taught me about motion and how motion could be used to create answers — not to get answers that you would call words or explanations or advice, you might say, but motions that create. And if a change is needed for a person or a place or a thing or all the people, then certain motions might be able to accomplish that. It is in the motions that things are done — not the motion itself, but the effect of the motion.

Motion Can Transform Fear and Suffering

I will be more specific. There was a time (this was after Grandmother passed over) when a child of our people had visions, and we were not sure whether the visions were correct because our person who had visions had died some considerable time before that and had not been able to pass on that ability — died unexpectedly, you see. So the child had visions, and we were not sure — some of the visions were so strange, odd — so I needed to find out (they asked me, of course) whether the child's visions were true. If they were, we would have to move unexpectedly. This was at a time when we were in the cave, but it was before we would normally move. It was not snowing outside but still cold at night.

So the child was seeing some danger coming. The child (very young) could not describe the danger but would shudder — no, shake! — at the danger and cry. I went off to part of the cave, a deep part, where I could do my oracle. It was not about a dance, though I think a dance may have come from it, some dances. And I started by just standing upright, and the ground under my feet was very fine dirt. That's the only way I can describe it: very fine, not sand but dirt, very comfortable, soft. And I stood and faced the direction that felt the most comfortable. Then I imagined the child — not *be* the child, but imagined the child. I would be the imagination of the child is the best way to describe it. It is like an energy, a feeling, you see.

Then I started to move, and I moved. You would say it looked like a slow dance. I moved and continued to move until I stopped, and then I felt much better. When I walked back, the child was happy and smiling. In this way, I discovered that the child's imagination was like a waking nightmare. The child was all right. The child was happy and smiling and before had been seriously frightened, afraid. The visions came no more. This was, you could say, like a spiritual cleansing of the child's imagination, but at the same time, the motions themselves expressed that nightmare. It turned out there was no danger, and we did not have to leave, so we stayed in the cave until the spring came, and then we went to our other place.

I bring this up because I want to pass this on to those of you who may already be doing some of this. You may think that some of the precise motions are the most important — perhaps somebody taught you some of these — but it does not always have to be that way. What may appear to be a dance, certain steps and certain exact motions, might be fine for some other way of spiritual expression (you say). In this case, it was a child, someone innocent (yes?). There were no other manipulations — you say "agenda." Nothing else was involved, so it was very clear that what was being expressed was no lie, see. So I was able to express the fear and transform it just by motions.

Now, those of you doing dance for the purpose of perpetuating or changing or creating whatever you do to create the dance (most of the time to keep things as good as possible), don't be afraid to express. I think some of you are doing this, see, in your groups or in your teaching or with your teachers, but it is not always well received. Don't be afraid to express, as I mentioned. I use the child as an example because this is an innocent. There were no lies, no other schemes, okay. That is important.

The Desire of the Spark of Creation

Now, another situation: An elder of our people with great wisdom (not all knowledge having been passed on yet but working with several young people to pass it on) had fallen and been injured in a way that could result in death. Nowadays you have ways so that these injuries do not result in death: a broken leg is severe — the kind of thing that could result in infection, you would say. I was off gathering some materials to make a tea — not a cure, just a tea that is pleasant to drink — and this is when it happened (during the summer).

Someone, Swift Runner, came up to me and said what happened, and we ran back, but halfway there, I stopped. Swift Runner ran back to me and said, "You must hurry," but I realized there wasn't time. I had to do my healing work right then and there. So I told Swift Runner to run back and say I would be doing what needed to be done, and then I would return.

I felt into the moment before the elder tripped over whatever it was (a stone or something), and just a moment before, the elder had been thinking briefly about his death. So I got in touch with the moment before that, when the elder's students were all asking him questions at the same time [laughs]. This happens sometimes. Elder was weary in that moment and thought briefly, "When I am gone, who will they ask?" — worried, you see, whether the elder had enough time to teach. In that moment of considering death, the elder tripped, and death was upon him. So I began moving on the basis of the moments before and found myself leaping into the air. Only afterward did I understand what that meant, the moving slowly, turning, and leaping into the air.

After this, I stopped for a time and just sat down. Within a little while, Swift Runner ran up to me and said, "It's wonderful! It's amazing! Elder no longer has a broken leg, no blood. It all went away. Everything is fine." And then Swift Runner, being an observant young person, asked, "Why are you sitting down? Are you tired?"

I said, "Yes, I am. I am resting. I will return soon." I gave him the herbs for the tea, and he took them back.

I stayed there for a time, and I realized what it was, the leaping. When a person dies, the spark of creation — you say "soul" — goes up. It doesn't go any other direction. It goes up. I realized that that spark of creation in the elder wanted to go, wanted to rejoin all its brothers and sisters that had passed before and wanted to see its father and mother, grandfather and grandmother. It missed all those from his generation who had gone on before him and for a moment was lonely even though besieged by students he loved dearly.

My leaping into the air expressed the spark of creation inside the elder, and he was becalmed and then comforted, and it transformed his injury. When I got back, I smiled at the elder, and he smiled at me, and we had a nice cup of tea.

We didn't talk about it because it's not so good to go back. Sometimes people in your time, I think (maybe more than our people), talk about things in the past, even things that were of suffering. We did not do this because it can bring it back. Sometimes when suffering, one feels bet-ter when the suffering stops or when somebody came to help as an act of love. If there is no love in your life since then, in those moments of talking, you might feel affectionate toward those good moments. So you go back and talk about the suffering because you want to remember the good part. But we did not do that because we felt that it could bring the suffering on. You tend, in your thoughts and memories, to remember the good things but not so much the bad things. You have to be careful what you remember so that you don't bring on the bad with the good.

That is absolutely beautiful. So you just let your feelings express through your body, right? You express your intuition?

Yes, exactly. In that case, the elder lived on for, oh, another year, I think it was (using our year, which is by the Moon). The elder was able to pass on all his wisdom, and that's what he wanted. So when death came, it was the most blessed kind. He died in his sleep, which is always the good way.

Think the Sun Will Come

How were you trained? How does one train someone to use their intuition in situations like this?

It is quite easy, especially when the teacher is very wise and knows how to communicate. Keep in mind that I was a child. My teacher was my grandmother, but I was a little girl. You would say five years old. So I was completely enraptured by being with Grandmother because she was the oldest person I'd ever known — gray hair and some white hair, very old, ancient! Just being with her was a joy. She would not immediately start teaching me. We would do nice things: maybe have a little tea, maybe have a little something to eat. We would often go for a walk; she was old but still able to move around. We'd walk somewhere. Sometimes someone would go with us, sometimes not. If they went with us, they would sit down at some point. I think maybe Grandmother must've nodded to them or something, and they would just sort of keep people away from us. Grandmother would ask me to sit down, and she would sit down. Then she'd talk about things that at that time seemed like play. She would ask, "Do you like to dance?"

I would say, "Oh, yes. I like to dance a lot," and then I'd get up and jump around a little bit [laughs] and do what a child would call dance.

She would laugh, and she'd ask me to come sit down in front of her again. She would ask, "Do you know how to imagine being the deer?"

I would say, "Oh, yes."

"Why don't you imagine being the deer, and then do the dance that you think the deer would do if you were a deer?"

I would do that. Then she would smile and ask me to sit down, and she would go through all the different animals that we would sometimes see. We would see deer often because there were a lot of them then in that area. They came and went. Sometimes there were antelope (I'm using your words for them, you know), and they're a little different. I would do that dance, meaning my childhood expression of what I would be like if I were an antelope dancing. We went through all that, including lion and bear, who we would see sometimes, but we tried to see them from a distance [laughs].

So I did all of that, and then she taught me how to be something else, how to express something else but in an innocent way, because lions, bear, deer, antelope, all these beings are also innocent. They are what they seem to be, nothing else. They are not trying to lie to you. They are who they are, and our people were like that too.

After a time, she asked, "Do you know what it would be like to be an old man like any of the old men in our tribe?" Then I would do the dance [laughs], childlike, trying to look like an old man trying to dance and continue on like that. And she would have me jumping around all the while (I'm using my imagination, see). This went on for days and days. It didn't happen all at once, and it didn't happen day after day after day because other times I went with Mother and my brothers or sisters or friends and did other things. But it happened, to use your measurement, maybe three times a week, maybe two times a week, something like that, for a few hours or however long felt right. This went on for some time.

Eventually Grandmother asked, "Do you know what it would be like to be the rain?" And I'd do my expression. By this time, I had gone through a lot of training. Then I tried to be in my childhood imagination, and I knew my job was to express a thing as a motion, so I did that and then the Sun. Then I'd do other things like that — the Moon, all kinds of things like that. After a lot of training like that, she asked me, "What would it be like to be any healthy young person?" Okay, all kinds of things.

She sat me down one day after all these kinds of trainings, and she said, "Some day, you are going to be able to do dances that will make things better. Maybe there will be too much rain, and you can go out and even when it's raining, you can do your dance that welcomes the Sun." Grandmother said, "You might find that this welcomes the Sun, but when you're doing it, remember, even if you're wet and it's raining very hard and you're standing in mud or water, that it is your job to be only the Sun expressed as Sun when you are doing your motions. Sometimes it will seem like a dance, and other times it will be very slow. Be only the Sun, nothing else. Then you will find that the Sun will want to come to be there with you, and very soon after that, we think, eh?" She looked to me, and I nodded, and she nodded. "We think," she said, speaking for both of us, "the Sun will come." Understand I'm using your words here, your type of words.

She talked more about these things. "It's all in expressing needs," she said. "There will be times when people are injured. When they are injured, imagine them in good health before they were injured."

We did all of that, and eventually she showed me how to do the expression of life as in the case of the elder before the injury. You see, all these things are learned, and it was very gradual. By the time I was eight years old (using your time measurement), I understood all she had to teach. And by that time, all her hair was white, and I had never seen a white-haired person before, but she was determined to stay alive to pass on all she could to me.

Envision People at Their Best

I, of course, am no longer on Earth anymore, but I speak to you of those times so that I can give you such details as I am now. I am not sure whether this fits in with your time, what I'm sharing with you. I think your people like to express themselves but sometimes get too caught up in the observation of other people's expressions and sometimes get caught up in some big thing done with lots of people, even if they really don't want to do that. So this can be used in other ways. Say that you are with some people or can see people at a distance. They are doing things that you know could be harmful to them or others, and you are worried. Don't get caught up in worry. If you're doing these kinds of things, what you can do is imagine those people in their kindest way.

If you know them and you have been around them when they are kind and happy and full of life and just enjoying life (not harming themselves or others), maybe you can express that portion of what they were. And if you do that for a time, it will possibly — it cannot be for certain because there are so many people in your time — remind them of happier, more innocent times, and they will perhaps then express that, remember it, feel good about it, and be influenced. It does not (how can we say?), you know, flip something in them. It reminds them of a better time in their lives, and then they can experience it once again because you have reminded them of it. You can be far away when you do this, maybe not even in sight of them. They could be far, far away, yet they perhaps need to be reminded of being younger, more innocent, and (most likely) happy and harming no one. Then they might be that. It is possible.

I feel this is a way to cure many ills in your time, including what's called mental illness. People in your time ask, "How can you do that?" or "Why did they do that?" Maybe they need to be reminded of earlier times when they were full of life and full of happiness and completely themselves without getting caught up in something that they regret — if not immediately, then shortly after it.

Yes, we have a lot of people doing crazy, violent things now. So you were able to use long vision or somehow tune into their actions before the time to go back, right? You could see it, feel it?

Yes. As you say, the term "long vision" is a good one because they were a long way off, but I could still see them, yes. And something that had occurred, I could see it, yes. I think this teaching has been given, this long-vision teaching, so I will not teach you that.

Time was no deterrent because you could go back before the incident you were seeking to change. You were not limited to connecting to them at this moment. Correct?

It was not that I wanted to connect to them, such as in the case of the elder, because the suffering did not need to be expressed. It was being expressed by the elder, who was in terrible pain. I needed to go back to the point before the pain happened, try to get in touch with what the elder felt, why he tripped over something when he was actually very sure-footed. You see, it was out of character for him to trip over something.

So there had to be a reason?

There had to be a reason, and the reason was essentially that the elder missed all those in his generation, such as his parents and grandparents, just in that split second and wanted, with his spark of creation, to go visit them. He had been visiting them, of course, in his dreams, but in that moment of weariness [laughs], he made a little mistake.

Life Ways of the People

What was the average length of life in your time for your people?

Well, we didn't do "average." It's just a number. I would say that, using your measurements, if life was comfortable and no unexpected things happened, a person could live until they were forty-five or close to fifty, whereas if the unexpected did happen, it could be at any time.

How old was your grandmother when she passed?

Grandmother was, in your years, forty-eight.

I just wondered how long you had with her teaching.

Oh, I was twelve. I had her in my life for twelve years.

Did you, in turn, teach others?

Yes.

Do your people still exist in Colorado or some place?

Some place.

Did you have children?

Yes. I had two girls.

Were they your students?

No [laughs]. As parents know the world over, your children do not always want to follow in your footsteps. No, the students were a girl and a boy. What I do is not always a woman thing — a girl and a boy in our people. But my own children, they did something else.

Okay. How many people were there in your group at different times?

Well, I'll have to think. [Pause.] Well, never more than 220.

Your grandmother taught you to do these motions with imagination. What did you learn on your own that you could pass on that she didn't teach you? Were there other things that you were able to do?

No. I had my skill, and that's what I did. Other than that, we all did some things like gathering food, although when meat was needed, the hunters did that. But we would dry meat. We would do other things. We would survive as well as possible. But everybody had some kind of skill. So you would have something that you would be called on to do as needed, you would say. If I wasn't needed for that, just surviving required a lot of effort every day.

So you were married, and I assume it was a happy union.

Yes, to someone I knew from childhood, naturally, and we were always drawn toward each other — a good man. We had a good life together. And [laughs] he was funny too. He would do funny things. It's good when you have a mate who is not only someone you love and loves you but someone you can have fun with, befriend — so important. Many times in our lifetime, when we were not just being lovers or helping each other to survive in our daily life, we would laugh and tell stories.

It was all right to tell stories about the past as long as they were fun and happy. But our people did not tell stories about the past, even if those lessons were important, that involved suffering and unhappiness because if the lessons were important, then they were already acted on. It was wisdom and knowledge that existed in the tribe that was always available. (I'm using your term "tribe"; we didn't call ourselves that.) And it was available. We didn't need to bring it up again, you see? Bringing it up again can re-create it. When you have something good, like I said before, associated (you'd say) with something bad, sometimes when you bring up the bad thing so that you can remember the good thing, you can, without meaning to, re-create that whole thing again. That's how you can — as a person, an individual (you'd say), or a group — get stuck going around and around in something like that, because of bringing up the bad thing to remember the good thing. Try not to do that. That's very important if you're going to be happy and if you're going to teach the children how to be happy as well as teach them how to survive and maybe help others to survive too, even if they are not part of your people. Maybe they are good people or they helped you, whatever the reason. You might want to help others sometime if it feels right.

Did your mate help others in some way as a medicine person or as a shaman?

He was a hunter, very important. We wouldn't have had any meat without the hunters.

Right. I agree with you about mates who make you laugh. That is so important.

It is good; you know this. Be sure to pass it on to young ones when you have the opportunity, especially young girls. Sometimes young girls get (you say) dazzled about what their mates will be like. Tell them that they might overlook the mates who would be the first-pick for them just because they're friends and they get along so well together and they laugh together. Don't overlook these people as mates even if they're not maybe as good-looking as the one you have eyes for.

[Laughs.] Yes. Did you have others in your group who did other things, like a medicine person, someone who gathered herbs, midwives, and things like that?

We had those people, yes. And I gathered the herbs, like I said before, for the tea, the comfortable tea that was not medicinal (you would say), as far as I knew. Actually, I had been taught by the person in our group. She did not want to complicate my life — "complicate," that's a good word — because I already had what I did, but she took me with her one day and showed me the herbs for making this nice tea. It is sort of a comfortable tea. I don't know how to describe it in your terms, but it's very mild, and after you swallow it, once it's already down your throat, it leaves a slightly sweet taste in your mouth. So you not only enjoy drinking it but also, after you drink it, it leaves that little sweet taste, and it's very nice. I wish I could tell you what that is. But maybe one of your special, knowledgeable people about tea will know what it is.

That's a good thing to say about people too: They leave a good taste in your mouth [laughs].

[Laughs.]

Did you have spiritual teachers who were not physical that you contacted? Did you have spirits and guides you were aware of?

I did not, but there were several people who did get their teaching that way. They were introduced to those beings by their teachers, meaning their grandfathers or uncles or grandmothers or aunties (you would say), but that was not my way. But, yes, that existed for some people.

Did you have an oral history or stories about coming from some place else or where you came from or your origin or anything like that?

I would say no, not exactly, but at times, the elders, when they would get together — I would only see this from a distance, and it wasn't just the male elders; there were female elders too — they would walk out in the night with a lot of stars. We could see they were very beautiful, you know. It was pitch dark, but we could see these stars. The stars were so bright that even if there was very little moonlight, you could see them well. You could see where you were going very well. You didn't need anything else to see with. The elders would stop, and they would point in the sky. I saw this several times. I would look to that point in the sky, as I thought maybe there would be one of the moving lights we'd see sometimes. But, no, it was just stars. They didn't talk. I don't know what that was about. So maybe that had something to do with it. But it could be something completely different. I don't know, and no one ever told me.

The moving lights: Did you ever see beings in a craft? Did any beings in a craft ever land and talk to you?

No, but one of our people said that the moving lights might be spirits or perhaps even people in something. But we weren't the sort of people who would make up stories if we didn't know for sure, and they were just very pretty. Sometimes they were blue, sometimes green, sometimes sort of a red color, you'd say a red-orange color, and sometimes a combination of those colors. And they were very nice. Sometimes they moved very slowly; other times, they were very quick. Of course, there were always the little streaks of light. Those were very pretty. We hoped it was a good thing, meaning we weren't the sort of people to imagine bad things. So I remember when we'd see streaks of light, the elders would smile and say that the creation was trying to make us happy with the dances and the light.

Everyone's the Same in Spirit
Did you ever meet other groups of people as you traveled?

We never met anybody else. We don't really know why. Several times the seers in our group (I use that long-vision but only when necessary) said they felt other people around, but we never saw them. And it's all right. We were comfortable with ourselves. Of course, sometimes we would see groups of nonhumans (you'd say). Like I said, the deer or the antelope, or sometimes we would see a mother lion with her young ones or occasionally a mother bear with a couple young ones. But we kept our distance [laughs].

One time I remember we saw a lion. She was very sad. We could tell that she was a mother lion and that she was hurt. Maybe she was dying; I'm not sure. But she was very sad. The hunters went over, but they knew not to harm her because it looked like maybe she might have lost her young ones. She had this very sad look in her eyes, so the hunters came back.

Medicine woman and spirit man — meaning he was with Spirit a lot and did Spirit things — brought special herbs over, and they sat with mother lion for some time until she died. Medicine woman sprinkled some special herbs on the mother lion, and spirit man, all during the time of mother lion's dying, helped her to see her babies and that she would join them. He helped that, and then we left her. We did not use her for meat because it was sad, and we wanted to leave her. That was when we were traveling, see, so we knew that some other (you say) animals would come along and do something, so we left her. And medicine woman told me that the herbs she sprinkled were to keep other animals away from the mother lion's body while she was going slowly. She said spirit man could see her spark of creation very slowly moving out. Medicine woman felt that the mother lion needed time for that slow travel out, so that's why the herbs. And then we went on. We had done what we could do, and I am sure the mother lion appreciated it.

That's beautiful. It makes me cry. They were very brave to do that. They had a lot of courage and compassion.

They had courage, but first hunters went over to make sure, and the mother lion did not try to cause harm to the hunters. The hunters knew she was dying, so they came back and put their weapons away so as not to make things worse for her. They stayed far away, but they could have rushed up if it was necessary. Of course, it wasn't. We made time for this because this was important. This was a mother who had lost her loved ones, her young babies, and she was suffering. She was hurt. We did not know who caused this, but we think probably another animal (you'd say). It happens sometimes. There are disagreements.

I did not know a lot about the animal world, but there were people in our group who knew all about it. Spirit man knew many things, and medicine woman knew many things. That's why they went. They knew things, and they knew what to do and how to do it. We all stayed at a distance. So I'm just reporting what I saw. They didn't tell us. Spirit man didn't tell us, and medicine woman said just a little bit, what I said before, but other than that, I'm just telling you what I saw.

I think the reason our people did not do that is because here was something that had happened, even though only a little time ago, but still it was a being suffering and dying and sad, all of that. So why bring that up? We saw what it was, and in life, there is death. This, we know. It comes for everyone. But we all come from the same lights in the sky and beyond. We all have a spark of creation — human beings, yes, and animals too.

We believe all come from the same place. Spirit man said he had seen the spark of creation leave many, many people, our people, many, many. And he said it looks exactly the same coming from animals as it does from human beings, so we must be the same. We just look different. But we're all the same in spirit. I liked that, what spirit man said.

The Reincarnation Experience

You're speaking from that time now, but since you left, have you reincarnated, or are you some place else or close to Earth?

I have reincarnated. I am on another planet. I am able to do this thing I am doing for you because on the other planet, I am asleep.

Can you say anything about that planet?

I do not wish to do that because if I do, I might wake up, and then our conversation will be over.

Ah, okay. What was the process? Did you choose to go there? Did you meet guides who recommended you go there? How did that happen? After you left your body in the time you're speaking from?

No, I understand why you are asking. When I left my body, there was another who had come for me. I remember looking at my body and feeling grateful to my body for having served so well as a vessel for me to express my life with. Then we moved into the light, and there was only love and light and great comfort. I felt as if I were surrounded by all those who had passed before me, yet I felt as if I were also surrounded by those I did not know in my physical life but who felt very familiar to me in other ways. It was a long time, but it wasn't time as we know it on Earth. It was a wonderful series of "just is," and I was there for a long while. Afterward, I remember being like an Earth human a bit, walking somewhere on something soft and talking to someone but mostly listening. Then not long after that, I was born on the planet where I am now. I better not say any more, or I could wake up.

Thank you so much for that. People want to know what happens when they leave their bodies the final time, so thank you.

In your time, I see that you struggle much, and people have objects that they look at or hold. These objects erupt with words that are not always kind or loving. They don't support and nurture life. They sometimes bring up anger in you. I want to suggest that instead of looking at these objects and believing what these objects say, walk away from them. If they are saying good things, loving things, then they might be all right, but if they bring up anger in you, then that can ultimately cause harm to you and others.

I recommend that you talk to your elders. Ask them how they lived. Ask for their advice on how to live. If their advice makes you angry or upset, then talk to a different elder until you find an elder who can tell you about good things in life, good things that you can look forward to. Learn that way how to be spoken to by a loving elder who can tell you about good things. And you will learn from your own elders in your family not only about these things but how to talk to the young ones. This is something that is being lost in your time. Learn again by seeking it out, and then if you feel it has value, pass it on to others. This I say to you in my farewell. May you have the best life that you can have, and then as you move on, I guarantee you, it will be better.

Thank you very much. I so enjoyed it. Thank you.

CHAPTER TWENTY-ONE

Hold in Your Heart the Value of All Life

Being from Africa

April 14, 2016

There is a method to know where a person is from or what that person dreams about or will experience in the future. It is taught through a very long process, so it is not something a few words can bring about with magic, all right? But they can help. Very often you dream of home, and home will feel, in that moment, exactly like what you are missing in your physical life. It might be a home you knew in other lives, or it might simply be a place that will be home at some point. Your visit will allow you to be nurtured and healed to the extent that is possible in those physical moments for your body even though you're deeply asleep.

It can also work in other ways. When a child is born and it's not clear what he or she will be good at because the child is versatile or perhaps just not very interested in what's happening ("detached," you might say), it is possible to look at his or her past life or dreams. What is the child dreaming of? If you can understand those dreams, you will know that the child either feels lost in the physical world or experiences a dream world that is very similar to the personality he or she has in life.

Another thing can be done. Often, elders of whatever culture or place are concerned about loved ones they will leave behind or wonder on a personal level where they will go or what will happen to them. If they are of certain religions, they might experience fear and anxiety because they think "this" or "that" will happen (or so people told you because of the unsavory aspects of the religion).

Sometimes religions intentionally or otherwise become encumbered with these beliefs to encourage people to stay with the program, whatever it is. Often, they start in a very slight manner, but because Earth is polarized at this time, they tend to become extreme. Very often people who guide the religion — the ministers or what have you (I'm not singling out any religion here) — don't know how to handle it because it's not part of what they learned about the religion, so it goes unchecked. As a result, there's a lot of fear and anxiety from change, old age, and feeling unsure about what will happen next.

So what can be done is essentially parting the curtains — or veils, you would say — to look at what the next life will be. Many simply will be spirit for a time, which is completely comfortable, relaxed, and nurturing, and it has an overwhelming feeling of unconditional love. That alone is much of the home that one might be missing. It will even transform, in only a few seconds, all misery and suffering that has ever happened in the person's life. You know this, but I have to give you this background so that you will understand.

The nature of this work during most of the time in my life in Africa was to simply reach forward very slightly with my hand and a little further with my energy field and move the veils just a little bit not so much to part them but to get a glimpse through a thinner portion of the veil as to what this person would do in the next life and where he or she would be. Sometimes, of course, the person would be on another planet. Other times, he or she might be a completely different form than expected. For example, there are many life forms on your planet now who do not identify in any way with how they look because they identify with who they were before. They had souls and personalities of course, but they didn't know what they would look like on Earth. That is typical, actually, for all forms of life here. However, once you are "physicalized," you immediately discover the benefits and the beauties of your form.

The culture for human beings is different, so the feeling of beauty and joy is compromised. When it comes to elders you can reassure them that their next lives will be completely happy or joyous, and you might tell them how long and where it will be. There will be such highs of joy and happiness and love that any unhappiness will be quickly moderated. Many beings who found themselves in water worlds, for example, had never been water beings before and suddenly and unexpectedly happened as water beings. Sometimes in universes where there are many water planets, a surprising number of water beings actually look more humanoid in other lives and sometimes even human. There is the belief that human beings will always be human beings on other worlds, but of course, that's not true.

Politically speaking, you might say in your time that human beings are the predominant species on this planet of yours, Earth, but that's not true. When taken within the entire panoply of life forms on Earth, human beings, even in the number you exist now, are still miniscule compared to the amount of other beings of all sorts, including at a molecular level. So there's that. But do not make it so complicated. The vast majority of elders are reassured that they will have a joyous life in total or at least in their maturity.

Examples of Future Earth Living

Generally speaking, Earth life is challenging in your times. My physical life (since you are interested in these things, eh?) happened about 1,200 years ago from your time, when Africa was a largely beautiful and benevolent place that was relatively undisturbed in terms of any invaders, you might say. I lived in southern Africa where we were largely insulated from anybody who might pull a boat up to the shore. There was not much worry about such things as an invasion. For that matter, there was not really an awareness of it.

I don't really call myself a seer (speaking as if I was still there) because the seeing I did was very specific to help people individually. I knew of another seer (not with our group) who looked at the bigger picture, you would say in your times. That seer could look around the world, see things, and understand the comings and goings of the human heart. While we did not discuss these things because we were at a distance from each other, I had dreams occasionally with this person in it. And I believe that the seer might have had the same dream connection. I learned a bit about what that person could do, and perhaps the seer learned what I could do.

I had three children, all of whom grew up to be strong and pursued their own interests. That was fine. I learned how to do what I did from elders, not parents or even grandparents. So they learned to do what they could do from the same stream of knowledge and education. I was with my mate for about thirty years, and if you are going to ask how old I was or how long I lived, you might be surprised to know that I lived (in terms of your measurement of time, yes?) to be ninety-six. And the people I was with, my people, all lived to be such ages. It wasn't unusual.

I think in this book, you have heard otherwise about people who lived in more hazardous circumstances, but our people got along well with all other species. We rarely ate meat and then only in the form of the occasional fish. It was difficult to do that since we would have known the fish's family, its loved ones. Sometimes fish jumped out of their pond, and the elders I was raised with said this meant we were supposed to consume them but we should wait until they died on their own. Then we would take the body away, and we would try to eat it. We would cook it, but no one could really eat very much, just a tiny bit. As I said, we knew their parents and their children and their siblings, you'd say. So it was difficult. The other life forms were similar. They occasionally ate each other, but we tried to avoid seeing that. When it happened, they would come to visit after a time and apologize. They would explain to our people that it was what they had to do to survive. They said that when they came to Earth, they were very surprised that they had to do that.

It was a different time and place. We weren't what you would call backward people. We were advanced in our own ways. We didn't have much need for machines or tools. If we needed to move something, which was very rare but occasionally happened, we simply moved it by interacting with the personality of what might be a problem. Perhaps somebody got a foot caught or something, and we might ask a rock or boulder or tree branch that had fallen to move off it. You know, if we could lift it, that would be one thing, but if it were too heavy, we would ask it to move. There were people in my group who could simply move their hands toward an object (I'll call it a tree branch because that happened once when I was in that life), and it just lifted slightly (not too much because there was respect for the fact that the tree left that branch there. It was supposed to be there). We lifted it up just enough to get it off of the young one it had fallen on. Fortunately, the person wasn't injured too badly, and the healer in our group rapidly repaired the leg and foot.

We lived fully engaged in the energy world as well as the physical world. Looking back on that life and at the world now in which you live, we (don't mind my saying "we"; I'm talking from the perspective of my now personality, my immortal personality you understand, like yours, so I'm going to say "we" sometimes) feel that the lifestyle we had in those times at that place is very much the way people will live on Earth in the next version of Earth that you strive toward and that we are still living in, you might say. Not living in the future, but in the way Earth was originally before all of this discomfort and (you say) negativity spread all over the planet. There was some slight discomfort, such as when the occasional branch fell on a youngster and caused some suffering, but most of that was fright.

Generally speaking, we didn't experience too many of the extremes you have now. I don't know whether you're comfortable with me saying this, but I pity you for living in the times and the way you must in your world. It must be extremely uncomfortable to be around people who are suffering and to be unable to cure their ills, whatever they may be, whether an attitude or pain or disease. It must be (you say) frustrating to be unable to transform that. You have to do the best you can and know that the world you will be in next will be more like the world I lived in.

Were you female in that life?

Yes.

Did you travel to find food to eat, or did you domesticate plants?

It wasn't necessary to travel, nor was it necessary to domesticate plants. Wild fruits and vegetables grew all around. I'm classifying them as what you would say. We simply would have said, "This is food." In our group of never more than forty people, there was always at least one person who knew whether a plant was safe to eat, how much would be all right to eat, and so on. These things came under the heading of what you would call fruits and vegetables.

You could communicate with all animals, then, all other species?

We did not consider them to be what you call animals. On Earth, we considered them to be other species, other people, all right? They all indicated that they were people. Human beings were people, and they were people. The word "people" just means an individual of a type of appearance; that's all. So there was no classification of human beings and animals, nothing like that. It will be that way for you in the next version of Earth that many of you choose to live on, and it will be very relaxing as a result. There won't be any sense of greater than or less than. All will be of the same cloth, you might say.

Did you interact with other groups of humans?

We weren't migratory, and we didn't live in a place where other humans migrated. I remember once being on a hill and seeing people moving in the distance. But it was well in the distance. Keep in mind that I was able to see from one life place to another life place, so when I saw the people moving, they were about twenty-five miles away, you might say. I could tell they were humans, so perhaps I was using my ability you call "seeing," meaning I could see beyond what was readily apparent. That ability allows you to see beyond your normal physical capability. You understand?

I think they call it long vision.

Some people call it that, yes.

So in your ninety-six years, you never saw any other humans except the group of about forty that you were with?

Yes. It was enough. [Laughs.]

To See Beyond, You Must Have Love

Can you tell us anything about your training? You say you can't just say it in a few words, but can you say anything about how you were trained?

Yes. A lot of the training had to do with love, what we would call heart. To see what is beyond for someone, you have to have the same amount of love, an unconditional love that one feels beyond the physical life now. The closest you would normally come to that love is when you were held by your loving mother (if you had a loving mother) as a child, a baby. Beyond that type of love is the love you experience as spirit, which you visit (I think everyone most likely visits) in your deep sleep. It is how you survive. I don't think it's possible for a human being to survive in your world without such visits of your personality and your soul to such places in deep sleep.

You must have the kind of heart to commune and to look beyond. Even looking beyond, you bring a portion of your energy, so it must be equal to that through which you are looking to find a person's experience — his or her life stream, where that person is from, where he or she is going, and that type of thing. You must be equal to the energy around you so that you do not disturb anything. Do you understand?

Yes. Did you have that naturally, or did your elders help you achieve that?

Everyone has that naturally. You are born with it even in your times. You often see babies smile, and they don't just smile with their mouths. Have you seen this? A baby smiles with its whole body, and when you see it, it's pure joy. Everyone is born with that even in your time. Even in our time, we wouldn't always feel that. You might be called on as an individual, as I was, to interrupt whatever you are doing and to help somebody else through some discomfort they are experiencing, such as an elder might feel or that a child who doesn't seem to fit in at the moment might experience. You would have to be able to experience that natural joy and complete unconditional love that all people, including yourself of course, are born with. So you don't have to learn something you don't know how to do, but it is good to try to remember it.

Explore Parallel Dreaming

How would you get into children's dreams? How would you join them in their dreams or see their dreams?

It would not be difficult at all! I would simply sleep near them, within about five feet (you would say) but not so close that we would roll over and bump into each other — five to six feet away, something like that. I would lie down and simply say, "I would like to experience, in some safe way, the dreams of this person so that I can know about him (or her)." (You might say "benevolent way." We wouldn't say "child"; we didn't really have a word for that. I'm using your words, you understand, answering your question in the way you asked it.)

This is something you can do now. You can, for instance, do that when a child seems to be having problems. You don't exactly accompany people in their dreams because they are with their guides and so on when they sleep. You follow a parallel course, and you can experience it as long as you keep a distance. You could do this even now by sleeping near some other life form. You, I think, experience certain four-legged life forms that you like, and some of them are actually wild. You seem to like that sort of thing. You could ask to have a parallel dream time with them, something like that, and you would ask in the most benevolent way. In this case, you wouldn't necessarily ask for a specific individual but just for the one with whom this would be the most compatible, you might say.

Perhaps you are a farmer or a rancher, and coyotes or foxes or other predators are causing harm and problem for your animals (you would call them animals). You could ask to have such a parallel dream time with a member of that group of predators so that you could understand not only that it is hungry and migratory but also when it will leave. That would be helpful. You could also request that the animal experience your dream and do it in a way that reminds it not to stay near your ranch (or farm) all the time and that moving on is good. You can ask for something like that and for it all to happen in your sleep, because in your deep sleep, there is no separation between you and the other being. You are equals. You are all from the same place, and you will experience the parallel dream as equals and as loving beings. Perhaps then they will cooperate and move on.

Can you give me an example of how dreaming with children enabled you to help them?

If they need help, you understand, the parents or an uncle (of course we are all related) someone would ask me. For example, a child who didn't seem to fit in was always looking at the stars. I was asked to dream with the child, as my people would say in our own language, and I discovered that this child had never had a life so far from the planets he normally lived on, and he was missing home. I found out that on his home, music was not only a language but also a constant background sound, and this child felt lost on Earth even though he was treated very well. He felt lost because there was no music. Although we talked softly, our people did not sing. So the simple cure was we learned to sing so that when we spoke to this person, even as he became an adult, everyone knew that it was important to sing communications to him so that he would feel at home.

Just knowing something like that can change someone's life for the better. And then he fit right in! When he had children, they knew to sing to him, and they knew that they didn't have to sing to others. Sometimes they did, and sometimes they didn't. So it just added what you would call a cultural element to our people. Sometimes we would all sing a little bit just for fun.

That's beautiful. Did you have an oral history about your origins? Did the elders talk about where you came from?

No, they didn't. Actually, one of the elders mentioned to me once that he was happy that we were celebrating and enjoying our lives on Earth because, of course, we all knew we had had lives other places. But you see, this elder understood something very important that many people in your time do not, and that's the more affection you feel for some other place or the more you miss something you were told was at another place (whether it was there or not but you believe it because you were told), then there is less connection, attraction, and involvement in the life you are in. It will be a constant comparison in your mind between your place now and the beloved place that you are no longer able to be in for whatever reason. It is a competitive thing. "Why can't it be 'this' way? Why can't we have 'that'?" In short, oral history (as you describe it), whether good or bad, was never a portion of our people because we had a natural, real, good life where we were. Why would we want to celebrate some other place where we had been or where we might go while we were living in a place we loved?

That is so interesting because in Europe, those times (ca. 800 CE) were considered the dark ages. For many people, it was a terrible time to live. It sounds as if you had a little Eden there in Africa.

Here's the thing you don't understand because of the times you live in: Much of the reason suffering continues in your time is that people feel, whether justified or not, that there is not enough. Therefore, one must compete to get more. This belief is often supported by statements you were once told and, as I referred to before, some other place you lived, which is often glorified as to how wonderful it was when in fact it might not have been that wonderful. It is idealized, you see. So the belief that there is not enough perpetuates much of the strife and suffering. This is a problem that will go away, but it's good to be reminded of it.

Remember always that you have the capacity. If you don't have enough food but you have a pail, you can put dirt in it and plant a fruit or vegetable to eat or share with your family. If there's enough, share it with your neighbors. If others do this, even on a very small patch of earth, much can be done to alleviate hunger. Apply that, if you can, to shelter for others, and do work that causes you to feel good. Please do not look down on anybody for his or her work. Always hold in your heart the value of all life forms. Live as well as possible with beliefs like that if you can come to them on the basis of your own experience — not just from what I (or others) say, but also from your own experience. Good night.

Thank you very much.

CHAPTER TWENTY-TWO

Establish a Sense of Equality for Beneficial Communication

A Shaman from Antarctica

May 13, 2016

Are you a shaman who has some wisdom that was lost to us that you can share with us?

Possibly. Do you have questions? What is your question?

We'd like you to share with us whatever it is that you do. I don't know whether you're in spirit or from your time, but we would like to know wisdom you gained that you could share with us.

The main thing that might be helpful in your times is a means for people to see past the surface in each other so that no matter what another person looks like, sounds like, or acts like, it will still be possible to communicate in a way that benefits both people and others. This is particularly helpful when interacting with a group of people that is so culturally different from you that you don't have many shared similarities. In our time when we came across such people or they came across us, the elder or the shaman would step forward first. If that person was acceptable, then communication of a sort would begin.

Whoever stepped forward would simply wave his or her hand, one or the other (different groups waved different hands), toward his or her own people, and then the shaman or elder would usually put the right hand on his or her chest or solar plexus, and then that person would just wait. The other person representing the other group would usually do the same thing. Then either at the same time or taking turns, the representatives would point to or reach down and touch their own legs, then touch their arms, then touch their bodies, and then touch their heads. Then they would put their hands back on their chests or solar plexus areas and wait. Then they would have a basis because that means, "I am a human being with two legs, two arms, a body, and a head." This established communication.

Next, if our group was camped near water, we would make the sign for drinking water: we'd cup a hand and reach toward the water or just cup a hand and tip it slowly toward the mouth. This was very important because that's how people drank (and still might in your own time). If the people in the other group nodded vigorously, we'd get out of the way and let them make a line for the water so that they could drink. After that, if we had enough food to share, we would make a gesture as if grabbing something with the thumb and forefinger and putting it toward the mouth. If they nodded their heads, then we would share a little bit of what we could. Whenever we shared with the people who were visiting, our people would eat at the same time so that it would be clear the food was safe to eat.

I'm not going to continue; that's sufficient. I'm mentioning these things because what you need to do in your time is something that many diplomats already know: It is easier to establish a sense of equality from one human being to another than it is to act superior or demanding or commanding. When you do that, it eventually comes back to you. If it's not through the person you are interacting with, then it will be through their friends or family. Why make trouble for yourself?

Keep in mind that sometimes people act in such ways because they are afraid, so if you encounter someone who acts demanding or commanding like that, you can suspect that underneath it all is fear. It is possible to soothe that fear, but it needs to be done in a way that is comforting for you both. Be gentle, and do not touch each other. Now, I know that these things are understood by diplomats in your time, but it is surprising how few people in positions of business (speaking of small business here) or in (how can we say?) hostile camps — meaning, different religions, different nationalities, and so on — are in flow, you might say, with that.

Work with the Moon and the Sun to Establish Common Ground
You're asking what I can share with you that you can use in your time. Basically, you're asking for something intellectual because the herbs that we used, that I used, do not exist in your time, and it won't help to use them if you try to synthesize the chemicals. That kind of thing doesn't work. It might work to soothe a symptom, but it does not work to create a chemical reaction in your body. It is a natural product. We could work with what you have that is natural, but the soil — not everywhere but almost everywhere where people live — has been greatly adulterated due to the process of your living on it. It's not easy to find soil in its natural state where people live.

I'm talking about being practical. You don't all live on mountaintops. If you lived on a mountaintop with your people, then I'd say, "Oh, you could do this," but you couldn't take the dirt down to where the vast numbers of people live and say, "Oh, you can use this dirt." You would have to use it where you were a resident because the dirt, the stones, the sands, and the pebbles, all of that, would understand that you are a part of that land.

The issue is that what we used in our time doesn't relate to your time, so we have to consider what is the same. Even the rain is not the same because your skies are filled with chemicals. It would take a long, hard, steady rain that is natural and that is not in reaction to something, all right? Mother Earth, in your time, is largely in reaction to something, so the only place you could find a long, hard, steady, natural rain right now is perhaps down in the southern end of the planet. Various continents are down there, eh? You call them Africa or Americas or Australia or something like that. But it is the southern end, and it's more likely to be natural if there are not too many people there. Of course, there are a lot of people living there.

So what then, if not the rain? How about the air? The air, of course, is filled with those chemicals of your time. What's left? Most likely what is left is the sunlight — all right? — the sunlight or the moonlight. That's what you have to work with that is still 100 percent natural and is the same in our time. So to those of you who can do these things, get used to working with the Sun and the Moon in order to be certain that what you are working with is completely natural and the same all over your Earth for all life. There are some forms of life, certain worms and so on, who live underground. But if they were to come above ground just for a moment, the moonlight or the sunlight would be the same for them. There has to be a sameness; otherwise there's no basis for common ground.

As I said in the beginning, what you need is a way for groups who are hostile toward each other — for reasons that can be proved or because they are simply suspicious because of "this" or "that" belief sometimes fostered by others and sometimes just made as a wrong guess — to relate to each other. So begin with an average person because you asked what "we" can do. You didn't ask what shamans or mystical people would do, and I agree that "we" is better!

When you meet people in the daytime who wish to communicate but don't have a common language or culture, point to the light is in the sky. If it's cloudy, point to the brightest spot you can find. Or if you are a mystical person and you know how, you can part the clouds slightly in that area so that you can point to the Sun. An average person probably would not know how to do that, so just point to the sky because it will be light.

If it is nighttime and there is any sign of the Moon at all, point to it and wait for the other person to do the same. If it is a night when there is no Moon because it is a new moon, then point toward the ground and do the thing with your feet. Point toward or touch your feet, touch your legs, touch your arms, touch your body, and touch your head, and hope that the other people understand. For those of you who use words, ask in prayer or whatever you use for help from your angels or guides, as you call them. But for those of you who have the Sun or the Moon available, simply point to the Sun or point to the Moon. Then say this: If you're certain the other person cannot understand your language, make a sound (I was going to say, "Say this," but it's a sound) like "ahhhh" and point to the Sun. When you point, don't point with a finger, all right?

Using your hand (I recommend your right hand, but feel free to use your left hand), hold your palm toward your body and point (with your fingers not straight out, but sort of loose) toward the Sun, and make that sound. Then with your arm extended (not straight out, but sort of relaxed) and pointed clearly toward the Sun, make that sound. Bring your arm back slowly until you touch either your chest or your solar plexus, whichever feels best for you. I recommend the solar plexus, but if the chest feels better, then do that. If you touch the chest, make it the center of the chest, all right? If the other person or people do the same, you've made a beginning. I feel it is important to make a beginning because the foundation of that beginning has to be common ground.

Lessons of Forgiveness from the Seals

Can you say something about when and where you lived?

I will say a little. When I was on the planet, I lived in an area that was very cold. Looking back on it now, it was at the extreme southern part of the planet. I do not know where my parents got their clothing, but it was warm and fur-like. The reason I do not know where the clothing was from is that when I was born, the garments that were available (which were handed down in families) were clearly other people's garments. It was not hard to understand, as one got older, that they must have been part of animals' bodies at one time. But by the time I was born, my people did not hunt for these animals anymore. Fortunately, the clothing was very sturdy and kept us warm. Also, the elder shaman, you would say, knew how to keep the clothes permanently as good as when they were first made. They were warm and snug enough so that we could stay warm.

The shaman also knew how to teach us to warm ourselves. I think some of you might know how to do that. It basically involves just remembering when you were the warmest in your life and focusing only on that memory. Do not move while you focus on that memory because memories are geographically located. If you move around, you'll run out of the memory, so when you bring up the memory, try to stay in the same position if you need to be warmer than you are. Stay completely focused on remembering. First, you'll remember it as a thought, then you'll remember it as a feeling in your time, and then gradually you'll get warmer, okay? So anyone can do this. That's what worked for us: We remembered being warm and having garments that were essentially very durable and that remained warm.

That's where I was raised and spent my life. As I say, when I was born, my people were no longer killing those animals for warmth and food, but they continued to fish. When fishing, they did not try to harm any more than what they needed. We had boats of a sort. I do not know where they came from, but they definitely looked like someone made them. So a shaman did things so that the boats didn't rot and didn't fall apart and could float — all of this.

When I became older, it was recognized that I could apparently do things. When I was younger, I used to follow the shaman around [laughs], and people figured out pretty quickly, you might say, that it was something I could do. So I learned what the shaman used. I will not share all of it because in your times, people could abuse it. But the shaman interacted with the water beings, the ones we didn't kill anymore, and these beings taught the shaman what he needed to know to learn how to stay warm in cold places. These beings could jump into the water, swim around, get the fish they needed to eat, and live off those fish. But the waters were … you can imagine perhaps. You drink water with ice in it. You can imagine jumping into water like that and swimming around. Well, really, it's like magic. You still have some of these beings with you, and they can teach you many things if you know how to listen and observe. They are magic in action.

We learned, the shaman and I, sometimes at the same time. The shaman taught me what these beings showed him: how to fish, how to use the boats in such a way (boats were there when the shaman was born too), and how to keep the boats strong and tight and safe. When people sat in the boats, they'd distribute themselves by size and weight, see? If the weight wasn't quite right, they'd bring along a youngster who was strong enough to balance the boat, and that youngster would have to be old enough and wise enough and light enough that if the boat shifted in the water, the youngster could move around so the boat could rebalance. It had to be a youngster so that there would be room to move about; the boats resembled something you would call canoes.

All this was learned from the water beings. I think you call them seals or something like that. They're wonderful beings, wondrous. They are perfectly happy. They share knowledge. It is very important to look at them and notice what they do and how they do it. They are marvelous beings. They were our teachers; we could not have survived without them. And it was very kind of them to forgive us, our people (whoever they were, those who came before us), for killing their people to eat them and make clothes and so on. Imagine some people killing your people for such a thing! Would you be as kindhearted as to forgive them and teach them how to survive? Think about it. If you think you could, then that says well of you. If you think you couldn't, then that means you need to learn from beings like this because they also taught us how to be patient.

If the fish we needed to catch were not available or darted away before we even reached them, it meant that they needed to live for their people. Perhaps they were going to give birth, or perhaps their wisdom was needed. Then we would wait and ask for those who could sacrifice themselves so that we would be able to eat. We learned many things from those beings.

Interactions with Travelers

Now, you asked when this was. Well, I will round it off, all right? About 1,200 years ago from your time is when I lived. And you're going to ask how long.

Ha-ha! Yes.

In terms of your measurement of years, well, we used the Moon, but we didn't need to measure time. What's the point eh? We didn't need that. I'm going to use your Sun years, though Moon years make much more sense. Why you don't use Moon years, I don't know; the planet — you know, Earth, the cycles of life — everything is set to the Moon. It's not set to the Sun. Anyway, about thirty-three to thirty-five years is the best I can guess. That's how long I lived, and it was long enough.

How many people were in your group?

Oh, about twelve — never any more. I was told by the elder that it didn't vary. (The elder was not the shaman, by the way.) I was told by the elder that once it was ten and another time twelve. It was believed that twelve would be enough. It was never more than that. Occasionally it went down. They think it might have been nine at one time, but generally it was twelve or fewer, usually between ten and twelve, something like that.

You mentioned other people. Did you interact with other groups in that area?

Sometimes people would come. We don't know how they came other than that they arrived on boats, small boats. But they looked around and could see that there wasn't much, so they moved on. They were travelers. Sometimes they looked a little cold, so our shaman taught them (it's very easy to do without spoken word) how to make themselves warm. Being people of nature (you would say not technical so no machines), they understood what it meant for a mother, say, to hold a baby, and then the baby snuggling in. You use your arm like that to say, "So warm." Then the elder or shaman would point to the people in the boat so that they would understand. He'd point to each one, first showing them the sign for a baby held by mother. He'd show them the sign, and they would all sit in the boat for a while and get warm. You could tell because if they were a little funny looking, a little frosty looking, they would warm up.

I remember a particular time when I was still young when such people really looked as if they were lost. They had food, and they could eat. Somehow, they could drink the seawater. At that time, I didn't understand that sometimes our water came from the sea too. We also had the snow, so we could use that. We melted it and, of course, gave them some, but they didn't have drinking vessels. They knew how to drink the seawater and be safe. Perhaps 1,200 years ago, it was safe to drink. I don't know. I remember seeing them get warmer and warmer, and when they were completely warm from using the baby example, they smiled and gave the sign for friendship but didn't get out of the boat. There was no touching. They paddled away. That's the instance I remember the best, and other things I was told about.

Did you drink seawater directly, or did you filter it through something or do something to it?

No, we don't use filters, but I understand you're a technical person. We did not do technical. You either did it directly or you didn't do it. [Chuckles]. Do you have humor in your time? I don't wish to seem like I am making you —

No, no, we have humor. You sound wonderful! Keep it up.

As for drinking seawater, our elder shaman didn't think it was safe but couldn't ignore the fact that when the people in the boat were thirsty, they just reached down to the sea, cupped their hands, scooped up the water, and drank it. They actually pointed to the sea! And then the shaman had to do it. When the shaman did it, he looked up in the sky at the Sun and raised his hand toward the Sun, asking it to be in his hand. The shaman would see the Sun in his hand (not hot of course), and as he drank the seawater, he would be drinking the Sun and then be completely safe. Shaman said later (understand "say" because we didn't really have much spoken language, but I would hear "no"; you would call this what I don't know, but it wasn't worded communication so much) that the people in the boat were doing that too, and the shaman believed that the people would see the Moon or the Sun in the water but just did it so fast that the water was safe to drink. But we had snow, so we would just melt it.

Did it snow year-round?

Well, yes. Isn't it that way in your time?

It might be down there. I don't know.

Well, that's what I mean. Yes, I am assuming there is snow. If there wasn't snow, you could break off a piece of ice, and it would melt. You might wonder, "What about it being cold?" Well, you have to remember that we knew how to be warm, so it would melt in our hands, and our hands would remain warm and comfortable, and then we would drink it.

Appreciate Your Environment

Why were you in that area? Do you know how your people got there?

I do not know, nor did I ask. Why are you where you are? "Why are you on Earth?" is a better question because in your time, people can travel. So, all right, why are you on Earth? You don't have to answer that question, but that's actually what you asked me.

Okay.

If you think about it, the simple answer is to experience Earth life. That's it. That's the answer.

I know, but it's such an inhospitable area, and there are so many places on Earth that are not like —

Wait. Where did you get the idea that it was inhospitable?

Well, it's cold all year round and you don't —

Oh, why is that inhospitable?

[Laughs.] I like to be warm, I guess.

Well, it's what you know. You have known the contrasts of cold and warm, and you chose warm.

Yes.

You can do that in your time. I was born to the cold, and it was very hospitable. I had all the water I needed to drink, and it was fresh and pure. I had all the food I needed to eat, and it was fresh and pure. I had love, I had friendship, I had companionship, and I had knowledge and wisdom. I had dreams, I had air, and I had light. What more do you need?

Were you male?

Yes.

Did you have children?

No. Others did. We had to keep our people to a certain number because there was only so much we could do. We were warned by the elder not to forget these things. There was always at least one woman who could give birth, and we were all a family in that sense. We were all close, but we didn't do sex, as you call it, in the actual completion of the act. Speaking for your general audience, we did not do that unless we were trying to make another member of the group. We had hugging and all this love but not the completion of the act. We understood where children came from. [Laughs.]

Good. You said you had herbs. Did you have a growing season, then?

No. But we had something that resembled herbs. I'm calling them herbs, but they're hard to describe. There was a spring, but we kept our distance from it. In our world of ice and snow and what you call cold, it was so different that we kept our distance. But there was a small spring of warm water, and around the spring was green. They were plants. So sometimes (very rarely but sometimes), we were allowed to go there. Elder was the one who was allowed to go there. In my time, the elder was either a woman or a man. The woman went there, and sometimes she would come back with some of the green. It was like magic, the green. We wouldn't touch it, but she would hold it in the palm of her hand (sometimes both hands) when we were going to sleep.

Oh, this is important: We did not have much in the way of shelter. I'm going to step away from the green for a moment. The elder and the shaman both felt it was not good shelter because it would keep the Sun and the Moon away from us, and they were part of our existence. We are light, and that is something we understood. When we slept, one or usually two people always remained awake so that they could remember being warm. They would get uncomfortably warm while we slept because when you sleep, your body goes somewhat into a different realm. You understand? So these two people (or one person) would remain very warm. It was a bit awkward because they would have to move around. Underneath their feet, the snow or ice would begin to melt, so they had to move around. If they stayed in one place, they'd sink into the ice. They would get that warm. So they moved around. At times when they needed to sleep, one person would be assigned to them who would be warm. That warmth would radiate, and the people who were asleep would be warm, you see? I thought that might interest you.

Now to get back to the green. The green was used to accentuate our dreams and when we didn't know how to resolve something. The water beings — it wasn't part of their world. They could come up to the land, but they didn't live on the land. They could be both places, so maybe you could say they lived both places, but they loved being in the water. We'll say that.

When the elder had the green, she would hold it out in the palm of her hand (or sometimes both palms), and she would bring it around to each person. And then we would dream, all right? In our next sleep, we would dream, and one or more of us would get an answer to the problem. So apparently, what I understood in those times from the shaman was that the reason we couldn't think of the solution was that the solution must come from the warm world, the green world. You understand? That's why the elder (I guess, as I would not know because elders passed on their wisdom to other elders, not to the others, but the shaman and I discussed it; my teacher and I discussed it) would be able to have a special relationship with the green, and the green would allow her to take certain parts of it. The parts were very small, but it was enough so that we would dream and remember the answer.

After such dreaming times, we would get up and discuss what we dreamed. We often discussed our dreams, but after such dream times, we would discuss them, and the elders would understand from hearing all the dreams of all the people when the green was available. Then the solution would be known. I do not know, to this day, what happened to the green. After the elder showed the green to everybody — no one got closer to it than what you would say is the length of an adult — I do not know what the elder did with that green. Did she take it back? I don't know. Only the elder was allowed to approach. I was told smoke came up from the place, but now I understand that it was steam. At the time, it seemed like smoke though, so it was very different from our normal life. There was always an elder who knew what it was and what it meant. Sometimes the elder, I was told, was a man, and sometimes the elder was a woman, so apparently it didn't make a difference. But I don't know that for certain.

Love Creates a Bond

Was this hot spring in a cave or volcano or something? What was it?

It was an exposed spring. There was nothing around it other than the water that came up, the steam, and the green.

So it was hot water.

No, not hot. I only saw it once and at a distance. The elder said the water was warm but not as warm as a baby.

Why couldn't you live around the water and be warmer?

You are asking a technical question. You are asking, "Why didn't you move?" That's what you are really saying. We lived where we liked to live. We were close to the water beings who were our great rescuers. They helped us in so many ways. I was told we lived before they became our teachers, but it was a struggle. Once they became our teachers, we lived much more comfortably. Why would we want to leave them?

I see. Was there a story told about the people who changed from hunting them to being their students? How did it happen that there was such a dramatic change?

It wasn't that dramatic. It was just that a young one in the group at the time and a young one of the water beings became friends, and they loved each other. The young water being would come out of the water and waddle up to the young one, and they would just, as you might say, hug each other. They were inseparable. Then the young one started teaching, sharing the knowledge from the young water being. That's all. It happened because of love and friendship. It wasn't anything so mystical. In your time, I think you have other life forms that aren't humans that you love. Is that not so?

Yes, definitely.

So it makes complete sense (doesn't it?) that a young, innocent child and a young, innocent water being would love each other, and from that would come this great change over time. Love is the answer, but it has to be actual love. That love between two children of different types of beings — there is nothing more innocent and pure than such love. Always remember that, if you can. Have the most benevolent, good life you can, and treat each other as kindly as you can. It will come back to you and be passed on to others in stories, in song, wisdom, and the very air you breathe.

Thank you very much. Thank you tremendously much!

CHAPTER TWENTY-THREE

Honor the Wisdom of Children

A Being from Mongolia and Speaks of Many Truths

May 16, 2016

Greetings.

Welcome.

Now, I know you like to have a location. This is what you would call Mongolia about 9,000 years ago in your time, give or take a decade or so. At that time, there was an area in Mongolia that had a warm (what you would call balmy) weather pattern: never any snow and with a light misting of rain almost all the time except for bright sunshine for an hour or two each day. As a result, the area was very lush and green. I'm looking for the area now, and I do not see it, so it is possible that it's either in a slightly different version of Earth. Where I am looking in your now time (using you as a guide, meaning where you are in this time), I can see that this was a different dimension. You are apparently between dimensions, correct?

That is correct. About halfway.

That explains why I cannot see the place we lived. There were no more than 1,200 people there at any given time. It is not a big place. If you were to see it, you would say it is an extraordinarily deep canyon, but it was more than that. There was a canyon, yes, but that led to an underground passage that led to a big opening that had, you would say, a phosphorescent glow. It was almost always light — not bright light, but phosphorescent, meaning there was something in the walls that glowed. I'm not sure if it came from creatures. I don't think so. I think it was strictly the makeup of the walls. I was born there, so it was a good place to be, and perhaps it will reemerge in the version of Earth you're moving toward. But that's enough about that.

Musical Healing

I was musical. We had music, all right? And we even had some instruments, something like a small piccolo and something like a small flute, you might say. (I think your words are amusing, okay?) There were also sticks we could tap together to make rhythms. That was it. Still, between that and singing, it was music. This was something I was apparently born to do. I think maybe even in your time, children are born with certain rhythmic capacities. It might not always be obvious to parents, but it might become so even without a radio (or some such thing) on. It can be noted in a child by the way the child moves. It might flex its legs in a way that is clearly rhythmic (meaning so many beats to the measure) as it lies on its back.

The elders could tell that I was musically inclined. I liked the flute-like instruments, but I was particularly attracted to the sticks we tapped together. The sticks were made of bamboo. Bamboo grew there, and it grew very tall in the valley, but it did not grow underground. I liked to use the sticks and create rhythmic sounds before I was even exposed to the music in a way that I could imitate.

One of the elders, being an older person, noted that when I tapped with these sticks, his knees felt better. They had been a bit stiff for him. He would come by and visit when I was tapping on the sticks every day, and his knees felt fine then. He could climb and do the things that were necessary, for he was a gatherer in the valley. Some mushrooms and fruits and vegetables grew there. We did not plant them, but we appreciated the food. This elder had been trained to climb to gather mushrooms, fruits, and vegetables, of which there were quite a bit, and my stick-playing extended his time of doing that. Of course, his work was also fulfilling because he contributed to the people.

So it was understood by my parents that I could do something different with the sticks, tapping them in such a way that it created some kind of compatibility that generated what my parents felt reminded the elder's body of its youth. So this was the case.

When I was a child doing that, I did it without thinking, okay? But as I grew older, I had to memorize something with thought that I already knew. So I did that. It was a lot to memorize — not just the sound, but also the rhythm of it: how many taps quickly, how many taps slowly, loud or soft. Like that. The amount of time it took for, say, the betterment of the elder's knees was about three and a half minutes of sound.

Over time, I could help the other old-age illnesses that elders had, and if I did not know how to make the sound that would help whatever they had, I would just look at the sticks, and I would do something that you would say was a relaxed state of being. I could go to the elder because I was old enough. The cavern we lived in was quite large, and it was easy to find our way around in because it was always light. I could find the elders.

One time, an elder had something quite different, something in her back. She was gradually losing the ability to grasp things strongly with her hands and to have agility in her feet. I relaxed into that feeling and did the tapping with the sticks, and then she was all right. So I tended to serve elders because they were the only ones who had conditions that were the sort of thing that happens before death, when your body signals that it is time for it to return to the earth and to move on as a light and become someone or something else. It happens in your time too. So this is what I did for my lifetime there.

A Peaceful Life in the Canyon

You are going to ask more about me. I was a woman in that life, and because of the demands of serving the elders, I was only able to have one child of my own, also a girl. I loved her very much. She did not follow in my path with the sticks, but two others in our group followed, and that was all right. My little girl became one of the climbers who gathered the fruits and the vegetables, and she loved learning to do that. The valley was very deep, you might say from above, but it felt very protected where we were. She could climb very high and very safely. There were a lot of vines. They were what the fruits and vegetables grew on, as well as on some trees that grew out of the sides of the cliffs that hid our valley. I don't remember any strangers coming to the valley during my lifetime, so I think it must have somehow been hidden, I had heard that it was different above. One of the climbers climbed up there once and said that it was uncomfortable and very white. Now I realize that it was snow and ice up there, so not surprisingly, no one found where we were.

That's wonderful. So the first healings you did with tapping were totally spontaneous. You just did it.

Yes, that's correct. Spontaneous without any thought when I was just old enough to grab something. You know, babies are fond of grabbing. They can do that pretty early, but they might not be able to manipulate things very early. So it was really when I was about two years old that I was able to pick up the sticks and use them. I think I told you that the sticks were instruments. That's right, part of the music.

Do you mean they used them on what we would call drums or something? Or were they meant to click together?

No drums. We just had the flute-type instruments, two different kinds, and the sticks.

But the sticks beat on each other. They didn't beat on something else.

Exactly. We tapped the sticks together.

You said that when you were old enough to think, you remembered some of the spontaneous methods. How did you know what to do after that?

Well, I think I already said. Remember what I said about the elder who had something wrong with her back? I said that I would just relax and then — that word you used, "spontaneous" — I would do that, and then I would try to remember it. If at any time I couldn't remember what was right for one of the elders, I would relax, and then it would come to me without thinking. But some of the things I did — "sequences" is your word — I remembered, so I could just reproduce it from memory. But if I didn't remember, then I would do the other.

Did you work on elders only, or did you work on the whole tribe?

I worked only on elders because they were the only ones who suffered. Oh, I see. In our time when women gave birth, there was no pain, so there was no suffering other than what elders would get. Also, people didn't get in what you call accidents, so there wasn't any need for care except for the elders.

No one ever got broken bones or diseases or anything?

Nothing like that existed.

You must have been a very special group!

I think maybe it's not that we were special. It's that we didn't know disease existed.

So you didn't create it! [Laughs.] Did you have any stories? You talked, didn't you? You had language. Did you have an oral history of where you came from?

We spoke, yes. We didn't speak a lot. We spoke when something wasn't understood. For a great deal of the time, things would simply be understood, so we didn't speak philosophically. We didn't talk about ideas. It was less conversation than your people apparently have. Your people have forgotten what you knew when you were born. Babies, I believe, are born with all their wisdom intact. But in your societies now, this is not encouraged, and other things are taught. Perhaps there are exceptions. Some parents might be sensitive to that. That would be good because you do not have to learn anything; you just have to be encouraged to remember what you were born with. That way, I feel you would be able to reconstitute our type of society. If you did not learn about disease and the people around you did not know about disease, you would say you would have to forget or become ignorant, but sometimes what is judged as ignorance is simply people focusing on other matters that have to do with health and thriving. I am not saying you are wrong; I am saying you live in times that are very harsh because the natural wisdom you are born with is not encouraged as wisdom to live by as a child and as you grow up. Perhaps what I am saying will be of interest to some.

Well, we had to forget who we were to come here.

Keep in mind what we're talking about, okay? We were here during that time. What I am talking about today is not unreachable for you.

Right, right.

Ancestral Connections

Do you know where you came from or how you got there?

I do not know that we were ever any place else.

Do you have descendants?

You are asking whether we have an origin story. No. When you have an origin story, there is always something else, maybe some place you are missing or maybe some place you would rather be. We would rather be where we were. That's a joke.

Have you been in spirit since that life, or have you reincarnated since?

I have not reincarnated physically, but I have experienced different versions of spirit life, nonphysical life. Nonphysical life is just as varied, if not more so, than physical life.

Were there animals then? Were there other species of beings in that canyon?

There were birds, multicolored birds — not big birds, but small birds. Lots of different colors. They did not make much sound, though. Occasionally we would hear little sounds, but they were very quiet.

Did you describe your source of water? Was there a river or something?

There was a spring in the valley. And it misted quite a bit. It misted a lot, and there were a couple of hours, you might say, during the day when there was bright sunlight, so plants in the canyon thrived in a moist environment with a couple of hours of no misting and some bright sunlight to warm them. All along where the plants grew was warm, warm and moist. The cavern where we were was not as warm, so during the day, the people went outside to enjoy the warmth. It was warm even when it misted. Of course, when the sun came out, it was warmer. There was a rocky place where we gathered and sat and enjoyed the warmth. It was all right to sit there, the elders said, because we were not harming the plants. The plants were our friends, and the sunlight was clearly for them. Yet we felt it was also for us, and we would go out and sit on the warm rocks and enjoy the heat. Then we would go back into our place slightly underground and enjoy our life there.

Did you live in family groups, or was everybody all together?

Keep in mind that the cavern didn't have any walls or sections. It was a large space. Does that not answer your question?

It answers part of it, but did you have a mother, father, and some children who sort of slept together? Or were the children considered everybody's? How did that work?

I see. Well, yes, people were mates and had children, but we were always encouraged by the elders to not have too many children because the elders thought that there would not be enough food or water for us. So we always had — well, when I say 1,200, it was sometimes fewer but never more than 1,200. And yes, men and women would fall in love and be attracted, and then children would happen, but people understood how children came to be. So there was care, and people avoided doing what would bring children when there were enough. They would still love each other, hug and so on. The children, of course, had their mothers and fathers, whom they loved, but they would also mingle with others, so it's hard to answer your question.

I understand. There were families even though you were all together. What about the children? Nobody ever left that place, right? You all stayed there your entire lives.

Yes, that's right. That's where we lived.

What about the fruits and vegetables? They just grew? Did you plant seeds, or did they just come up every year?

We didn't. I didn't know anyone, and the elders didn't know anyone. There was no awareness of where they came from, but of course, the fruits and vegetables had their own seeds, so they seemed to understand how much could grow and how much would be best to be consumed by others. It was a life in balance, all life in the valley. We copied life in the valley. We noticed that everything grew in balance with everything else or didn't grow, what stayed the same or even sometimes less so. It seemed so perfect. If we were ever in doubt, the elders would sometimes wonder about things, and they'd gather together and sit on those rocks to observe and think about what the plants were doing in the valley or sometimes what the birds were doing. The birds had their own part. They lived very high up on the ledges, but there were still plants that grew there, and the birds would eat them. That's what I remember.

Incarnated Wisdom

When you did that with those sticks, was that the first time in your group that anyone had ever done that?

No one else remembered at that time. No one else remembered that having been done before, so I cannot say "ever." I can only say no one remembered it being done. My feeling is that someone must have done that, but it's hard to say. Perhaps I remembered that from another life. That's why I made that remark about children being born with wisdom. Our children were not talked into some other cultural belief. You know, "You are from 'this' place," "You are from 'that' place," and so on. Our wisdom was honored. So perhaps it was from another life and was wisdom I brought in when I was born.

Did you then train somebody to do this when you became an adult, or did someone else remember it after you?

There were two others. My child did not do that, but there were two others who had the ability. One followed me around when she was just about two years old, and she was naturally good at doing these things without thinking. The other one was more of a thinker and memorized the sequences.

How long did you live on average?

Using your measurements, we lived maybe about seventy years.

Ah, that long!

There was a place in the cavern where it was possible to place elders who had passed into spirit, and we would place their bodies in this distant area. That was not my job, and I never saw it, unless you say that I saw it when I was placed there, but of course I wasn't there. I understood that there was a place where the bodies were taken, and it was apparently a distance away, so there were tunnels, you might say — "passages" is what I say — that branched off from the big cavern. I never went into them, but some other people did. When the shell remained of a person's life (the body), those people knew where to take the body. They would never go alone; four always went even though one person could often carry the remains. They went in fours because they would do ceremonies. For other passages, sometimes other people took them, but I never had to, so I was never really sure where they led and what they did. It's not that we had secrets from each other; it's just that everybody had a specialty, and there was often a great deal to remember in our specialties, so we didn't really want to be distracted by other people's specialties.

You mentioned those who gathered the fruits and vegetables and mushrooms. There were no grasses or wheat or barley or any grains like that, either?

No.

Okay. So there were people who gathered, and you worked with the sticks, and other people took the deceased. Those were specialties. What were some of the other specialties?

I don't know what they were. I only told you about the ones I know about. Everybody didn't know how to do everything. If we didn't know how to do something, we didn't do it, so we wouldn't know about anything associated with it.

Did you become an elder? Was the elder anyone who was old, or was just a very small group called elders?

Everyone who was old was an elder, but there was a group of elders who solved problems by thinking about them, and that was a group unto its own. Usually people in that group had not been necessarily all the time focused in any one thing, as I was. It's hard to describe because in your times, everybody seems to know everybody else's business, you might say.

[Laughs.] Yes.

It wasn't that way for us. We lived together and contributed to each other's lives, but we didn't investigate what they were doing. The only ones I could tell you about are things I observed or someone told me. People didn't gossip.

Okay, you probably had midwives to help with births and people who cooked. How did you clean? Did you have the most elemental things — clothes and blankets?

I have to go back because you said something that wasn't so. You said "people who cooked."

Oh, you didn't! You didn't use fire for anything?

No. There was no need. It was warm. It was light. What would we need that for?

Okay, so all the vegetables could be eaten raw? They weren't tough or needed to be cooked or anything?

There was no cooking.

Okay. Did you have clothes or blankets or something to sleep on?

No. We slept on the ground. The floor of the cavern was powdery. It was not sand, but it was sort of powdery, so it was soft. We slept on that.

Do you think you have descendants today in that or any area?

It's possible that there are some, but I wouldn't know how. I cannot say for sure. As I said, no one ever remembered that I — no one said. I shouldn't say they didn't remember; they might've and just didn't say anything. No one said, and I never saw anybody come from other places to visit us, but I cannot say that didn't happen. On the other hand, I cannot say one way or the other. If you're asking, though, whether it is possible that the place was discovered by others, then I really don't know. I am a little confused because Earth is not the same where you are, and I cannot find the place. When I look from my own vision back to our time, it is there. It is on Earth. It is just apparently a different Earth from where you are. Perhaps it's because you're between dimensions and that's why life seems so — how can we say? — tenuous for you.

The Flow into Spirit Form

When it came time for you to pass from the body, what was your experience? How did you choose what you were going to do?

I didn't choose; I simply became my natural, full self.

Right. But you said you were embodied as spirit. Did you choose the next spirit life, or did you just find yourself there?

It's like a river, and you flow into it naturally. It's not something that you stop and think, "Now what do I want, 'this' or 'this' or 'this'?" It's not like that. It's a natural flow, and it feels wonderful. There's no authority that says, "Now you will do this." You just flow, and you become something wonderful.

As a spirit being now, do you have a physical or spirit body that you are attached to or responsible for or connected to in any way, or are you just you?

I am me.

Do you have a sense of sequence, of past and future, or does everything happen at one time?

It is now.

So you don't have a sense of past or future except when you look into this life?

I don't consider it the past. I looked into my life as I remembered it there, and it is part of my flow. I looked into your time by looking at you, but I'm keeping my distance so that I am not affected by it.

By the discomfort?

Yes, but even just now I got a little. I don't see how you bear it.

Okay, so there's only now. Do you have knowledge of any other life except that one in the canyon?

I don't have to have knowledge of it. The only reason I have knowledge of it is that you asked. You made a request, and I was available to respond to your request. When I am no longer communicating with you, I will not remember that life. My recollection is a tie. It is a tie to the past, and in flowing in my natural life, I do not wish to be anchored. I wish to continue my flow.

All right, it's nice to get a few words about how it works out there, about how life ends, you know?

Yes, of course. I will say a few more words. In your time, there is a tendency to overlook things that children do or sometimes misinterpret them because in your family, your culture, and your place of residence, such things are not acceptable. As a wise and observant mother or father or uncle or aunt or grandmother or grandfather or other, a family friend, take note of what children do on their own. Could their activity reveal some wisdom that is not present in your time but could be helpful? You will see this particularly when they are very young, two years old or younger and sometimes up to three years old. You don't have to stare at them, but just notice. "What is that she's doing?" or "What is that he's doing?" Talk it over among yourselves. You might feel some connection to it, a resonance, you might say. If that happens for you adults, don't push it aside. Maybe this is an attempt by the child, who has been born with all its wisdom, to communicate.

Remember, when you are born with all your wisdom, it is from all your other lives, and there might be a great deal you wish to communicate, but you cannot speak the language, you see? Still, you can be as a child. You can show things just by being. So when you have the opportunity, pay attention to what the little ones do, especially if they are in your family, because they looked forward to being born with you, being with you, loving you, and being loved by you. May you have a most enjoyable life.

Thank you very much for coming. Thank you.

✳   ✳   ✳

A Protected Existence

Speaks of Many Truths.

Hey, welcome! This lovely lady talked about a life in Mongolia 9,000 years in what sounded like Shangri-la in a beautiful canyon, but when the being went to look at it now, she couldn't see it. Was it 3.0 or a higher dimension? Where is that now?

It's in 3.0, but even at 3.0, it is not there. It has been covered over with ice. This does not mean that the valley has been filled in. The valley is still there; it's just that the opening to it is a little smaller because of earthquakes. So the opening to the valley would require exploration. It would not be possible to find under all the snow and ice.

Oh, it sounds like such a wonderful place.

If people knew where it was, they would go there. How many times have you seen people in your day go to a beach or a lake and pick up a stone for a souvenir? How long would everything be there if everyone picked up a stone?

So it's protected.

Remember that when you pick up stones. When you go to the beach or are on a trail, you might pick up a stone to look at it, but don't be attached to taking it with you.

Okay. In the future when life is more benevolent, will that area open up again?

I do not know whether the opening will get wider, but it will be revealed. There will not be much ice or snow in the future Earth you speak of, but there will be some at the top of mountains because it is beautiful, and beauty will be welcomed. So the definition of beauty will expand. Some people in your time think "this" or "that" is beautiful, but it is not a thought; it is always a feeling. Good life.

Thank you very much. Thank you.

CHAPTER TWENTY-FOUR

Recognize the Timbre of Life

Future ET from Unknown Planet

May 18, 2016

Greetings.

Greetings!

Now, this may not be exactly in your chosen place to search for lost wisdom, all right? That's because from my point of view, in my time, it is a past life for me. Okay? But from your point of view, it would be about 1,800 years in your future. It isn't the future of the planet, so it is not necessarily the future of where you all are, but it will give you some idea of how the rhythm of life is folded into the continuity and turnover of life as you move toward this.

Right now you live in tumultuous times, and these times do not appreciate life in the human culture. This does not mean there is no happiness and joy and pleasure, but it means that people very often have to prove they are of value — within their own families, even — even though the fact that you exist is already proof that you are of value. In your cultures now, you do not necessarily focus on the beliefs you have religiously, philosophically, or educationally. On the feeling level, those beliefs in common are the most important ones. The differences, however major or minor they might be, are not particularly important. It is the common ground, which you have so much of (but it is not accentuated), that is important.

In the world I'm remembering that is in your future, that common ground is what everyone relates to. This does not mean that the birds do not fly and the fish do not swim; obviously, those are major differences. It means that the senses one has (physical, you understand — sight, sound, all of that) are acknowledged and appreciated even though some do not see the same way others do, physically speaking, and some do not hear the way others do, physically speaking, and so on. There are senses in that world I'm speaking of.

There is also a sense of awareness, the awareness of each other's value and the appreciation of what I will call (to use a musical term, if you don't mind) the timbre of life, which is associated with the tone. You may or may not know this, but every human being and every other being has a musical tone. Sometimes it's very high in the scale, so you cannot necessarily listen to it as a human being. Sometimes it's very low, and that does not have anything to do with value, high or low or whatever. This tonal element has to do with your physical self in resonance with your spiritual self, thereby allowing all other life forms to instantly know whether you are a friend or a foe.

You might wonder how instinct works when it happens at such a distance. That is how. That is how you know whether something is dangerous. That is how you know whether something is attractive or safe or wonderful and everything else. I bring this to your attention because your book is attempting to retrieve wisdom that has been lost. Even though this is a little outside that purpose, it is in your own time that wisdom is not understood or has, at the very least, been lost. This idea of tone — that the physical body, in concert with the spirit or lightbeing, self-manufactured this tone all the time per individual — is not something you now practice as a science (a loving science, mind you, but a science). It was practiced in your distant past. The tone does not mean that it is the only tone you experience. Quite obviously, there is music, and other life forms make sounds, such as the birds I mentioned before.

Relationships Will Develop through Common Tones
All other kinds of life forms, including beloved pets, make tones that don't necessarily refer to worded language but have to do with the feelings in the individual at that moment. Ultimately, feelings are your most common

connection between one life form and another. Since you, as human beings, are on Earth now to learn, you don't necessarily remember these things from other lives, but the other life forms do. This is why a dog, for instance, might bark a warning or make a growling sound at an approaching human being. Even though there is a fence and the dog does not represent a danger, it will react to the person's tone because perhaps that particular tone was not meant to be friends with the dog in that life. Perhaps that person's friends will be horses or birds or cats or some other such creature that brings him or her happiness and he or she, in turn, gives joy to.

I want you to know these things because a time is coming very soon when some of you (and I believe a few of you already have had this experience) will begin to hear, very faintly at first, tones when you approach other people. Some of you will think that this is a reminder of a song, and you will manage to find a song to put the tone to. Others of you who are not listening to music or are simply open to possibilities will recognize that the tone has to do with a passing being. Others who are tremendously sensitive to the hearing level will, in a group of people sitting on a bus or a train (largely people you don't know though you see them every day if you commute), hear these tones as a chorus, not unlike hearing people harmonize. Even though people might be talking and there might be noises from the vehicle or in life around them, the background tone will be present as that chorus sound that is not unlike what you might find in musical theater or perhaps in a religious institution.

I wanted to bring this to your attention because those of you who will hear it (and are perhaps hearing it now) will notice that some tones feel particularly harmonious. These tones will just feel good. This doesn't mean that you can necessarily approach the individual, as you cannot be certain that the person hears the tones too. However, there will be those moments when you meet someone who is able to hear the tones and is drawn to you while you are able to hear the tones and are drawn to that person. This will be the rare occurrence now, but it will happen increasingly over the next four to seven years until people acknowledge the relevant truth of it. Granted, it won't take place in every country or in every situation, but it will be something that becomes more established. If you know about this, it can make a huge difference in terms of struggles and warfare and so on because you might find that you are in a position to recognize that a great many benevolent-feeling tones from other people (who may or not be known to you) feel wonderful, feel marvelous. And it will reduce the difficulty in creating peace, whether a dispute is simply from family or neighborhood differences or control issues or even neighboring-country squabbles. These common-ground tones that feel good to you all will let you know that there is indeed something very special happening.

The Creator of all life intends for you to be some kind of a benchmark so that you will be able to recognize the inevitable re-creation of your natural self as your physical day-to-day self. These tonal elements are absolutely known in spirit. So it is not that you have to learn something; it is more that you will be able to acknowledge the reality. The reason you will have the reality is that your spirit, your soul you say (some of you), will be more and more in residence in your physical body and more and more compatible with your conscious mind and your brain and with other functions in the nervous system. So if you understand this, then what's coming could bring about in time (perhaps not instantly but in time) world peace because you will notice these similar tones.

Word will spread that this is a wonderful thing, and it will become more known and understood when people travel from one neighborhood to another, as I said before, or one country to another, and certain people, members of the group in travel — whether family or friends or a group tour — will be able to hear these tones and will compare notes and realize this is not some strange thing that only happens to them! It is something that is unusual. The words "strange" and "weird" will pop up, but after a while, especially in countries where receptivity to things of the senses are more approved or appreciated, there will be the awareness that this is something that is a gift and not just weird.

That's wonderful! And it's totally new.

Well, we felt it was important to let you know so that you can have a glimmer that this is coming. In fact, some of your people on Earth, human beings, are beginning to have this experience. And we feel that it's important to know that it's not a background tone (though, granted, such things do exist for "this" or "that" reason). This is something associated with other life forms, human beings and other nonhumans. In time, it will be possible for a person walking down a path after a hike, for instance, to suddenly hear these little tones, almost like little voices, and realize they're from ants walking by or a worm or a small creature waiting to cross the path, and you will stop. Then you will hear the little sounds calm down, and before you know it, a quick stream of ants will run across the path, or perhaps a spider scuttles across, or even a caterpillar moves as quickly as possible because of the large beings who tread the path, and that will be that. When this happens, you will know that your spirit wants you to know that other life forms exist and that you now have something in common with them.

As you discover more human beings who can do this, those of you who may be lonely will discover that friendships might be possible where you never thought to look. Sometimes you don't think about certain types of people. Young people tend to congregate with each other, and old people with each other, and so on — not just in families, but in general social interactions. But perhaps two beings of a similar tone will be attracted to each other, and one might be very old, and one might be young. You will find that you can have friends this way as well as having friends who are closer to your age.

Tell me about this tone. Is it a one-note tone, a chord, a harmony? Is it a repeating note or a continuous sound? How do we hear it?

Those were many questions! It is one note. It won't necessarily be a perfect tone, meaning it might be sharp or it might be flat, but it is one note. I mentioned before that it would not be possible for you to hear some of the tones. Some of the tones will simply be above your register to make them out. You will feel those tones that are impossible for you to hear (as you are hearing so many other tones) as vibrations, and then you will begin to recognize that the nature of tonality is vibration, the connection to what you have been told in the past about different vibrating rates and so on (as you might have heard yourself speak of), and you will understand that tone and vibration are two words for the same thing.

So we will hear the vibration! Wild.

You will not hear it; you will feel it. You will hear the tone. But if the tone is above your ability to hear, you will feel the vibration. Creator of all things has thought of everything.

[Chuckles.]

You Are in Precreation

Tell me about the life that you lived 1,800 years in the future. Did it have to do with tone?

No, it has to do with a library. The library is the knowledge of the future. It is not, however (I know you're briefly smiling), the knowledge of the future of your people. It is the knowledge of the future of our people, so it may not be particularly relevant to you. "Our people" means the people I was among in that life, you understand, speaking in terms of the past for me because 1,800 years in your future is still my past.

You mentioned something about a fold or folding into — what? — a turnover of life or something, continuity. Can you say something more about that?

I did already. That's what I was talking about.

Okay, but it doesn't have anything to do with our people, yet it's on Earth?

What are you talking about? I'm talking about my life. You asked about my life.

Was your life on Earth?

Oh, I see. Ah, no, but it was nearby.

Was it on another planet in this system?

Yes, but I won't say which one.

Okay. What dimension was it?

If I say a number of a dimension, no matter what I say, it will be other than the dimension you are in because you are not in a dimension. Your people right now are not in a dimension.

Right. We're transiting.

Yes. So whatever dimension I say, it is like this (you may not understand this, or perhaps you do): You as a people on this planet and, to some extent, with a resonant effect on the rest of the solar system (not the Sun), you do not exist. The reason you do not exist is that you are in a transference point. You could go, since we're using arbitrary numbers for places of existence, to the third dimension, or you could go to the fourth dimension. You are in a transference point where you could go either way, so this is a point of precreation. Precreation can also be expressed as nonexistence. You do not exist. Yet quite obviously to you, you are physical. You can prove it. You can touch things. They are there, but they are encapsulated in the transference point also known as precreation. You will make a choice the more often your spirits are with you, which is regularly happening these days. Your spirits want to go to a more benevolent dimension, so they urge you along in a patient, loving way.

This is marvelous! I'm just trying to soak it in. I know we're transiting between dimensions, but nobody ever said we didn't exist before. [Laughs.]

Keep in mind that when I say that, it means you do not exist to the rest of the universe. Anything in precreation does not actually exist because it is in that moment before becoming. When Spirit manifests a life, perhaps a life as what you call spirit, and it is a life of purpose, identity, friends, and so on, there is a moment of precreation. It is something that cannot be measured by your current instruments because it is extremely quick, but you are in that moment. As a moment of precreation, you are in — how can we say it? — the soup of all time.

This universe is so old and so new, so permanent and so transitory. It is many things. The moments of precreation are constant, and they are stable. It is so small of a split second, yet in the very full experience of it, it is the orchestra playing every tone at once, and it sounds like a harmony. All these things and more are the moments of precreation, and this precreation is what you are in now. However, precreation in the universe does not exist for others who are also in precreation or in creation. Otherwise, it would be a distraction to their perpetuation of their creation or their creation of their creation. It is the way the Creator of all things has of keeping all people in their own uniqueness.

It sounds as if we're in some sort of bubble that protects the rest of the solar system from our discomfort.

Your discomfort has nothing to do with precreation.

But at the same time, the solar system is protected right now from our vibrations, isn't it?

Yes, and you are protected from their creativity. If you were able to feel everything else happening in the solar system, the galaxy, and the universe, you would be overwhelmed and not able to create for yourselves.

Does that mean we're getting much more sensitive because we weren't in precreation in the 3.0 dimension?

You are becoming more sensitive. I am not going to comment on that other part. I must ask you to keep your questions benevolent. You are becoming more sensitive because your souls are in your bodies in a more committed way. This is why some of you have more misunderstandings and why some of you have greater (the other way) understanding of what other people say to you, whereas even just a short time ago, they could say the same things, and you really did not understand what they felt or meant. The more your soul or spirit, you might say, is present and in a full-bodied manner (not just floating above your head trying to get out but completely in your entire physical body), the more every fiber of your physical body is infused with your lightbody, and you can sense much more.

Your Body Knows Your Tone

Is it important now to feel our own tone, to know what it is?

No. It is like this: Your tone is what keeps you on pitch (you might say, musically speaking), but it is not something you have to study or, if even possible, make the tone. It would be like trying to create another right hand when you already have one. So no. It's like singing a song and saying, "I'd like to be able to hear the song I'm singing," when you can.

We can hear it. Okay.

Your body reacts to it. Your body maintains its individuality when, in truth, you could ask yourself. You eat food, and you drink water. There is no question that atomically, on a molecular level, that food has been something else. Why does it transform into being you? Because of the tone. Your body makes the tone, and everything that enters your body as food or water, and even air for that matter, becomes you while it is in residence in you. The moment it passes out, it is free to become another person, place, or thing.

Is it our responsibility to make the tone more benevolent? Are there ranges of benevolence and not benevolence?

It is not your responsibility. There is no willfulness involved in whether it is benevolent or otherwise. You do not have to make it "this" or "that." It is. When Creator tells you, "I Am," it is the same for you (though perhaps not as Creator). You are for yourself. Your tone announces who you are. Other life forms understand this. Maybe you go to the pet store, and you're interested in getting a puppy. A lot of puppies run over, but there's one who looks at you, and you know that's your puppy.

It's because of the tone.

You recognize its tone, and it recognizes yours.

I like that. But as we become more loving and sensitive, does our tone become more harmonious or more attractive or more anything?

Now, I understand that more is attractive to you as a human being in your culture, but no. It will remain the same.

As a walk-in, I have my own tone. It is not the tone of the birth soul, is it?

It is not that, but it is partially that. It has to be. You walked in to what? Did you walk into a table? What did you walk in to?

[Laughs.] A human body. I would really like to know what percent of my tone is the original soul's bones and what percentage is the walk-in.

You are asking me? You understand that I could give you a percentage right now, but two seconds from now it will change, and forty seconds ago it was different. It depends. Now we're going to have to stop, or I can make a closing statement.

Closing statement, but can we continue? I'd like to know more about you and the life you've lived and other things you can tell us. Can we continue next time?

Probably not. You do not always get to mentally know everything in a physical life, and that is actually a great gift.

[Laughs.] All right.

So now maybe those of you reading this understand that part of the reason you are attracted to different songs or types of music is that the music resonates with your tone. Tones are everywhere, and as you begin to hear them, know that your resonant world is becoming broader, more open, and more loving to you personally as an individual as you become part of the universal conscious forest.

Thank you very much. Thank you.

CHAPTER TWENTY-FIVE

Build a Relationship with Light

Fire Reader

June 1, 2016

Now I am here. In my time, I was the fire reader. We lived in the Himalayas, and it [fire reading] had been known before simply because someone who had a small fire was able to tell the events of the future by looking at the flames — not at what was burning, but at the flames and the way they moved, the way they danced. Fire, then, was not the prediction in itself, but it was the motion of the image in the flames. We all knew this because it had been almost like a myth, one based on truth, that several generations previously, there had been a fire reader.

Children Who Move between Worlds

I was a child when it was noticed that I could read fire. I recall it vividly. Someone had built a fire, mostly just to keep the cave warm, and I remember glancing at the fire — not at the material burning (wood of some sort), but just at the flames — and suddenly saying, "The child that will be born will be a girl. When she is born, she will have blue hair, and it will turn white shortly thereafter. Then it will turn a pale red color. Because of this, we will learn that we can have children who can move between worlds and still be in our world." I remember saying that, and afterward everybody looked at me. It was as if I was standing outside myself and looking at myself, and I thought, "Why did I say that?" There was one among us who was just about prepared to have a child. I remember she hugged herself where the baby was and said, "And she will be just who we need."

At that time, our people — and there weren't that many of us; we were not what you would call a tribe but more like an extended family — felt as if we needed to move, but we didn't know where. Because more people had started moving through the area, we realized it wasn't just a place where we and the animals were, but it was apparently a passage. We discovered that because it was a passage, people could see us, though they hadn't yet. In those days, it wasn't necessarily good to be seen because some people had weapons. We did not have such things. It is hard to describe how we were, but we were what nowadays you would call spiritual people, I suppose.

So then it happened. She gave birth to such a child who, for the first few hours, had blue hair and then, with a gentle washing (not that something was washed out of her hair, but something seemed to change), she had white hair. When her hair changed, we all felt the change. It wasn't just that the baby changed, you see. In a couple of days, her mother washed her again, which was possible because there was a stream of water in the cave, then came the red hair, and we changed again. You see, when I saw what I saw, I looked at the flames and I saw an image, which is the only way I can describe it. When the image was present, I apparently knew the future. I say "apparently" because this happened a few times but not always and not every time we needed it.

I am going to say her name the best I can say it. I will spell it phonetically for you: M-E-H A-H-H. We called her that because that is the sound she made. She never cried, but every once in a while, she would say, "Meh Ahh." When she was old enough to speak, she told us that she was talking to someone from another world, and when she said, "meh ahh," she was either talking to or answering a person named Meh Ahh. [Laughs.] But by that time, the name had stuck, and she was Meh Ahh. We all thought that was a little funny. I know you want to talk to someone in this case who can read fire. I am telling you about Meh Ahh, but I don't think she is prepared to speak at this time, maybe next time.

Okay. You're doing great.

Thank you. I will continue. I will describe what I can about what I saw in the flames. It wasn't the type of flame so much or what was burning, but near the top part of the flame was something that was oval shaped. It was white, and it remained in that position even when the flame was just briefly not there. The shape was still there, and it exuded light itself. I am not sure to this day what it was, but it was something unusual. You might ask, reasonably, "What do you mean by 'to this day'?"

I will jump ahead in my story a little bit to say that I am still alive and my people have moved from the world we were in to the world that Meh Ahh could see. Now we are safe at home. We are in a world that is different. When we were on Earth, it was about a thousand years ago in the Himalayas, and it was as I described. Now we are all still together, and Meh Ahh is still with us, alive and well. She has had a child of her own who was born in the normal way. [Laughs.] We all thought the baby might be like Meh Ahh, but no. Meh Ahh looks young. We all look fairly young, for we are on a different world.

Welcome the Light in the Flame

You are asking for beings to speak who can advise you on things you can do in your time. This is what I think you can do if you like to look at fires burning in a stove or a fireplace. I believe that some people have had this experience already — some people in your time sometimes see a bright light at the tip of the flames. I think the people who see this often see something that is round, but the light is so bright that they blink a little bit and don't know what to do when they see it.

If you have that experience and see that light somewhat as I described already (maybe it's a little different for you. It might not always be white light; it might, in your case, be pink or some other color), as long as it is a light that feels good to you (that is the really important part, not just that the light is exciting but that it feels like love), don't try to touch it because the fire will still burn. If the light in the fire feels good — you must feel it for it to work well — this is what to say: "Welcome." That's all. Say it in your language because the word "welcome" in your language will have a feeling associated with it.

It is possible that the light will not only be seen in the flames but also might show itself at other times. If it looks as it looked in the flames and it feels good to you (it is very important that it feels good to you — not exciting, just good, such as a feeling of friendliness or love), then say,

"Welcome," and build a relationship with that being. At some point, you can ask to have a quick picture of something important in the future, or you can ask to see something that will happen in the future or something like that. You might see yourself. It would be as if you are standing outside yourself, and you see yourself maybe meeting the perfect person for you to marry or maybe see yourself somewhere you always wanted to be, and you look happy. You can ask for something good for yourself.

Don't ask the being to show you something bad. It will only show you good things because that is compatible with it. If you have loved ones, you could say, "Show me something good, if you would." You can say, "Please show me something good that will happen for my son" or "my daughter" or "my husband" or "my wife" or "my friend." Like that. But don't do that every day. You need to build up a relationship.

Now, you are asking for the being to show you something, but what can you do for it? To have it feel good about working with you, you can have a feeling such as welcome or gratitude or happiness or encouragement — a physical feeling that you can practice and feel strongly. Be that feeling that is encouraging or happy or something like that, and just feel it for a moment. You will know that the being has felt it because the light will get stronger for a moment. This doesn't mean it is taking the feeling; the strong version of the light, the brighter light, is the acknowledgment that the being felt the feeling. The being likes that, and that is what you can do. It is important to know how to give as well as receive.

The Light Is the Being You Love Most

Welcoming the light is an engagement with a being from a world that you once occupied. Before you come into physical life on whatever planet you are born, you have a time when you enter something like a passage to transform from whatever type of lightbeing you were in spirit to what you will familiarize yourself with for the form of life you will take in, say, a physical world like your own.

Just as you enter that passage, the being you love the most will be there with you. It is hard to describe how that is in spirit, but it will always be, and many of you will be happy to know this. There will always be one really special loved one, and that loved one will be there — not saying goodbye or hugging goodbye because in spirit you are immortal, but just to lend support. It will most likely be that being who will come to visit. It is not unusual for such a being to have the opportunity to check on its loved one. Even here on your Earth as it is now with all the struggle and strife, there is still love and happiness, so the being can appear for a moment. It can be here a little longer but just not visibly. And of course, when it appears briefly, not everyone can see it. Very often the person who was its special best friend, you might say, in spirit form, will be able to see it, but just briefly, either out of the corner of his or her eye, like a twinkling light. Or sometimes, if that person is more involved in spiritual studies, the being might appear directly in front of him or her as a sudden, intense but small light of various colors.

Don't try too hard to make it happen. It is not something you can invite and make happen, but you can say this in your own language and in a way that makes you feel good. You are not trying to impress anyone. No one else will be there when you say this; you will be alone (if you are never alone, you can whisper it to yourself). Just say, "I welcome my spirit friend to be with me." That's all. You don't have to say anything fancy beyond that. Welcome is an important feeling, one that you don't always feel these days in your world, but it is a very important feeling. This will allow you to feel good about your spirit friend being with you. Just experiencing the feeling of welcome is a way to attract what you want to enjoy in your physical world. Perhaps a best friend would be nice if you don't already have one. If so what to do is this:

Hold your left hand in front of you just in front of your mouth. Speak as if you are speaking to the palm of your hand. You can open or close your eyes. If there is something you need in your life — not an object, but a best friend or a mate or something like that, or perhaps the feeling might be identified with an object, for instance a warm, safe bed to sleep comfortably in, which would suggest a place to live or at least a bed for the night — and you say first, "Welcome," and have an image of what you would experience if you were in that warm safe bed. It will give you a good feeling, so imagine being there, and then again say, "Welcome." Then from time to time — you don't have to repeat that; once you have said it, it will be in the palm of your left hand — take your left hand and [laughs] (you will think this is funny) just aim it at the ground. If you are sitting on the ground, touch your feet with the palm of your left hand, and remember what you welcomed. You can also shake your hand gently toward the ground because it is Earth, your planet, that helps to bring things to you. You don't have to touch yourself, but as I say, you can touch your feet because those are the parts of you that most often touch the land, unless you lie on the ground very often. So it is like dropping seeds into the earth in the hope that what you want and need will sprout, physically, in the form you would like.

Life in a Different Dimension

How old were you when you first saw the flame and saw the future?

I was about nine years old.

So where you are now, time is different. Is it a different dimension?

It is a different dimension, as you would say, but it resembles Earth. I cannot tell you whether it is the same place, the same space. I can say that at night, there are stars. During the day when it rains, there are rainbows. So there are things that are the same. There are plants. There are creatures like butterflies, only they are a little bigger and friendlier. And there are — I can't describe them exactly — water beings. We live on the land. We do not need to eat. That's the one big difference. We don't need to drink water (but occasionally we touch it to our lips), yet we are human. This is how we know we are in a different dimension. There are beings (and we did not see these beings when we were on Earth) that resemble deer or antelope, but I don't see any horns or anything sticking out of the top of their heads (probably because they don't need them because this is a peaceful place). We did not see these beings when we were on Earth.

So we are not alone, which is nice, because we like to have interactions with others. There are many flowers, and very often, very big trees. There is a tree that I particularly like, though it is not exactly near where we live. I like to walk there. It takes about a day and a half to walk there, in terms of your time, and it is a pleasant journey.

It is a magnificent tree. If I start at one point near the tree — it has roots that come out, so I want to be respectful because the tree does not like us to step on its roots — and go across the tree, it is about thirty-eight feet, using your measurements, to the center of the tree, so it must be another thirty-eight feet beyond the center to the other side of the tree.

It is a very old and wise tree, and sometimes when I am near it, I hear stories or a voice speaking. I don't think of it as a teacher. It is as if this is a voice talking about things in other worlds. I think of the tree as the tree of wisdom, but I have on occasions spoken to it and asked, "Is this your voice?" The tree says, "No, it is something that seems to reside in this space that I grew in." The tree remembers itself as a seed and all the years that followed. So apparently the voice was there originally, but when the tree's seed landed where it was, it grew there, the tree became friends with the voice. It just talks about everything — never anything unpleasant — but I like it especially when it tells stories. That's fun. I believe the person who is allowing me to speak through him knows of this voice, though it has been years since he has tried to listen to it. The voice just speaks. It is hard to describe. You hear it out loud, and it is very comforting. It is like an educational program, but the voice is friendlier than that, not saying, "Now learn this." It's not that. It's more as if someone sits down next to your campfire and tells you who he or she is and where that person is from and what he or she is doing and all of this. You learn things.

Are you the only one who hears this voice, or do others of your people hear it when they go to the tree?

They hear the voice too, but you don't have to hear it. You have to focus on the center of the tree. What is in the center of the tree is the original seed energy, and the seed landed on that spot where the voice was speaking. So if I think about the center of the tree, I can hear the voice immediately, but if I don't think about it, I don't hear it.

Can you tell me something about the circumstances of your move from the Himalayas to where you are — from Earth to that world?

Yes. As time went on, more and more people were traveling, and we could see them in the distance. We spent a lot more time in the cave, and we were careful about never building fire at night. Other people, including travelers, would build fires, so we weren't too concerned about smoke, but that was an issue.

When Meh Ahh got a little older (but she was just a toddler, maybe two years old or a little less), she would point. By that time, her mother knew that she was talking to someone called Meh Ahh, but like I said, we had gotten used to calling her Meh Ahh. She pointed at Meh Ahh, and her mother said at one point (I'm using that word two different ways), the child pointed at Meh Ahh and then looked at her mother — not to be rude but so that her mother might see Meh Ahh.

Although her mother could never see the Meh Ahh from the spirit world, that day the mother saw a hand reach out from the spirit world. She saw it. It wasn't exactly a human hand, but it was a beautiful hand. I think she said it did not have as many fingers as we have, but it was very beautiful, just illumined with light coming off the hand. It touched the little one's hand, and the little one smiled, turned around, and held hands with her spirit friend, and she looked at mother and said, "Meh Ahh," with a big smile.

One day, one of the people — not the soldier types with the weapons, but one of the children — came up to the cave and saw us. Fortunately for us, it was a happy child and not one who would run and say, "Look what I found." It was a happy, thinking, studious child who smiled at little Meh Ahh, and she smiled back. The child climbed back down and continued on with whomever he was with. I don't know whether that child ever spoke about it.

We took that as a sign that we needed to move. In other situations, we would have welcomed the child and his family, but that wasn't the situation at the time. Because we were worried, the little one reached out and said, essentially, "Meh Ahh, go there." So it was not difficult. There were nine of us at that time. It is hard to describe, but Meh Ahh reached for spirit Meh Ahh, and they held hands again. Then spirit Meh Ahh got closer to the floor where we were in the cave, and we got closer, and the closer we got, we just merged into that other world. Then along came child Meh Ahh, and we were there. It all happened in light, and it was very quick and comfortable. We were in this world.

How old was Meh Ahh, the girl, at that time?

Not quite two years old.

You were only about eleven then? And the rest of your life has been in this new place?

Yes, I suppose so. But the years on Earth, in a place that was originally beautiful and comfortable and safe and then became dangerous, those years are — how can we say? — louder in some ways, meaning more intense. So I try not to think about those years because in the beginning, they were beautiful, but toward the latter part of my time there, they became very frightening.

How did you get there in the first place? Why was your small group there in the Himalayas? Where had you come from?

We came from farther down — not flatter areas, but not as high up —

and we were always exploring, looking for places where we could sleep comfortably, where there was water, where there was some kind of food we could acquire — a comfortable place to reside. We found that in that cave. If you went farther into that cave, there was a stream of clear, drinkable water, and there were — I feel very uncomfortable speaking about this now because we don't eat living beings where we are, but there we had to — fish in the stream. We ate as little as possible because we liked them, and they liked us. When we were hungry, one would jump out of the stream and just lay there for us, and we knew it was okay to eat it. But I always felt bad about it at the time because they had families and loved ones. So we appreciated the sacrifice. We never ate them in front of the stream; we always took them away. When the eating took place, it was always away from the stream, as far as we could get, but still in the cave. That way, the loved ones didn't see what happened to the fish.

Ageless Time

Do you have origin stories? Do you know where you came from and how you got to the Himalayas?

No. We don't have stories like that. Where people came from in those days wasn't as important as who they were. I don't know when in your time where a person came from became important, but in those days, it was who a person was in that moment that was important — what skills he or she had to share and how he or she behaved with others. All of that was important, and when we met people, very often they would immediately let us know what they could do. Maybe they knew how to make fire. Not everybody did. Or they might know how it was done, but they might not be good doing it. Or they knew how to fish or something. People would quickly reveal their skills, and that is how they would be identified.

I am curious how nine people got up in those high mountains. Did they split off from another group or land in a spacecraft?

Well, how did you get here?

I was born here in the usual way. My grandparents came here on a ship from Norway and Sweden.

We didn't really think about that. By the way that I described how we would introduce ourselves, you can see that we lived in the immediate moment. We didn't dwell on the past. So why would we even think about that?

Do you think you were the reincarnation of the person who was the last fire reader in your group since you just knew it; you weren't taught how to do it?

It is not relevant.

Is there time where you are now?

Yes, there is time, or there wouldn't be day and night.

So you have a Sun and an orbiting planet? Do you have a moon?

You understand on other planets, from what I have heard from the voice from the tree, sometimes there is only light and sometimes there is only dark. But it is not unusual for there to be day and night. So don't assume that there isn't time. My understanding is — and this is unusual because I can still remember my time on Earth — our day times are longer and our night times are longer. I don't know if your scientists could then figure out how big or how small our planet is, but that's the difference. There is time here, but we just don't age. This could possibly be because of the way we arrived here, but I have friends who are not human beings, including one of the butterfly people, and they don't age either. So we apparently have been welcomed into this world and have become a portion of it. Even though there is day and night, we do not age. But I still think that with day and night, there must be time of a sort but maybe not. Maybe there is just the time of the light and the time of the night sky, and so on. I will say I have never seen a moon, like with Earth there is a moon and moonlight. But the stars are very bright. Our eyes adjust as yours would, and we can walk around and see sufficiently.

There is one thing I miss. On Earth there were these cats, Himalayan cats. They were so beautiful, and I miss the cats. One was my friend. It was apparently born around the same time I was, and we used to visit with each other. And I admit, I miss that. I can picture her sometimes. I know that she finished her life on Earth, and she must be in spirit form.

Do you reproduce there? Have you added to your group?

We do not reproduce. We are who we were when we passed through that opening. We do not re-create, but we love each other. We make love, you would say.

So even here you have never seen another group of humans or humanoids or a spaceship or anything like that? Are you the only humans on the planet as far as you know?

I have no idea. We don't wander that far. You have to remember who we were when we lived on Earth. We stayed together. We were never out of sight of each other. If we were in a flat place, we might be off a ways, but we could always see each other. We are like that. We haven't wandered all over the planet. We came to a beautiful, wonderful place. Why would we want to leave? It is certainly possible there are other beings on the planet, but we do not know. Perhaps someone will wander by someday, and we will find out. But if other beings on the planet are like us, the way deer and big butterfly are — I think deer and the big butterfly are the same being — there are not different butterflies and different deer. So I think on that planet, people reside where they are most comfortable and stay there. It is not a prison. You can go where you like, but we like it here. It is wonderful, and it is safe. It is welcoming. Why would we want to leave to go any place else? It is paradise. Why leave paradise?

[Laughs.] What about fires? Do you still look at fires? Do you have fire there?

We don't have fire here.

What about the girl? Does she have special abilities there, or you don't need those either?

She does not need them, but she still talks to spirit Meh Ahh, and every once in a while, we can see a hand reaching out, and she will hold spirit Meh Ahh's hand and then look at us and smile. Then she will walk off by herself, and we know that she is talking to her spirit friend. We thought when we came to this place that spirit Meh Ahh would be present, but she is spirit and has remained so.

Is Meh Ahh still two years old?

No, no. It has been about a thousand years here or something like that, and we have matured. We mature to the age where we are the most comfortable. Right now if I were on Earth, you would say I was about seventeen years old in terms of my size and the way I look. It is not impossible that we will get older, but I have noticed that the very young get to look right around my age, and those who are older have remained looking the way they look.

So if they were elders, they stayed at that age?

We didn't really have elders per se at that time. We had beings who were in their twenties. I don't think anybody was beyond their twenties. There had been elders, but they had moved over.

Okay, you have explained as much as you know about all of this. Could we talk to the girl Meh Ahh or the spirit Meh Ahh to get their perspectives so that they could add more to this story?

Perhaps, yes. Request it. I won't make a closing statement since this is not the end. Good Night.

Thank you very much.

CHAPTER TWENTY-SIX

Humans Have the Ability to Traverse Dimensions

Mmm Ah

June 2, 2016

This is Mmm Ah. If you were to spell that, it would be M-M-M A-H. When the little one tried to speak my name, she said it the way she said, but actually one makes the sound initially with the lips closed, and then as you open your lips, out comes the "ah."

Welcome.

Now, I will tell you the story of these people. These people did not think of the past, and when you asked the origin story question, they really didn't have a response. It is because, well, they were very focused in the present moment, and that is not unusual for people of the Inner Earth. That's where they were from, but they did not know that. They lived a very benevolent life, as you could tell from what was described. They went back into the cave — way back — and found the stream, and that was an opening to Inner Earth.

The reason they were alarmed when the little boy ran up was that they didn't have encounters. Think about it. They rarely saw anybody, and here was an encounter with a person, even though he was a nice little boy. He looked into the cave at the people and smiled, as any child would. The people could tell there was something different. It was as if the little boy could see them, but that didn't startle them because they thought they were part of that world, you see. But when they saw the little boy — imagine this: They saw him as if they were looking through glass. That was the experience they had even though normally they would look out and see everything as it was, including people going by in the distance as they described. But here was this instance when they saw this child who had run up to look around and see things, as any child might, and they saw him through something like glass even though there wasn't an actual object there.

They knew something had happened even though the encounter with the child was pleasant. When the little one [Meh Ah] was communicating with her spirit friend, they were able to — and this is what happened — return to Inner Earth. They thought they went to another planet, but actually they returned to Inner Earth. That's where they went. And the opening that went back into the cave and to the stream, which was from Inner Earth, all of that was erased. So if you went to the Himalayas today, you might very well find the cave, but the opening that went back about a quarter of a mile is no longer there because, as you know, this is a different dimension.

The people did not realize that even though they were living on Earth in that thousand-years-ago time, they were not of the surface, really. They had forgotten that they had gone to that place on Earth as an outing, as a family might. They liked what they saw, and then they forgot where they were from because, when you think about it, they were always functioning in the present moment, so the past was not available to them as a memory. That's how they got lost. They lived very well, considering. Keep in mind that they didn't need much to eat. They had water and occasional food. People from Inner Earth do not need to eat very much, so a little bit goes a long way. I thought you might be interested.

What about the people they left behind in Inner Earth? Didn't they miss them?

What people they left behind?

The people they interacted with in Inner Earth before they went on their outing, other parts of their family or relatives or friends. Didn't these people miss the ones who came to the surface of Earth?

To miss someone is to go into the past.

Oh. So everyone in Inner Earth lived only in the present?

Yes, so there is no "missing." This makes for a constant state of calm, peace, and happiness.

How long were they in that cave? The same generation? Many generations?

More than one generation. Although they wandered around some-what, they had been in and around that cave for, in terms of Earth time, about 900 years. So yes, they had generations that came and went. However, in Inner Earth, while such a thing might take place, there wouldn't be so much turnover. Of course, the turnover on the surface of Earth — and in a different dimension, I might add — is quite a bit more frequent for obvious reasons.

Embrace Your Pure State

Are you the being who was talking to the little girl?

Yes.

Those people are gone now, aren't they? There are no people now in Inner Earth?

There is no one in the location where they were, but keep in mind that Inner Earth is in a different dimension. You can have multiple dimensions in the same space, and they do not disturb each other because of the separation, the veils, you understand. Inner Earth civilization still functions, but the location has shifted. If you seal up a passageway from one dimension to another, very often you will simply move that passageway from one place to another, just to be cautious.

The location has shifted even now. This is perhaps why there is a prevailing concept among some people that Inner Earth still exists. It does. It is just not some place you can go hunting or caving for, you might say, to find. Some people, the very young and occasionally the very old, have access to that if they are imaginative in a pure state, meaning their imaginations are not complicated by fears or worries. They are just completely open to what is benevolent, you might say. This is why a child can interact with a young one of another species in a completely open and friendly way whereas an adult might say, "Oh, get away from that; it is dirty," in the case of a child interacting with a many legged, as you say, or with a mouse or something like that. The adults won't see the young child and the young mouse for their pure states. They will just see themselves as adults trying to protect their child. But it is possible.

In the case of the little child who came to be known as Meh Ahh, that child had that completely pure state. It wasn't that the other people didn't, but that child, who was so young, was able as a toddler to see that.

It was also where she stood sometimes. It was the space, it was the place, and it was the person.

This kind of phenomenon is not unknown in your times. Very often when a person has the ability to see what others call phenomena, that person could be standing right next to a person who doesn't see what the first person sees. On occasion, this has led to sad consequences because the person who doesn't see decides that the other person is crazy and tries to prove it by taking a picture that shows nothing is there. However, with today's high-speed cameras, that person might very well take a picture and see something on the image — maybe not exactly what the other person sees, but something. So notice that.

This is particularly important: There are still people institutionalized simply because they can see things that others cannot see. They were born with the ability, and they never lost it. When people are born, they can see things like this. But most people are talked out of it — not in the sense of, "That's just your imagination, dear," but they become more engaged in getting along in life and learning the language, the culture, and so on. Some people remember, and if their parents are loving and conscious and all of these sorts of thing, they might encourage their children to remember. But most of you know this, so I will simply say that such a thing is possible.

Why are these people alone? They feel they are alone on a planet with a butterfly and a deer, but they haven't seen any other people.

They haven't seen any other people *yet*. It is better for them to have a transitional experience. They don't remember, and why would they? They were on the surface, and they personally were not the ones who crossed over into the other dimension that you would call your Earth dimension. Even though when they crossed and those who came after them, you understand, were born, they had a cord, you might say, that was available to them. The cord was stronger for some, less so for others. For little Meh Ahh, it — the cord to that place, an energy cord, not a string — was strong. So they — what was your question again?

Why aren't they interacting with other people in Inner Earth since there are other people there?

Yes, thank you. They weren't interacting because they themselves were not from there. So there needed to be time, and it will continue for some time, where they are gradually exposed to other people. Then eventually they will be told what I have just told you, but in greater detail.

Humans Are from Inner Earth

Even though you say they had no memory of the past, the boy who talked to me, who said he would say his name later but he never did, said he remembered from the Earth life the cat that he played with all the time since he was born, so he did remember some of the past.

Yes, that's interesting. That is my response to that. Keep in mind that there are always exceptions because some people will just have that experience. Also keep in mind that cats have that connection to other worlds and access them. So he remembered the cat because, of course, the cat could traverse from one world to another. So the cat was part of that world. Cats are with you even now to remind you that this is something that is natural for you. All human beings on the surface of Earth right now actually have the ability to move from one dimension to another because you are all from Inner Earth. This is the missing link, you see — to your ancestors. I am not saying your souls; I am saying that all physical human beings on Earth, in all their varieties, were originally beings from Inner Earth, and cats are in your lives in all their forms to remind you that this is something you can do. That's why cats are cute, yet they have aspects that aren't so cute. They can (those of you who are fortunate might see them, to the extent that you are able) traverse from one dimension to another. Most often this will be seen by the very old, the very young, or those who have the ability to do so (they learned, or it remained from childhood), the sensitive ones, you might say. Not to say that other people aren't sensitive, but sometimes life has a way of covering that up. So cats are with you now not to take you back to Inner Earth but to remind you that it is where you are from.

So how did that work? When the first humans came here, they came to Middle Earth or Inner Earth before they came to the surface? Why did they go to Inner Earth instead of going to the surface?

No, no. The first human beings that came to the surface — human beings as you recognize yourselves, not some pre-version that walked somewhat stooped over, none of that, but as you recognize human beings today — didn't come *to* Inner Earth, okay? Eliminate that from your thoughts. They were *from* Inner Earth. They were always there. They came to the surface just as the family that we were talking about did. That's where human beings are from. Not all human beings on all planets are from Inner Earth, but all human beings on Earth genetically, you might say (but I would say in light), are from Inner Earth and can be traced back there. When your scientists get a hold of the quantification of light particles and can track light on the basis of the pathway it has taken, they will discover that the human genome interacts very nicely with light — not condensed light as in lasers, meaning unnatural light, but actual natural light. And its pathway can be traced back to its point of origin. They will discover that the point of origin of human beings is somewhere under the earth, but they will not quickly adapt to the idea that it is Inner Earth at a different dimension. In time, they will.

So our physical bodies came from Inner Earth. When did the beings first start to come to the surface?

It happened the very same way it did with others. The surface was at that time an adventure, you might say, but it wasn't covered with dragons [laughs], meaning no dinosaurs and so on. They came up to the surface of the planet. You know, that planet that was here?

Oh, yes, the first planet.

That's where they came, and there were no dinosaurs there. They came much later with the planet that followed.

That was the loving planet, the one that was too gentle, the second one.

Not too gentle, it can never be too gentle. Keep in mind that gentle is good because it does not harm ever.

Then how did the human body get to this planet, the third Earth planet in this orbit? Is Middle Earth of the three planets connected in some way?

I don't think you understand, and apparently it is difficult to make myself clear. It is not your mind; it is my poor approach to explanation, apparently. Imagine, for a moment, that the planets you identify as the planets in this solar system didn't exist, okay? Just imagine that. But something is still there. What is it in the space where Earth is now? What was there before Earth? Inner Earth.

Oh, I see. The one Inner Earth was in this orbit where Earth is now before Earth planets were here, but it is at a different dimension.

Inner Earth is simply *Inner* Earth because Earth the planet is in that space. Inner Earth is part and parcel of its own place. It just happens to be small enough to be *inside* Earth, the planet, but it is not actually Earth. It is its own place at its own dimension. Even if the solar system that you know and understand and is physically here were not here, Inner Earth would still be there. Earth occupies the same space as "Inner Earth."

Okay, that's brilliant. I understand it now. It preexisted. It was here before the planets in this solar system. Do any other planets have a similar other-dimensional place within them?

No, I asked you to imagine that the planets weren't here so that you could get that part aside, but other planets were here. I just asked you to imagine it so that you could understand, not that there was a sequence there.

Okay, but do other planets have something similar, an Inner Saturn and an Inner Jupiter, or something like that, or is there only Inner Earth?

Some of the planets have that. I am not able to tell you at this time which ones, but it is not because of some higher-dimensional group of planets. It is just that at other dimensions, life exists in abundance, so one wouldn't expect to find empty space very often. If you think about it, you think about dimensions in terms of numbers and even mathematics because to some extent in your mathematical world, dimensions are real. But in fact, we are using the term "dimensions" simply as a way to explain that life forms and entire cultures and communities can exist in exactly the same space without interfering with each other because dimensions are inexhaustible. There aren't just the eighth and the ninth dimensions.

These things, when numbered, will seem to be hierarchical perhaps, or you understand that some are denser and some are better. It is not that. It is just a way of categorizing. It's a file system, but if you set that aside, you can simply say that all life exists in all varieties you can imagine, as well as those you cannot imagine, at this time in your experience and in exactly the same space.

It might be something you can put on the head of a pin, as in the old story, or it might be something that is so large that it cannot be quantified. Space is not that which is between things. It is as a mother who loves things in all of their varieties, and such love welcomes all life in all varieties in the same space. Big or small, it is only relative in thought but not in deed.

Synchronistic Reincarnation

What is your connection with Inner Earth? Are you a guide or a teacher to the beings there?

Teachers are not necessary. [Laughs.] Teachers are only necessary when something that isn't known needs to be known. Always remember that. In your culture, things need to be known that aren't known by others, so teachers are required. But if you were to live in a world that is completely benevolent and everything that you need to survive and thrive and live and love is known by all beings, teachers are unnecessary, as are guides. They are also unnecessary.

So who am I, you ask, to those people? I am their friend. I cannot describe it any other way — a personal friend. How can you have a personal friend who knows you as a person from thousands of years previous? After all, the people in the cave were not the ones who went through that space and found themselves on the surface of the planet we have been talking about. No. So how could I, Mmm Ah, know them? The answer is very simple, isn't it? The synchronicity. Those souls were finally synchronized. All those souls who were there at that time, including little Meh Ahh, were the same souls who went through that opening to the surface, and they were the same souls that I knew in my place in Inner Earth. I was able to help them come to their natural place of existence because we were in complete synchronized harmony at that time. But it only happened when little Meh Ahh was born, so she was the last of the original souls to reincarnate. They were all reincarnated as those souls who originally left. That's why it couldn't happen — they couldn't come back — until they were all the original souls simply reincarnated in their time.

I see. So they are immortal in Inner Earth? They incarnate in mortal physical bodies? They die and are reborn on the surface of Earth?

All souls are immortal. You are mistaken there. You said in the beginning that in Inner Earth, their bodies were immortal. They are not. They live a long time, but the length of time — which I won't say but it is a very long time — changes because souls like a certain amount of variety. So there is no suffering in the body. There is a change, and the body returns to its origin of makeup. You have heard perhaps (and this story is a real thing) that when elephants are about to die, they go where other elephants have gone, yes? They attempt to bring their bodies back to the place of transition for them. In Inner Earth, when it gets to be someone's time, the person returns to that place where he or she was born so that the body, when the soul leaves it, will return to the earth from which it was made (speaking of Inner Earth here, even though it is its own place).

Let me change my question. These beings lived a very long time in Inner Earth, but the boy who talked earlier said that when they came to the surface of this planet, the older ones of the group were in their twenties. So they had short lives on Earth?

Yes, they had short lives then because, well, the surface of Earth was not the same as Inner Earth.

Fascinating. There are humans all over the universe, but you're saying that our original bodies came from Inner Earth. In other channelings, we were told that our bodies were deliberately changed to have vulnerabilities for the Explorer Race experiment we were involved in.

Keep in mind that I am not going to rubber-stamp what you are saying. I am just going to say that the human body, if living in a completely benevolent circumstance — you have to understand what "completely" means: not 99 percent, but 100 percent. One hundred percent of the apple is the entire apple. Understand that mathematically. If you live in a place that is 100 percent benevolent, you don't have to eat because everything is benevolent. You eat when you are hungry, and it takes only a little bit to satisfy you. You might, for instance, be walking along and notice that you are hungry, and you go over to a tree and interact with the tree and ask if it is all right for you to pick a berry. You walk around the tree until you see an area that has a little more light around a berry or two, and then you hold your hand up to them and very slightly touch them. They fall into your hand because they are ready to be consumed. You eat one berry and then the other berry, and you feel completely satiated. You do not need anything else, but you are a human being. This does not mean everybody is horribly skinny; everybody looks fine. They are slim, that's all.

So were the bodies we inhabit modified from those bodies for our experiment?

No. It is just that you are living in a hostile environment. By hostile, I don't mean that everybody you meet on the street wants to punch you. I mean that survival has become difficult because you have forgotten who you are, and when you forget who you are for whatever reasons, you will get along as well as possible.

Do you have memories from before interacting with the beings on Inner Earth?

Excuse me, but you do not understand something. You are thinking of me as a spirit.

Yes. What are you?

I am not a spirit; I am a resident of Inner Earth. I was seen by the beings on the surface of the planet as light. They could see my lightbody. You have a lightbody too, and under some circumstances, somebody might only see your lightbody as light. I am a resident of Inner Earth, and I reside there today as a human being with a lightbody.

Have you reincarnated there, or is this a very long incarnation?

In terms of your dimension's years, you would say that one of our incarnations is very long indeed, but in terms of our years, it is just a regular lifetime. That is all I can say.

As a soul, you have had incarnations in many places. You don't restrict yourself just to Inner Earth, do you? That is just where you are now?

Yes, I am in what we are calling Inner Earth, and I have resided other places. On your planet, there is much difficulty and strife and struggle, but know this is not who you really are. When you pass over, when your time is right for that, you will gradually rejoin your natural state of being. What I mean by "gradually" is that it will actually only take a few seconds, but it will seem gradual as your Earth experience just drops off of you, just as if you might get out of a suit of clothes, and you will move into your own state of being, and then you will gradually remeet people. Gradually will seem like a few minutes. You will be with your guide, a friend. You will know that guide immediately because it is an immortal friend that you have known forever, you might say. You will see loved ones you have known on Earth, and you will transition into your light self. Yet there will be a time when you will want to incarnate in some physical world somewhere else, perhaps somewhere far away that has piqued your imagination in the past. And there you will go to live a most benevolent life with happiness and joy and nothing to impede the beauty of life. Good life.

Thank you very much. Thank you.

CHAPTER TWENTY-SEVEN

Request a Benevolent Vision of Your Future

Shaman from South America

June 6, 2016

All right.

Welcome.

This is a time for people on Earth to consciously create. You have to be strong with yourself now. When you find yourself worrying or imagining that something bad might happen or recalling when something bad happened or even thinking of something that was uncomfortable that is a memory, you have to discipline yourself, pull yourself out of that, and just be in the present. The present may not be good for some of you — this is a reality in your time — so simply saying, "Focus in the present moment" is not sufficient for many people, especially when the present moment is filled with discomfort, irritants, worries, or worse. These are important times, and people have to make an effort to create consciously — conscious creation. The simple version is to not dwell on the past and not focus on unhappiness. Try to be in your present if it is better than the things that are troubling you, worrying you.

For these minor irritants or discomforts in your life, this gesture will help: With your right hand in front of you, imagine sweeping the annoying events or uncomfortable thoughts out of the way. Use the back of your fingers, and move them as if you were whisking a paper cup off a table in front of you. When you are in a situation that is difficult, use this gesture: When you have a moment and are alone or with people who will look away to give you privacy, reach out in front of you and motion as if you were washing a window. Move your hand back and forth and say,

> "I ask to be able to benevolently reach into my good future."

Reach through the spot you were washing until you feel something good or all right. You have connected with a place from the future of your current physical life. Stretch it like a rubber band. Pull it to you, and touch the right side of your face. Then move the hand holding it back toward the place you washed. Let your future gently go back into that place. It should go back gently and carefully. You do not want to disturb that future so that it will be there for you, that benevolent future.

Life as you know it on Earth is not always easy. Old or young, sometimes you learn something, and other times it is just life with worries and feelings. You are in a temporary spot, as if you had pulled off the road on a long road trip to look around. Compared to the life of your soul, your lives on Earth are temporary, a brief moment of the total. A life on Earth is education you cannot get anywhere else. For your soul stream, this training is available only on Earth. Earth is a challenging school filled with choices, a tough place. These gestures will help you to focus on the pleasant part of your present.

Immortality Is Spherical

Can you tell me about your training? Did you have a teacher?

My teaching came from visions I saw. There were circles that turned into other shapes. They were colored and had symbols on them. I was about three years old when I first saw them. I did not have a physical teacher; the visions taught me. In the visions, the shapes were like blocks that children might have. Those blocks might have numbers or letters on them, one on each side, so that the child gets familiar with these shapes. But later on, the child is eventually taught numbers and the alphabet. It was like that, only they were not blocks; they were round balls. They would have different symbols on them. The closest I can come to describing them would be the symbols for geometry. So they were shapes and forms, and then after a while, the shapes would re-form themselves, not just be pictures on round objects. The spheres would re-form into those shapes. That's how it started.

Do you use those shapes now?

No, but it helped me to understand that things shaped in one way are often shaped in other ways, and they are the same things. You see, that's the lesson: You could have round balls of different colors, like toys, that in the end would have pictures on them, simple pictures one would have for a child, like on the blocks. After a while, the balls shape themselves into those simple things. The lesson being that what *is* forms itself into what it *becomes*. That's how you build an education: You start at the beginning, and you teach one step at a time.

So that's how I learned that all things stem from all things. It is very important to know that. In a culture of human beings, even though a human might look or act a certain way, you know that originally he or she was something completely different. It is sort of a way of teaching about soul, you understand, or immortality. Immortality begins with one shape, and that shape becomes many different shapes. Of course, that original shape is a sphere. You can trace immortality and the ongoing reality of immortality back to its point of origin. It is always a sphere. Spheres of origin are always complete. They contain everything and nothing because they do not have walls around them. They have infinity within them, and that infinity has no barrier, but the primal aspect of the infinite is spherical. This allows time, creation, and transformation to function compatibly and comfortably and generously, as is its nature. This is what I was taught.

What was your first act of helping someone based on these teachings?

I found an ant that somehow got one of its feet caught under something, and it couldn't move. I asked the little ant, "Can I help you?" The ant looked up, and I heard him say, "Gently, please." So I moved very slowly, and I did not pass my hand and arm over the top of the little ant. I walked very carefully around to the side of the pebble — to the ant, it was a big, heavy thing. I reached slowly, and when I touched the pebble, I made sure my fingers were on either side of the pebble so that I wouldn't accidentally press down on the pebble when I pulled it away. I moved my fingers up slowly, and in that gesture of moving it up, closed my fingers on the pebble and pulled it up. Then the ant moved its foot from beneath it and scuttled a couple of steps away, of course, trying to help the foot feel better. It sat there for a bit. I moved the pebble far away. Then I sat down very carefully, at a distance but close enough to the ant.

I pictured the ant in complete health and harmony. While I did that, I saw a circle of life: I saw the ant before it was that form, I saw the ant after it was that form, and then I saw the ant in its healthy form before the pebble rolled onto its foot. While I was doing that, I noticed that the light became golden and there were shimmers of white and all other colors, pink especially and sometimes a light green. All of that happened around the ant and me and the space we were in, which was not exactly a cave. It was more of a hollowed out area. Looking back on it, it looked as if it had been hollowed out by wind and rain — probably a form of sandstone that hollowed out over time.

The little ant and I sat there. Then I noticed that my eyes had closed, and I opened them and looked down. The little ant was standing right in front of me. The little ant bobbed its head. Then I bobbed my head, and the little ant turned around and walked off.

How beautiful. How old were you?

I think I was about five, maybe a little older. I mention these things the way I mention it to you because you all can learn to do these things now. Learn to help others, whether they are human beings or non-humans. Sometimes it is not good to run up to try to help. You have to be polite. Sometimes you have to let other life forms approach you if it is safe for them to approach you. Obviously if it is a mosquito, you might think twice. But maybe some life forms are just curious about life. Perhaps a caterpillar — it's very beautiful with a little green and maybe a little red or orange around it — walks up to you on its many legs. If you are not comfortable with it, then just tell it something good about it. If it is obviously not safe to be around, then get out of its way. But if it is safe and perhaps just being friendly, then tell it how much you love the beautiful green color (or whatever colors) of its body, and apologize for being nervous because you don't understand it or you haven't been introduced to it yet. When you say that, it will probably stop.

Introduce yourself in some way. If you are a child, just say your name — and your age, if you like — and then whatever you want to say. If you are an adult, you can simply picture what you did that morning, but make sure it is not anything that would frighten it. Say, "I woke up, and the sun was shining," or "It was raining, and there was a rainbow." Something like that, and keep it polite. Maybe say you had breakfast and now you are visiting with the being. Then pause. It will do the same thing. It might have already done so, and maybe you didn't notice. This is a good thing to do with other life forms because many life forms are leaving the planet now. Many of you might know about that; don't feel bad about it. You as a life form are also leaving the planet. This doesn't mean you are going to die immediately or something like that, but it does mean that the human race as you know it is going to move on to some other planet somewhere else. You don't have to go on ships; it will happen spiritually in some way that doesn't cause everybody to suffer.

So the other life forms are starting to move on first. Just so you know, even though they leave their bodies behind, they have moved on. This is why they sometimes do dramatic things. Your scientists might say, "Oh, it is because of pollution," or "Oh, it is because of 'this' disease," but it is a little hard to imagine how a flock of birds — let's say 150 birds — could suddenly fly into the air and simultaneously fall out of the sky. It is not because someone pointed an invisible ray gun at them and shot them down. They are showing whoever saw it or heard about it or read about it (any of those) that life goes on. It is not typical of these beings to die at the same moment. It is a lesson for you. Obviously, they are moving on to a benevolent world somewhere nice, their home planet, or wherever. The lesson for you is that life goes on, so don't worry about that.

Use Light and Love to Heal Others

Now you are going to ask me about some of the other things I did for people. Here is an example. I went to a place where a person was having headaches (I knew that because the person was holding his head). So what I did — and you have healers who can do this — was to ask that person to sit down so that his tailbone was essentially touching earth and then to lean back against something. He was still holding his head and grimacing. Then I did something that helped the person go to sleep. (So healers, just wait for the person to fall asleep. Don't give them anything; just wait for them to fall asleep, or help them go to sleep. You will know how to do this.)

While he was asleep, I reached into the top of his head right at the point where the most light is, where his soul is. But first, of course, I aligned myself with my true spirit and my source spirit, that point from which we all originate that I referred to before. That is why I brought that up. I knew that the person was aligned with that as well because I knew that everyone is. I followed that connection to the person's soul. We were both simultaneously connected to that point of origin, and his soul allowed me to enter his skull very gently and spiritually. Of course, I didn't create an opening in his physical skull, but I was able to find that a vein was blocked. I removed the block by something usually called transformation. It involves light and love. Love can transform almost anything.

Doing the light and love, I again saw those lights as I did before with the ant, and as the lights began to fade, I realized that the healing was complete. I could see that the vein was fine; the things that were flowing were flowing in it. I very slowly removed my hand from the top of his head and went back to that point of origin and stayed with him for a minute or two. Then I returned along that point of origin to the stream that was my soul stream. I sat with him for a while, another twenty minutes or so, and then he woke up and was fine.

Now I am saying this in this way because there are healers who have been working along these lines in your time, and all of them have a piece of this. I wanted to give you all the pieces, healers, so that you can know how to do this in the most effective way.

Would you say this was fairly typical of how you dealt with most of the physical ailments that your people had?

Yes, usually. Sometimes it was a broken bone, but in the case of a broken bone, the pain was so extreme that the person couldn't sleep, so I would do the same thing with him or her that I did with the ant. In a specific case of a young man with a leg that was broken below the knee but above the ankle, it was very painful — excruciating, of course — but it hadn't broken through the skin, so it was still in pretty good alignment. I did the same thing I did with the ant, picturing that, but I did it first by connecting through the point of origin. I came in through the top of his head, but I went down, energetically, through his body to his leg and then it was very much the same thing: seeing him before life, after life, the colors, and so on, until his bone moved forward in time, not back in time. If you move somebody back in time before the injury, there is always the slight chance that he or she would have the injury again. So it was better to move forward in time to when the leg was completely healed in a comfortable way with the surrounding tissues completely all right. That was the way to do it — the healing — but the rest of the body also moved forward about the length of time it would take in ideal conditions for the body to heal. So it was about two years forward for the person. The whole body had to move two years forward, so he looked almost the same but was essentially two years older. It was better that than dying, so the people were happy with that even though the young man was now an older person. He didn't have the maturity of an older person, but he had the body. They had to give him his education and get him caught up, but he was physically fine. That's what we did in our time.

That is amazing! I have talked to many shamans from times past, and anytime there was a broken bone, that person usually died.

Yes, but this person didn't. And I am telling this in such a way to speak to the healers in your time so that they know what to do and how to do it and to adapt it to what they are doing. Unless, of course, what the healers are doing works fine. Then don't change anything. For those of you who are looking for something extra, that's why I am telling you these things and trying to make it relevant in your time to others, which we did in the beginning.

Everything Is Connected

How long did you live in that life?

Well, let's see, I lived until I was about fifty-eight — very old. I was considered an elder, of course, and I had white hair. But I was full strength until I was just a little over fifty-seven, and then there was this need to have someone help me walk, and slowly my body declined. But I made it to fifty-eight and then passed over.

Did you have students? Did you teach them what you had learned?

Yes, of course.

So you were able to teach them what you had learned from the visions?

Yes, and I tried to give them the visions, but they didn't see them, so I gave them the teaching as best I could.

Was there a healer among your people when you were born? Did you have to learn through the visions because there was no one there to teach you?

Well, it was just my mother and father and me.

I mean in the group.

There was nobody else. You keep saying "the group" as if there was one.

There was just you and your mother and your father?

Yes.

But the settlements of people that you worked with as a healer had multiple groups of people?

Yes, the settlements did, but my mother and father were not in a settlement. When I walked to one or the other of the settlements, they remained where they resided.

Was there a reason you and they weren't part of an extended family, like grandparents and siblings and cousins?

I never asked them. I didn't ever feel lonely; I had mother, and I had father. Before they passed away, I met my wife, my mate, and had children.

Were the people who you trained your children, or were they from the settlements?

Well, I thought I would train my children, but they were meant for something else, so I trained a couple of people from one settlement and one from another settlement. When I first started walking, there were just two settlements, but then eventually there was a third, so I walked among those. They were located in a roughly triangular shape. I understood the triangle since it was one of the original shapes I was shown, so I realized that even though they were in three different geographical places, they were all connected. Everybody is.

How long did it take to walk to each one?

It was about four or five miles to the first two and about seven miles to the third settlement. A nice walk, enjoyable, and I often had company. Birds or other life forms would come by, and they were often the same ones I had seen on the last trip, so we were friends, and we would talk. I would tell them about my life, and they would tell me about their lives — not what they did, but what they were doing. It was nice. Sometimes it would rain, and there would be a rainbow. Very often there were fruit trees, and I stopped to have a piece of fruit — very nice, pleasant.

Did your parents have origin stories about where they came from?

I never asked them. It wasn't like that for us. They accepted me as I was, and I accepted them as they were. Keep in mind that we didn't have much of a worded language. We mostly used gestures, and a few sounds — just love.

Do you have descendants today on the planet?

I do have descendants in the same bloodlines, if that is what you are asking. I won't say where, but yes, there are descendants in my bloodline.

Do they have your abilities?

One of them does. In creation, all beings — the biggest, the smallest, the microscopic — all stem from an infinite source, a shape that is spherical. It does not have boundaries like walls. It is infinite, but it contains all potential for creation and creativity. Within it, you will see many shapes, forms, motions — things moving, things still, everything — and it can, at any time, combine with other things, forms, shapes, sounds, colors, anything. And it can emerge from that sphere. It is in the nature of immortality that the sphere is the point of origin whether it moves on an axis or on a slide, as in a microscope, or from place to place on its own, as water. Even when water freezes and becomes angular when examined, the sphere would be found deep within, just as scientists have discovered atoms. Know that the sphere is the point of origin of consciousness, and you will know what you need to know about the connection of all life.

Always remember it is best to be honest and speak as a human being, not as a teacher. That is what young people love these days. The reason they send so many pictures around is that they are sharing their humanity. They discover, of course, how much alike they are, and that ultimately solves strife and the world's problems. After a while, they do not want to go fight "them" because those people are who they interact with. It is like saying, "They are us."

Remember, I was shown those visions, but I couldn't make the visions be there for my students. I had to share with them what I learned from the visions, and it was more personal — human to human, as it were — and they liked it very much. You can do the same thing by making your teaching personal.

All of you in this life need to know only this: You all come from the same point of origin, and regardless of the soul stream and your many lives between lives and very often within lives, in dreams and at deep levels of sleep, you go Home, and you are with all life, and it is good. Good life.

Thank you so much.

☥ *Light Technology* PUBLISHING *Presents*

TO ORDER PRINT BOOKS
Visit LightTechnology.com, Call 928-526-1345 or 1-800-450-0985,
or Check Amazon.com or Your Favorite Bookstore

THROUGH ROBERT SHAPIRO

$19.95 • 6 x 9
512 PP. • SOFTCOVER
978-1-891824-12-8

Chapters Include

- Approaching Material Mastery through Your Physicality
- The Explorer Race as a Part of Mother Earth's Body
- Spiritual Beings in a Physical World
- Earth Is Now Releasing Human Resistence to Physical Life
- The Shaman's Key: Feeling and Five Senses
- Breathing: Something Natural We Overlook

Shamanic Secrets for Material Mastery

This book explores the heart and soul connection between humans and Mother Earth. Through that intimacy, miracles of healing and expanded awareness can flourish. To heal the planet and be healed as well, we can lovingly extend our energy selves out to the mountains and rivers to intimately bond with the earth. Gestures and vision can activate our hearts to return us to a healthy, caring relationship with the land we live on.

The character and essence of some of Earth's most powerful features are explored and understood, along with exercises given to connect us with those places. As we project our love and healing energies there, we help Earth to heal from humanity's destruction of the planet and its atmosphere. Dozens of photographs, maps, and drawings assist the process in twenty-five chapters, which cover the Earth's more critical locations.

Learn to communicate with the planet!

Light Technology PUBLISHING Presents   307

TO ORDER PRINT BOOKS
Visit LightTechnology.com, Call 928-526-1345 or 1-800-450-0985,
or Check Amazon.com or Your Favorite Bookstore

THROUGH ROBERT SHAPIRO

$25.00 • 6 x 9
576 PP. • SOFTCOVER
978-1-891824-29-6

Chapters Include

- Cellular Clearing of Traumas and Unresolved Events
- Dealing with Fear, Pain, and Addiction
- Life Lessons and the Vital Life Force
- Feeling Is Our Bodies' First and Primary Language
- Shame, Arrogance, Safety, and the Inability to Trust
- Using Gestures to Protect, Clear, and Change
- Communicating with the Natural World

Shamanic Secrets for Physical Mastery

The purpose of this book is to allow you to understand the sacred nature of your own physical body and some of the magnificent gifts it offers you. When you work with your physical body in these new ways, you will discover not only its sacredness but also how it is compatible with Mother Earth, the animals, the plants, and even the nearby planets, all of which you recognize as being sacred in nature.

It is important to feel the value of yourself physically before you can have any lasting physical impact on the world. The less you think of yourself physically, the less likely your physical impact on the world will be sustained by Mother Earth. If a physical energy does not feel good about itself, it will usually be resolved; other physical or spiritual energies will dissolve it because it is unnatural. The better you feel about your physical self when you do the work in the previous book as well as in this one and the one to follow, the greater and more lasting will be the benevolent effect on your life, on the lives of those around you, and ultimately on your planet and in the universe.

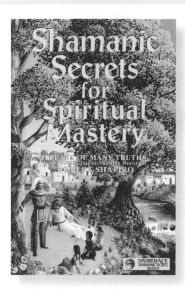

THROUGH ROBERT SHAPIRO

The Explorer Race
Book 1
gives you the foundational understanding of who you are, why you are on Earth, and where you are going.

Zoosh, End-Time Historian
through Robert Shapiro

$25.00 • Softcover • 608 PP.
978-0-9293853-8-9

"Welcome to the Explorer Race — of which you are a portion. What you are about to embark on now is a way to understand the entirety of your being as well as all that is around you.

"The Explorer Race series — what I like to call the Explorer Race history books — is intended to give you all the background you need to understand the value, purpose, and greater vision of what you are doing here on Earth. The information contained within is intended to remind you of your true capabilities and your true capacities. Don't let anybody tell you that you have to give up God or religion to do this. You don't. These books don't take that away from you.

"These books will give you the background you need to understand why you are here and help you to appreciate your true value. The Explorer Race books are intended — literally — to change your life, to put meaning where there wasn't meaning before, and to provide you with the insight and wisdom you need to improve the quality of your life and the lives of those all around you, maybe even on other planets.

"That's why you exist. That's why you're here. So enjoy the liberation you feel from the wonderful insights of Book 1 — and the others in the series you read. Welcome to the Explorer Race!"

— Zoosh

CHAPTERS INCLUDE:
- Origin of the Species: a Sirian Perspective
- Conversation with a Zeta
- The ET in You: Physical Body
- Coming of Age in the Fourth Dimension
- The True Purpose of Negative Energy
- The White Brotherhood, Illuminati, New Dawn, and Shadow Government
- Fulfilling the Creator's Destiny
- Etheric Gene Splicing and the Neutral Particle
- The Third Sex: the Neutral Binding Energy
- The Goddess Energy: the Soul of Creation
- The Heritage from Early Civilizations

THROUGH ROBERT SHAPIRO

ETs and the EXPLORER RACE
Book 2

The purpose of this book is to guide you toward acceptance of the differences among you all as well as acceptance of the wide variety of life that the universe has in store for you.

Know that we will look forward to meeting you explorers as you come out to the stars, and we will help you in every way we can. Please enjoy the book.

— Joopah

Joopah, Zoosh and others
through Robert Shapiro

$14.95 • Softcover • 240 PP.
978-0-929385-79-2

CHAPTERS INCLUDE

- The Great Experiment: Earth Humanity
- ETs Talk to Contactees
- Becoming One with Your Future Self
- ET Interaction with Humanity
- UFOs and Abductions
- The True Nature of the Grays
- Answering Questions in Las Vegas
- UFO Encounters in Sedona
- Joopah, in Transit, Gives an Overview and Helpful Tools
- We Must Embrace the Zetas
- Roswell, ETs, and the Shadow Government
- ETs: Friends or Foes?

Benevolent Magic & Living Prayer
$9.95 • 3.75 x 5 • Softcover • 96 PP. • 978-1-891824-49-4

This book is intended to cover, at least in a beginning way, manners and methods by which you can create for yourselves benevolently and create for others benevolently. This book is intended to teach you the ancient wisdom of gentle methods of feminine creation.

I want to remind you, to let you know immediately, that the purpose of these little books, what these books are intended to do, is to nurture, to support and — by their very titles, as well as how the books read — to serve you, to improve the quality of your lives and to support you in supporting yourselves and others.

—Isis

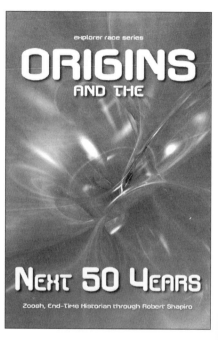

THROUGH ROBERT SHAPIRO

CREATORS and FRIENDS:
The Mechanics of Creation
Book 4

Now that you have a greater understanding of who you are in the larger sense, it is necessary to remind you of where you came from, the true magnificence of your being, to have some of your true peers talk to you. You must understand that you are creators in training, and you were once a portion of Creator. One could certainly say, without being magnanimous, that you are still a portion of Creator, yet you are training for the individual responsibility of being a creator to give your Creator a coffee break.

This book will give you peer consultation. It will allow you to understand the vaster qualities and help you remember the nature of the desires that drive any creator, the responsibilities to which that creator must answer, the reaction any creator must have to consequences, and the ultimate reward of any creator. I hope you will enjoy it and understand that maybe more will follow.

EXPLORER RACE

CREATORS AND FRIENDS
The Mechanics of Creation

Creators and Zoosh
through Robert Shapiro

$19.95 • Softcover • 480 PP.
978-1-891824-01-2

CHAPTERS INCLUDE
- Andastinn, Prototype of Insect Beings
- Kazant, a Timekeeper
- Founders of Sirius, Creators of Humanoid Forms
- A Teacher of Buddha and Time Master's Assistant
- Designers of Human Physiology
- Avatar of Sea Creatures and Quatsika, Messenger for the Dimension Makers
- The Empath Creator of Seventeen Planets
- Shapemaker of Portals
- Creator of the Inverse Universe, Our Creator's Creator

𝒥 Light Technology PUBLISHING Presents

TO ORDER PRINT BOOKS
Visit LightTechnology.com, Call 928-526-1345 or 1-800-450-0985,
or Check Amazon.com or Your Favorite Bookstore

THROUGH ROBERT SHAPIRO

PARTICLE PERSONALITIES
Book 5

All around you in every moment you are surrounded by the most magical and mystical beings. They are too small for you to see as individuals. But in groups, they form all of your physical life as you know it.

Particles — who might be considered either atoms or portions of atoms — consciously view the vast spectrum of reality yet also have a sense of personal memory like your own linear memory. Unlike your linear memory, where you remember the order of events you have lived, these particles remember where they have been and what they have done in their long, long lives and can access the higher strains associated with their experiences as well.

For instance, perhaps at one time a particle might have been a portion of a tree and it had access to all the tree's higher wisdom and knowledge, what it had been before or might be in the future. Or perhaps it might have been in the ocean. The knowledge of anything swimming past it or growing or simply existing nearby would also be available to it. So a particle has not only its own personal wisdom but anything or anyone it has ever passed through.

Particles, then, have a unique and unusual perspective. In reading this book, understand that some of them will have similar points of view. But others will have quite extraordinary and unexpected points of view. Expect the unexpected!

$14.95 • Softcover • 256 PP.
978-0-929385-97-6

CHAPTERS INCLUDE

- A Particle of Gold
- The Model Maker: the Clerk
- The Clerk, a Mountain Lion Particle, a Particle of Liquid Light, and an Ice Particle
- A Particle of Rose Quartz from a Floating Crystal City
- A Particle of Uranium, Earth's Mind
- A Particle of the Great Pyramid's Capstone
- A Particle of the Dimensional Boundary between Orbs
- A Particle of Healing Energy

THROUGH ROBERT SHAPIRO

EXPLORER RACE and BEYOND
Book 6

With a better idea of how creation works, we go back to the Creator's advisors and receive deeper and more profound explanations of the roots of the Explorer Race. The liquid Domain and the Double Diamond portal share lessons given to the roots on their way to meet the Creator of this universe, and finally the roots speak of their origins and their incomprehensibly long journey here.

$14.95 • Softcover • 384 PP.
978-1-891824-06-7

CHAPTERS INCLUDE

- Creator of Pure Feelings and Thoughts, One Circle of Creation
- The Liquid Domain
- The Double-Diamond Portal
- About the Other 93% of the Explorer Race
- Synchronizer of Physical Reality and Dimensions
- The Master of Maybe
- Master of Frequencies and Octaves
- Spirit of Youthful Enthusiasm (Junior) and Master of Imagination
- Zoosh
- The Master of Feeling

- The Master of Plasmic Energy
- The Master of Discomfort
- The Story-Gathering Root Being from the Library of Light/Knowledge
- The Root Who Fragmented from a Living Temple
- The First Root Returns
- Root Three, Companion of the Second Root
- The Temple of Knowledge & the Giver of Inspiration
- The Voice Historian, Who Provided the First Root
- Creator of All That Is

THROUGH ROBERT SHAPIRO

COUNCIL of CREATORS
Book 7

The thirteen core members of the Council of Creators discuss their adventures in coming to awareness of themselves and their journeys on the way to the Council on this level. They discuss the advice and oversight they offer to all creators, including the creator of this local universe. These beings are wise, witty, and joyous, and their stories of love's creation create an expansion of our concepts as we realize that we live in an expanded, multiple-level reality.

THE **EXPLORER RACE**
COUNCIL OF CREATORS
AND ZOOSH THROUGH
ROBERT SHAPIRO

$14.95 • Softcover • 288 PP.
978-1-891824-13-5

CHAPTERS INCLUDE

- Specialist in Colors, Sounds, and Consequences of Actions
- Specialist in Membranes That Separate and Auditory Mechanics
- Specialist in Sound Duration
- Explanation from Unknown Member of Council
- Specialist in Spatial Reference
- Specialist in Gaps and Spaces
- Specialist in Divine Intervention
- Specialist in Synchronicity and Timing
- Specialist in Hope
- Specialist in Honor
- Specialist in Mystical Connection between Animals and Humans
- Specialist in Change and the Velocity of Change
- Specialist in the Present Moment
- Council Spokesperson and Specialist in Auxiliary Life Forms

THROUGH ROBERT SHAPIRO

The EXPLORER RACE and ISIS
Book 8

"This book will address the Creator in all of you and speak directly to stimulate the benevolence of that energy you are all built on. Creator School is the place where the energy that precedes creators comes from in order that creators might create their ability, their energy, and their capacity to manifest. It is my intention to speak not only about the seen and the unseen, but also, from time to time, the unimagined."

— Isis

This amazing book includes priestess training, shamanic training, Isis adventures with Explorer Race beings — before Earth and on Earth — and an incredibly expanded explanation of the dynamics of the Explorer Race. Isis is the prototypal loving, nurturing, guiding feminine being, the focus of feminine energy. She has the ability to expand limited thinking without making people with limited beliefs feel uncomfortable.

She is a fantastic storyteller, and all her stories are teaching stories. If you care about who you are, why you are here, where you are going, and what life is all about — pick up this book. You won't lay it down until you are through, and then you will want more.

THE EXPLORER RACE AND
ISIS
THROUGH
ROBERT SHAPIRO

$14.95 • Softcover • 352 PP.
978-1-891824-11-1

CHAPTERS INCLUDE

- Isis and Your Creator
- The Biography of Isis
- The Planetary Influence of Isis
- The Adventurer
- Soul Colors and Shapes
- Creation Mechanics
- The Insect Form and Fairies
- Orion's Transition and Its Application to Earth
- The Veil and the Blue Portal
- The Goddess and the Natural Feminine
- Self-Violence and Self-Love
- The Concept of Mutual Benefit

Light Technology PUBLISHING Presents

TO ORDER PRINT BOOKS

Visit LightTechnology.com, Call 928-526-1345 or 1-800-450-0985, or Check Amazon.com or Your Favorite Bookstore

THROUGH ROBERT SHAPIRO

The Explorer Race and Jesus

Book 9

"In this book, I will make an effort to speak of who I really am, where I'm from, what I'm doing now, why I went to Earth, what I hoped to accomplish, what I really did accomplish, and perhaps other things. I want to try to explain why things happened, why people did 'this' or 'that' during my lifetime. I will try to fill in details."

— Jesus

The immortal personality who lived the life we know as Jesus, along with his students and friends, describes with clarity and love his life and teaching on Earth 2,000 years ago.

These beings lovingly offer their experiences of the events that happened then and of Jesus's time-traveling adventures, especially to other planets and to the nineteenth and twentieth centuries, which he called the time of the machines — the time of troubles.

It is so heartwarming and interesting that you won't want to put it down.

$16.95 • Softcover • 352 PP.
978-1-891824-14-2

CHAPTERS INCLUDE

- Jesus's Core Being, His People, and the Interest of Four of Them in the Earth
- Jesus's Home World, Their Love Creations, and the Four Who Visited Earth
- The "Facts" of Jesus's Life Here, His Future Return
- The Teachings and Travels
- A Student's Time with Jesus and His Tales of Jesus's Time Travels
- The Shamanic Use of the Senses
- Many Journeys, Many Disguises
- The Child Student Who Became a Traveling Singer-Healer
- Learning to Invite Matter to Transform Itself
- Inviting Water, Singing Colors
- Learning about Different Cultures and People
- The Role of Mary Magdalene, a Romany
- Jesus's Autonomous Parts, His Bloodline, and His Plans

All Our Books Are Also Available as eBooks on Amazon, Apple iTunes, Google Play, and Barnes & Noble.

THROUGH ROBERT SHAPIRO

Earth History and Lost Civilizations
Book 10

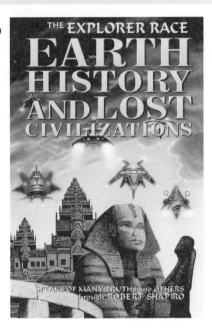

THE EXPLORER RACE
EARTH HISTORY AND LOST CIVILIZATIONS
SPEAKS OF MANY TRUTHS and OTHERS
through ROBERT SHAPIRO

Speaks of Many Truths and Zoosh, through Robert Shapiro, explain that planet Earth, the only water planet in this solar system, is on loan from Sirius as a home and school for humanity, the Explorer Race.

Earth's recorded history goes back only a few thousand years, its archaelogical history a few thousand more. Now this book opens up the past as if a light was turned on in the darkness, and we see the incredible panorama of brave souls coming from other planets to settle on different parts of Earth. We watch the origins of tribal groups and the rise and fall of civilizations, and we can begin to understand the source of the wonderous diversity of plants, animals, and humans that we enjoy here on beautiful Mother Earth.

$14.95 • Softcover • 320 PP.
978-1-891824-20-3

- Andazi Teach Jehovah How to Create Human Beings
- The Academy of All Peoples: Cave Paintings, Symbols, and Crop Circles
- Sumer, an Art Colony from Sirius
- Nazca Lines Radiate Enthusiasm for Life
- Easter Island Statues: a Gift for the Future
- Lucy and her Laetoli Footprints
- Egypt and Cats as Teachers of Humans
- The Electrical Beings
- The Andromedan Origins of Stone Medicine Wheels

CHAPTERS INCLUDE
- When Earth was Sirius
- Ancient Artifacts Explained
- Fire and Ice People and Multidimensional Lightbeings
- Early Civilizations on Earth: Mongollians and Desert People
- The Long Journey of Jehovah's Ship, from Orion to Sirius to Earth

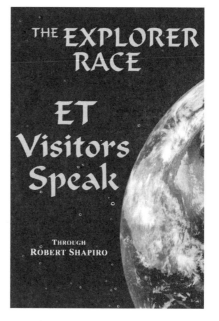

THROUGH ROBERT SHAPIRO

Techniques for Generating Safety
Book 12

CREATE A SAFE LIFE AND A SAFE WORLD

THROUGH ROBERT SHAPIRO

$9.95 • Softcover • 208 PP.
978-1-891824-26-5

The opportunity to change the way you live is not only close at hand but also with you right now. Some of you have felt a change in the air, as you say, the winds of change. Sometimes you can almost taste it or smell it or feel it. And other times it is ephemeral, hard to grasp.

It is the ephemeral quality that can help you to know that the good thing that is out of your reach has to do with the future timeline. The future timeline is also an experience line. It is a sensation line. It is associated with the way your physical body communicates to you and others. It is a way of increasing your sensitivity to your own needs and the needs of others in a completely safe and protected way so that you can respond more quickly and accurately to those needs and appreciate the quality of life around you, much of which you miss because the old timeline discourages you from observing.

The future timeline encourages you to study and understand, but it discourages you from feeling. And it is feeling that is the ultimate answer to your discomforts as well as the pathway to true benevolent insight and fulfillment. When you read this book, know that it is intended to give you the gift of ease that comes with the simpler path, the less complicated path — the path without attachments.

CHAPTERS INCLUDE

- Zero Four
- The Traveler
- The Fluid of Time
- Ordinator of Souls
- The Energy Three
- The Mother of All Beings
- Benevolent Magic to Move the Future to You
- The Love-Heat Exercise
- Creating Safety in Your Life
- A Lesson in Benevolent Magic

☽ *Light Technology* PUBLISHING *Presents*   321

TO ORDER PRINT BOOKS
Visit LightTechnology.com, Call 928-526-1345 or 1-800-450-0985,
or Check Amazon.com or Your Favorite Bookstore

THROUGH ROBERT SHAPIRO

Animal Souls Speak
Book 13

"The animal world will speak, if you prefer, through elders. This has certain advantages, since that way they can include knowledge and wisdom to a degree — not to a vast degree, but to a degree — about their home planets."

— Grandfather

Each animal brings a wondrous gift to share with humanity — enjoy it!

"Welcome to the footsteps of the loving beings who support you, who wish to reveal more about themselves to you, and who welcome you not only to planet Earth but, more specifically, to the pathway of self-discovery. Take note as you read this book of what resonates, what stimulates your own memories.

"Use it to inspire you and to encourage you, to support you along your path toward inevitable self-discovery — ultimately to support self-discovery in others that results in revealing the true and most benevolent heart of all beings. Good life."

— Creator's Emissary

$29.95 • Softcover • 640 PP.
978-1-891824-50-0

CHAPTERS INCLUDE
- Feelings Unite All Forms of Life
- Eel: Helping You Make the Unconscious Conscious
- Tortoise: Providing Inspiration for Solution
- Frog: Calling in the Rain and the Sun
- Snail: Representing Change in a Fluid Way
- Deer: Supporting Your True Heart Nature
- Elephant: Providing an Impetus for Change
- Phoenix: a Form of Life for the Future
- Cat: Transforming Your Discomfort
- Butterfly: Reminding People of Beauty
- Feeling Is the Common Ground for Animals, Humans, and All Life
- Animal Beings Help Anchor Your Pathway on Earth

♄ Light Technology PUBLISHING Presents

THROUGH ROBERT SHAPIRO

Astrology
Book 14

The planets and signs of astrology speak to us through superchannel Robert Shapiro — sharing not only **LONG-LOST INFORMATION** but also **NEW WAYS OF BEING** for an awakening humanity.

Astrology and astronomy are one. The heart is astrology; the mind is astronomy. But you would not, in your own personality, separate your heart from your mind, would you?

This book honors that pursuit of the lost heart. It demonstrates the personality of the planets, the Sun, the Moon, the signs. This is what has been missing in astrology ever since the heart was set aside in favor of the mind. Over time, such knowledge and wisdom was lost. This book brings all that back. It allows astrologers to feel the planets, to feel the Sun, the Moon, and the signs. This is not to abandon the knowledge and wisdom they have now but to truly include, to show, to demonstrate, to provide to those seeking astrological knowledge and wisdom, to provide the heart elements of personality.

As the planets and signs speak through Robert, their personality traits and interests (many of which have been unknown since ancient times) can be clearly heard and felt. In addition, you — humanity — have made such progress that other new energies and traits of the planets and signs are expressed through their words. These energies, traits, and characteristics were only potential in earlier times but now are becoming available to you to become aware of and to express within your life on Earth as you awaken to your natural self.

$29.95 • Softcover • 704 PP.
978-1-891824-81-4

TOPICS INCLUDE

• Planets Know Each Other by Feeling

• Sunrise Is the Most Balanced Nurturance You Can Experience

• The Real Measurement of Time Is Experience

• Astrologers Can Help You Fill in the Gaps

• Elsewhere Practically No One Has a Name

• Creation Is Always Personal

• You First Need to Learn About the Thirteenth Sign

• Desire Is a Direct Result of Earth Life

• Humans Need Optimism

Light Technology PUBLISHING Presents

TO ORDER PRINT BOOKS
Visit LightTechnology.com, Call 928-526-1345 or 1-800-450-0985,
or Check Amazon.com or Your Favorite Bookstore

THROUGH ROBERT SHAPIRO

ET Visitors Speak
Volume 2 • Book 15

THE
EXPLORER
RACE

ET
Visitors
Speak
Vol. 2

THROUGH
ROBERT SHAPIRO

**$19.95 • Softcover • 512 PP.
978-1-891824-78-4**

For those of you who've always wanted to meet somebody completely different, here's your opportunity. This book contains the continuing adventures of visitors to planet Earth. In a strange sense, you might include yourself as one of those, as the human race does not really claim the title of full-time and permanent Earth citizen.

So when you're reading this book, think about it as if you were visiting another planet. What would you say in reaction to the local population, their habits, and so on? Put yourself in the picture so this isn't just a meaningless travel log from various beings that you don't know and may never meet.

Make it personal this time because the time is coming, maybe even in some of your lifetimes, when you might just be one of those extraterrestrials on another planet. So you might as well practice now and get your lines down right.

CHAPTERS INCLUDE

- ET Greeters to Future Mars Earth Colony
- Harmony Is a Way of Life on Future Earth
- ETs Create an Alternate Path to Earth

- A Being from Planet Odin Visits the Iroquois Nation in the Thirteenth Century
- Odin, the Norse God: How the Myth Began
- Sirian Researches Earth Life Forms and Their Harmonious Interactions
- An ET Visitor from the Twelfth Planet Looks for His Planet in the Future
- Individual-Specific Communion Among Human Beings
- Predictions for the Past-Anchored Timeline and the Future-Anchored Timeline

THROUGH ROBERT SHAPIRO

Plant Souls Speak
Book 16

Planet Energies Available to You:
Live Plant 100% • Dead Plant 10%

"What we intend to speak about — if I may speak in general for all plants — is how you can interact with plants in a more benevolent way for you as the human species. For a long time, you have been clear on medicinal uses of leaves and stems and seeds and flower petals and so on, but you are only getting about one-tenth of the energy available to you that way. It is always better to interact with the plant and its energies in its live form, but you need to know how.

$24.95 • Softcover • 576 PP.
978-1-891824-74-6

"The intention of this book is to reveal that formula so that you can stop searching, as a human race, for the magical cures to diseases by exhausting the supply of life forms around you when a much simpler process is available. The beings in this book will not just comment on things you know about but show you what you are missing in your interaction with plants."
— Dandelion

Each plant brings a wondrous gift to share with humanity — enjoy it!

TOPICS INCLUDE

- You Must Form a Personal Relationship with the Seeds You Plant
- Sage Can Help Resolve Communication Problems
- Not All Plant Life on Earth Is Meant for Human Beings
- You Must State Your Intentions as You Approach a Marijuana Plant
- Plants Receive Most of Their Energy from Earth
- Silica Will Bring You Clarity and Purpose

THROUGH ROBERT SHAPIRO

TIME and the Transition to Natural Time
Book 17

"The purpose of this book is to provide a context for your lives in the sequence you find yourselves in now. This explanation of time — and, to a degree, its variables — is being provided for you so that you will understand more about your true, natural, native personalities and so that you will be reminded that you are, as you know, in a school, and that this school is purely temporary.

"You don't come here very often to this place of linear time; like in your own human lives, you are in school for only so long, and then you live your lives. When you exist beyond this school, you will find all those lives infinitely easier. And even as the Creator, your lives will be easier than they are in the single, linear existences you're living now because you will have all your components."

— Founder of Time

$16.95 • Softcover • 352 PP.
978-1-891824-85-2

CHAPTERS INCLUDE

- Time Is Now Available for Your Personal Flexibility
- Your Blinders Are Coming Off
- You Live in a Stream Hosted by Planet Earth
- Time Is an Application for Expansion
- You Are Moving toward Complete Safety and Benevolence
- You Can Transition to the Future in Warmth and Safety
- The Gift of Time
- Your Future Selves Are Linking to You
- You Are Here to Learn about Your Personal Physicality
- You are Making the Transition through Deep Sleep
- You Will Let Go of Conflict in the Next Focus

🜊 *Light Technology* PUBLISHING **Presents**

TO ORDER PRINT BOOKS
Visit LightTechnology.com, Call 928-526-1345 or 1-800-450-0985,
or Check Amazon.com or Your Favorite Bookstore

THROUGH ROBERT SHAPIRO

ETs on Earth, Volume 1 Book 18

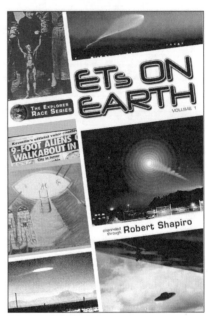

Greetings. This is Zoosh.

In the beginning of the Explorer Race adventure — that means you, all humans on Earth way back — ETs on Earth were a normal thing. In fact, you were ETs who came from many different planets those thousands of years ago, and you felt that Earth was a wonderful place where you could thrive.

I want you to keep that in mind when you read about these ETs that happen to be still visiting Earth. In this book, as well as in other books that have material like this, if you can keep that in mind, it will not be too surprising or shocking. In fact, for most of you, you will be ETs again in another life, and your youngsters just might be ETs from Earth visiting other planets in the future.

This should be a fun read and a gentle reminder that ETs are just friends from some place — you might say from another neighborhood.

Good life.

**$16.95 • Softcover • 352 PP.
978-1-891824-91-3**

Chapters Include

- ET Beings Use Green Light to Support Earth Beings
- Humans Are Going through Rapid Changes on Earth
- Update on ETs and UFOs
- Blue Spiral Light over Norway
- A Glimpse Beyond the Explorer Race
- Will There Be a Phony ET Invasion on Earth?
- Orbs Are Lightbeings Visiting Benevolent Spaces
- You Traverse to Your Home Planet in Deep Sleep
- The "Little People" Are Humans from Alpha Centauri

☥ *Light Technology* PUBLISHING *Presents*   327

TO ORDER PRINT BOOKS
Visit LightTechnology.com, Call 928-526-1345 or 1-800-450-0985,
or Check Amazon.com or Your Favorite Bookstore

THROUGH ROBERT SHAPIRO

Are You a Walk-In?
A New Form
of Birth Is Now
Available on Earth
Book 19

THE EXPLORER RACE SERIES

ARE YOU A WALK-IN?

A NEW FORM OF BENEVOLENT BIRTH
IS NOW AVAILABLE ON EARTH

Zoosh, Isis, Reveals the Mysteries, and More
through **Robert Shapiro**

"Walk-in" simply means the transfer of one soul out of the human body followed by the welcoming of another soul meant to come into that physical body. It is not random. It is not done without permission. Everything is done with sacredness and with permission.

"Usually when a soul leaves the body, the normal process follows: The body dies in a death, and you carry on as you're used to. In the past, it was rare for a walk-in to occur, but now something is occurring that requires more walk-ins.

"Many of you will identify with personal qualities that you couldn't really put a finger on before. You will be surprised to come to the realization that perhaps you are walk-ins. If you are, the information within will help you understand why your life has changed and perhaps what the sudden change is about. I just want you to know that this book is presented with love and encouragement, and we believe (speaking for our spirit in general) that it is timely and perhaps in your best interest to know now so that you can welcome the process, whether you're coming or going."

— Zoosh

$19.95 • Softcover • 304 PP.
978-1-891824-40-1

Chapters Include

- How the Body Prepares for a New Soul
- The Physical Effects of the Walk-In Experience
- Communication between the Exiting Soul and the Walk-In
- Walk-In or Soul Braid
- Walking in, a Benevolent Birth Process
- How the Walk-In Adjusts
- Your Walk-In Experience Is Supported by Your Physical Body
- The Personality Allows the Soul to Reveal Itself
- How to Live as a Walk-In
- The Walk-In Support System
- Mother Earth Welcomes Every Soul

THROUGH ROBERT SHAPIRO

TOTALITY AND BEYOND
The Search for the Origin of Life — and Beyond
Book 20

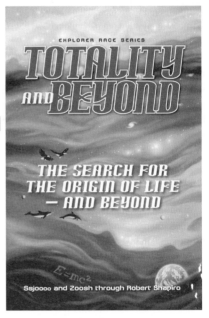

$24.95 • Softcover • 416 PP.
978-1-891824-75-3

"The book you are about to read attempts to explain and, to a degree, put an order to existence. You might reasonably ask, "What is the purpose?" The purpose is very simply this: In order for you now to be able to function in a world of responsibilities well beyond your own physical life, you need to be able to understand the functionality of creation and the confidence you need to have in simply emerging from seemingly nothing. "Nothing" is not really zero. Nothing is a matrix available to create something. It will always be that, and it has always been that.

"This book will explain, with some wide variety of points of view at times, those points, and over the next few hundred years, you can consider them as you blend with your total being, creating and re-creating what is now, in order to bring it to a more benevolent state of being."

—Ssjoooo, September 18, 2015

CHAPTERS INCLUDE

- The Thirteen Envision the Worlds Within Worlds
- The Loop of Time
- An Unending Parade of Existence
- Disentanglement
- Disentangling Cords of Discomfort
- All Creation Responds to Need
- Every Action Has a Reaction: It's Mother Nature's Plan
- Love and Care for Others to Embrace the Totality
- Feel Heat to Learn Oneness
- You Planned Your Journey
- The Reservoir of Being

ꭹ *Light Technology* PUBLISHING *Presents*   329

TO ORDER PRINT BOOKS
Visit LightTechnology.com, Call 928-526-1345 or 1-800-450-0985,
or Check Amazon.com or Your Favorite Bookstore

THROUGH ROBERT SHAPIRO

ETs on Earth,
Volume 2 • Book 21

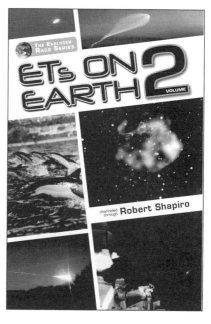

"You've noticed lately—haven't you?—that for the past few years, UFOs and phenomena in the skies are all over the place. Well, hold on to your hats! You can be pretty sure this is only going to increase in its frequency in the skies. In this book, you'll be able to read a little bit about who the beings in the UFOs are, where they're from, why they're here, and so on.

"In the future, it won't just be airplane pilots reporting on these things. You'll be talking about it among yourselves because regular folks just like you will be seeing these ships. This time, don't keep it quiet. Just talk about it with your neighbors or your friends online. It gives other people permission to believe what they saw. People have been taught, you know, not to believe what they see. So you can believe it."

— Zoosh

$16.95 • Softcover • 416 PP.
978-1-62233-003-4

Chapters Include

- Dolphins: Creators of Time Bridges
- Physical Feelings Are the Language of Physicality
- ET Sightings Will Increase as Earth Becomes More Benevolent
- Pleiadians Request ETs' Help in Project to Help Humans Awaken
- The Mountain Energies Are a Gift to Amplify Your Consciousness
- ETs Disarmed Nuclear Missiles
- ET Colonizers of Chinese See Promising Signs
- Fake ET Invasion: Why?

THROUGH ROBERT SHAPIRO

ETs on Earth
Volume 3 • Book 22

THE EXPLORER RACE SERIES

channeled through
Robert Shapiro

$16.95 • Softcover • 416 PP.
978-1-62233-044-7

M any of you are ready to welcome ETs — if not in your personal lives, at least interchanging with government bodies in large groups. Some of you are prepared to shake hands. Even a few want hugs. But it may not be that personal.

There are circumstances coming up in your now evolution toward your natural selves that make it almost imperative to have contact of a benevolent nature between Earth people and extraterrestrials. For now, many ETs are shy about coming here. They will, at some risk to themselves from time to time, show you images of themselves literally (in the skies you will see them defined by clouds), or you will see something that reminds you of ships. I'm not just referring to lenticular clouds. It will be a cloud form, often all by itself in the sky, that reminds you of a ship and has details that could be nothing but. So look for that all over the planet, and don't be afraid.

As your cousins, which is the way they see themselves (the ones you are most likely to meet), ETs recognize that you are a version of their extended family. So read this book. You will find many reminders of who you might have been or who you might be in other lives or who your extended family is now.

Chapters Include

- Beings Who Communicate through Mathematical Expression
- Hope Benefits the Pleiades
- The Road to Compassion Is Paved with Growth
- Change Represents Growth for You *and* Other Beings
- From a Light in the Sky to the Solution of a Great Mystery
- Sound Feeds Life
- Be Aware of Emerging Sense Communications
- Panda Bear Energy Helps Humans Resolve Conflicts
- ET Scientist Seeks Out Unusual Life
- Time-Traveling Orion ET Visits Future Jupiter

THROUGH ROBERT SHAPIRO

ANDROMEDA

The Andromedans and Zoosh through Robert Shapiro

The Andromedans who originally contacted the Professor speak through superchannel Robert Shapiro and give instructions that will allow trained scientists to construct a shield around existing Earth planes so that Earth astronauts can fly to Mars or to the stars.

The Andromedans also tell what really happened on their journeys and on Earth. They clear up questions one would have after reading the English or Spanish version of the previous book — the text of which follows the channeling in this book.

In addition, they supply a lively account of their lives on their home planet in the Andromedan constellation of our galaxy.

The eight-foot-tall, highly mental crew members of the ship who speak include

- Leia, the beautiful cultural specialist and social diplomat who so intrigued the Professor
- Cheswa, the cultural liason
- G-dansa, Leia's daughter, equivalent to an eight-year-old ET, Eloise
- Duszan, the Junior Scientist
- Onzo, the Senior Scientist and Crew Leader, the youngest (yet genetically modified to be the most brilliant) of the crew
- Playmate, a two-foot-tall, roly-poly Andromedan who teaches communion of heart and mind

$16.95 • 464 PP. • Softcover
978-1-891824-35-7

Ultimate UFO Series:
ANDROMEDA
Channeled Commentary by
ANDROMEDANS & ZOOSH THROUGH
Robert Shapiro

Includes the Text of UFO CONTACT FROM ANDROMEDA
EXTRATERRESTRIAL PROPHECY
UFO Books: Rodriguez • Hernandez • Stevens

✦ *Light Technology* PUBLISHING

Chapters Include

- Our Ancestors Came from Space
- Extraterrestrial Concepts of Energy
- Reviewing the Past and Feelings
- Early Visits to Earth
- Antimatter
- Our Explosive Atmosphere
- On Space Travel
- ET View of Our Religion
- Life and Death of Planets
- Changes Overcome Me
- The Extraterrestrial Photographed

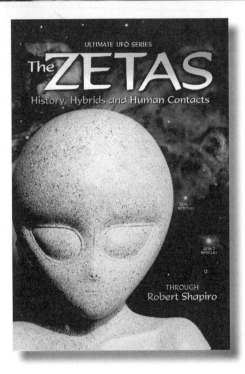